Men, Money, and Diplomacy

CORNELL STUDIES IN SECURITY AFFAIRS

edited by Robert J. Art *and* Robert Jervis

Men, Money, and Diplomacy:

The Evolution of British Strategic Policy, 1919–26

JOHN ROBERT FERRIS

Lecturer in History
University of Calgary

Cornell University Press
Ithaca, New York

First published 1989 by Cornell University Press

Printed in Hong Kong

Library of Congress Cataloging–in–Publication Data
Ferris, John Robert, 1957–
Men, money and diplomacy.
Bibliography: p.
Includes index.
1. Great Britain—Military policy.   2. Great Britain
—Foreign relations—1910–36.   3. Great Britain—
Economic policy.   I. Title.
UA647.F4   1989   355'.0335'41   88–47750
ISBN   0–8014–2236–1

To my parents, Robert and Gwen Ferris

Contents

List of Tables

Acknowledgements

I owe gratitude to many sources for assistance in the completion of this book. I am indebted to the copyright holders and also to the Birmingham University Library, the British Museum,, the Bodleian Library, the Masters, Fellows and Scholars of Churchill College, Cambridge, the Syndics of Cambridge University Library the House of Lords Record Office and the Trustees of the Beaverbrook Foundation, the Imperial War Museum, the India Office Library and Records, the Liddell Hart Centre for Military Archives, the National Army Museum, the National Library of Scotland, the National Maritime Museum, Nuffield College, Oxford and the Royal Air Force Museum, for permission to examine and, where appropriate, to quote from the papers listed in the bibliography. Documents in the Public Record Office and all other material under Crown copyright are cited by permission of the Controller of Her Majesty's Stationary Office.

I am especially grateful to the staff of all the archives listed above for their unfailing courtesy and helpfulness in the face of scholarly importunity. I must also thank Mrs Sylvia Smither, who performed the miracle of turning my typescript into a fair copy.

I owe much in terms of intellectual stimulation and correction to John Darwin and to members of the Military History Seminar at the Institute of Historical Research, London, particularly Brian Bond, David French, Andrew Lambert and Gerald Spillan. Without the kindness and criticism of Michael Dockrill and of Elizabeth Herbert this book could not have been written.

My Lords, it is the proud distinction of the policy of this country that its objects and its interests are those of peace—not only peace amongst ourselves, but peace throughout the world; and to promote the independence, and security, and prosperity—of every country in the world. Your Lordships saw the pains which were taken last year, and have been taken every year, and are now going on, to preserve peace throughout the world. Look at the acts of mediation carrying on lately, and even now, sometimes alone, and sometimes with the aid of other nations, to preserve peace throughout the world; and why? Because it is the undeniable interest of this country to maintain peace everywhere.[1]

Duke of Wellington to the House of Lords, 4 July 1844

Introduction

British strategic policy during the 1920s has not been seen as a coherent and specific topic in its own right. Historians have examined aspects of that policy, like the development of the Singapore base or the actions of departments such as the Admiralty, but they have treated each such issue and department essentially in isolation.[1] The strategic decisions of the 1920s have been regarded as a prelude to Britain's position in the 1930s rather than as an autonomous historical subject in their own right. Scholars have made these decisions seem inexplicable and unconnected by removing them from the context both of their time, the 1920s, and of their place, as part of strategic policy. This approach has led them to misinterpret the evolution of strategic policy during the 1920s. These errors in interpretation have stemmed from several false assumptions about the nature of the issues in question, indeed, from preconceptions which have shaped the very questions which historians have sought to answer.

Scholars have recognised that during the 1920s foreign, service and financial policies were interrelated and even coordinated. Although historians have not systematically analysed this inter-relationship, they have assumed that the policies of the fighting services were always dominated by financial policy, the pressure of which was reinforced by the imperatives of foreign policy. This view reflects a misinterpretation of the connections between these issues. It does not explain why Whitehall struggled so bitterly over them or why notable developments occured in strategic policy. For example, between 1922 and 1925 the government alllowed the Royal Air Force (RAF) and the Royal Navy (**RN**) to pursue expensive rearmament programmes. Any useful analysis of strategic policy must explain not only why these programmes were abandoned, but also why they were undertaken in the first place.

Historians have misunderstood the nature of strategic policy because of their preconceptions about its formation. They have assumed that between 1919 and 1931 two factors dominated service policies: the power of the Treasury and of the so-called 'ten-year rule'. Yet scholars have not analysed either factor. They have held that the Treasury always controlled the services, but have rarely examined its exact effect on specific issues. Actually, the Treasury's power developed very gradually and from a low level; between 1919 and 1924 it only moderately influenced the services. Although the 'ten year rule' has been deemed 'infamous' and 'notorious', historians have not studied its influence in practice.[2] In fact, it had a variable importance between 1919 and 1931 and did not always mean what historians have believed that it meant. The 'ten-year rule' had little effect on service policies between 1919 and 1924. It was only one of several strategic principles which the government formulated in August 1919, nor was it ever termed the 'ten-year rule' before 1926.

The Treasury and the 'ten-year rule' shaped service policies between 1925 and 1928 and dominated them between 1928 and 1931. They did not cause Britain's strategic decisions between 1919 and 1925. In fact, their power was the product of these decisions. Only after 1925, when the government altered the basis for its strategic policy, did these factors begin to have that influence which has been ascribed to them throughout the 1920s. Only then did the Treasury become the central department in the formulation of strategic policy, and only then did the 'ten-year period' become the 'ten-year rule'. Thus, historians have misunderstood the dynamics of strategic policy during the 1920s and have mistaken the results of a process for its causes.

This book argues that Britain did have a strategic policy between 1919 and 1926; that it did seek to coordinate in a rational fashion the diplomatic, financial and military elements of British strength in order to support its aims as a great power. These matters were dialectically related. Financial and foreign policies shaped British service decisions and at the same time were affected by the latter. The decisive issue in strategic policy was the need to balance the military strength which seemed necessary to support British strategic aims against what the British economy seemed able to afford. The imperatives of foreign, financial and service policies were individually important, yet collectively they pulled strategic policy in different directions. Throughout 1919–26 Britain followed many different strategic policies and there was nothing inevitable in its decision finally to select one of them. Only during the pivotal period of 1925–26 did Britain begin definitively to follow one strategic policy, which it retained until 1932.

This book is primarily concerned with how, during a lengthy period of relative peace, Britain developed a long-term strategic policy. It examines how the government defined and pursued its strategic aims and shaped its armed services to meet them. It analyses how accurately the government understood Britain's situation among the powers and how effectively its strategic policy suited Britain's requirements. This book considers whether something did go wrong in strategic policy during the 1920s and whether different decisions were practicable which in their turn could have strengthened Britain's position for the 1930s. These questions can only be answered after analysing how British governments formulated strategic policy.

1 The Politics of Strategic Policy, 1919–26

Strategic policy sprang from politics. It was made on the margins of power and responsibility of several elements of the government. The Cabinet defined the priorities between the government's aims and approved policies for each department. The latter executed these policies, which regulated their claims on government resources. The relationship between ministers and departments was dynamic and all of their decisions were inter-related. Two independent factors determined the evolution of strategic policy. One was the random evolution of politics and the other was the constant process of bureaucracy.

Although in the 1920s issues of strategic policy did not often shape the course of politics, Parliament and public opinion did influence aspects of strategic policy, sometimes decisively. Moreover, the ideological views of the political parties differed on aspects of strategic policy. Four different governments held office between 1919 and 1926 and it was during the politically most complex period, September 1922 to November 1924, that strategic policy fluctuated most dramatically, as each government started, but was unable to complete, new undertakings in strategic policy.

Each prime minister handled strategic issues in a different way. David Lloyd George, working with a few colleagues, always sought to dominate his government's policies. Ramsay MacDonald wanted to make his government's strategic decisions by himself. Stanley Baldwin, like Andrew Bonar Law, gave his ministers their lead, shifting support from one to another so as to further his own ends. The most important ministers involved in strategic policy were the Chancellors of the Exchequer and the Foreign Secretaries. The First Lords of the Admiralty were the most powerful service ministers, followed by the War Ministers, whose strength gradually declined. The Air Ministers, while initially the weakest, grew steadily in power. Most service ministers were influential politicians, although Lloyd George in 1921 and MacDonald in 1924 appointed weak ones.

No Cabinet could avoid strategic issues, but they were only one of its concerns. Few ministers attempted to influence the formulation of even critical decisions of grand strategy, such as the renewal of the Anglo-Japanese alliance in 1921, or of service policies, as in August 1919. Controversies on such matters were usually referred to arbitration by senior ministers, Cabinet committees or the Committee of Imperial Defence (CID). The Cabinet could initiate decisions, but rarely did so. Its involvement in strategic policy was sporadic, and it generally had less influence than the departments. Consequently, fundamental problems arose at the source of strategic decision making. The Cabinet alone could coordinate strategic policy, yet it rarely exercised this authority. Like an absentee landlord, it left the daily business of the estate to its stewards, the departments, who disagreed among themselves about the aims of the business. The formulation of strategic policy was dominated by two contradictory inter-departmental trends. As each department wanted to dominate limited aspects of strategic policy, it tended to become compartmentalised. As all these aspects were connected, strategic policy at the same time tended to become unified.

Each department believed that the issues for which it was responsible should be the central concern of strategic policy and that it should wield primary authority in that area. Thus, each sought autonomy, that is, control not only over its own area of responsibility but also over those portions of the concerns of other departments which impinged upon its own. For example, the Admiralty intended to run naval policy, which required power over part of RAF policy, naval aviation; financial policy, the size of naval estimates; and foreign policy, aspects of British relations with the main naval powers. These departmental areas of responsibility were interconnected. Since the services' programmes were expensive and linked to diplomacy, they concerned the Treasury and the Foreign Office. Aspects of the latters' policies, such as relations with France or reductions in spending, affected service policies. Thus, the Foreign Office and the Treasury indirectly influenced each other's responsibilities. Although complete departmental autonomy was impossible, all departments strove to attain it; and in doing so they sought to control strategic policy. They formulated their policies and influenced the evolution of strategic policy in a complex fashion.

Historians have argued that the Foreign Office's influence in the formulation of foreign policy declined in 1917 and remained weak throughout the 1920s, especially between 1919 and 1922.[1] While containing a kernel of truth, this view is distorted. This issue has two aspects: the influence upon foreign policy of the permanent officials of the Foreign Office (as opposed to that of the Foreign Secretary) and of the department itself. As regards the first, in the prewar era these officials had significantly affected the formulation of foreign policy for only a brief period. 1906–12. During 1919–22 their influence was small, owing primarily to the tangled relationship between them, Lloyd George and Lord Curzon. The Prime Minister was fascinated by foreign policy. The Foreign Office and Curzon disliked him and resented his involvement.[2] Yet on all strategic issues outside the Middle East, such as the Japanese alliance, Curzon and Lloyd George shared similar views, whilst Curzon rejected those of his officials. The latter could not hope to override the opinions of both the Prime Minister and the Foreign Secretary. However, after 1922 these officials increasingly shaped the formulation of foreign policy.

Even in the prewar heyday of the Foreign Office, the Cabinet and other departments had influenced the formulation of foreign policy. Postwar Cabinets were entitled to question the proposals of the Foreign Office in exactly the same way as they did those of any department. Particularly during 1919–22 other departments challenged Foreign Office policies, but the latter interfered just as much in their affairs. This reciprocal interference was inevitable, since disputes often concerned matters of strategic policy which were of inter-departmental concern. Thus, during 1920 troops were committed to untenable positions in the Caucasus. The War Office had a legitimate right to influence this matter, which was as much one of army as of foreign policy. In any case, between the armistice and September 1919 the Foreign Office had little influence in the formulation of foreign policy. It became increasingly influential when Curzon became Foreign Secretary and after October 1922 it became once more the most powerful department involved in foreign policy. By 1925 it had also gained a decisive influence over strategic policy.

During the 1920s the Foreign Secretaries had far more influence than other ministers over the formulation of their department's policies. However, they could dominate only a few such issues at any one time. Subject to their inclinations, foreign policy was shaped by the permanent officials: the permanent under-secretaries Charles Hardinge (to December 1920), Eyre Crowe (December 1920 to

April 1925) and William Tyrrell (after April 1925); the deputy or assistant under-secretaries, including Crowe, Tyrrell and Victor Wellesley; and by several departments, like the Central Department. Between 1919 and 1924 the Foreign Office consciously avoided any involvement in service policies. It did not even seek to influence the fundamental reconsiderations of these issues in summer 1919 and spring 1922, despite their effect upon diplomacy. Conversely, between 1925 and 1928 the Foreign Office decisively supported radical changes in strategic policy, simply to prevent the services from hampering foreign policy, just as it sought to do in the 1930s, if then in the opposite direction.

The Treasury has been considered the dominant influence on service policies between 1919 and 1931.[3] This misleading view hampers any understanding of strategic policy during the 1920s. The Treasury sought to become what Otto Niemayer called 'the central Department to view expenditure *as a whole*'; to have the decisive departmental voice in determining the government's priorities, to act as the government's general staff.[4] It always wished to control strategic policy and regarded the services as extravagant, describing their proposals as 'necessarily coloured by the prejudices of a lifetime', like those of a 'habitual toper' about the 'minimum cellar which it is reasonable to keep'.[5] The Treasury's clash with the services shaped the evolution of strategic policy. Yet until 1925 the Treasury did not dominate strategic policy or all the services. It gained control over all their estimates only by 1926 and over their policies by 1928. The Treasury's gradual rise to power constituted a decisive trend in strategic policy, yet its crucial victories did not occur until 1925, nor its final ones until 1928, and it won these battles only because of support from the Cabinet and the Foreign Office. The limitations on the Treasury's power influenced strategic policy as much as did its strength.

All the Chancellors influenced the Treasury's approach to budgetary issues, but only Winston Churchill among them did so on strategic ones. The most important influence on Treasury policy was its permanent secretary after September 1919, Nicholas Warren Fisher, a skillful bureaucratic politician. One of his favourite techniques was to set up committees of public figures rather than ministers to recommend cuts in spending. Another was deliberately to demand larger departmental economies than he expected to receive, so as to improve the Treasury's bargaining position.[6] Warren Fisher was a blunt and unbalanced man; at least once he almost suffered a nervous breakdown.[7] Complications arose from his lack of expertise in financial and service issues and from what he later called the Treasury's 'bizarre' division into three almost autonomous branches.[8] Niemayer, the chief of the Finance Branch, ran financial policy whilst George Barstow, the chief of the Supply Services Branch, dominated the Treasury's views on service issues. Barstow had an extraordinarily piercing mind but, like Warren Fisher's, his strategic judgements were often eccentric.

None of the services was as powerful as the Treasury or the Foreign Office, yet they all had real strengths, particularly the Admiralty. Their failure to establish their policies was partly due to their own political errors. The service departments had similar structures of decision making. Few ministers, Churchill being the notable exception, significantly influenced the formulation of their departments' policies. Each service had its own chief: the chief of the naval staff, CNS; the chief of the imperial general staff, CIGS; and the chief of the air staff, CAS. Each had a corporate decision making body, including ministers, service chiefs and other senior personnel: the Admiralty Board, the Army Council and the Air Council. The Board regularly determined policy, the Army Council did so to a lesser degree while the Air Council had little effect on RAF policy. Each service had functional branches for personnel and material and civilian elements for administration. The service chiefs and their staffs had the greatest influence over their services' policies.[9]

Of the two CNS of this period, Western Wemyss (to November 1919) was in many ways superior. He was an able strategist and one of the few admirals with the slightest understanding of politics. Despite this, his hold on the Admiralty was tenuous and his successor was a more effective departmental representative. David Beatty (CNS from November 1919) was a formidable, if arrogant and politically naive, spokesman for the Admiralty. He was not an original strategist and did not single-handedly create naval policy. He defined problems and let the naval staff, especially its 'Plans Division', formulate the solutions. The Admiralty's proposals were always exceptionally large and expensive, and it did not overstate them simply for bargaining purposes. When the Admiralty had no choice but to reduce its demands, it did so, but it always demanded what it thought it needed and wanted almost all that it demanded. It took an extraordinary line regarding its authority: that it and not the Cabinet should control naval policy. It often gave the Cabinet a choice between three alternatives: to accept the Admiralty's proposals, to replace the Board, or to state publicly that Britain would accept maritime inferiority to other powers. This last alternative was politically inconceivable. Contrary to Captain Roskill's assertions, Beatty and the Board often threatened to resign if their demands were not met.[10]

This uncompromising stance sustained the Admiralty through some difficult situations, but it finally alienated the Cabinet. Lord Salisbury, for example, disparaged the Admiralty's 'remarkable attitude'. Sailors 'are splendid people, but their notion of an argument closely resembles an order from the quarter-deck, and it puts them off if everybody does not fall in with it.'[11] This view reflected a common perception which ultimately crippled the Admiralty. Moreover, its attitude provoked a virulent conflict with the Treasury, that other department which wished to be the government's chief advisor on strategic policy. Warren Fisher believed that the Admiralty's claims for control over naval policy meant the 'negation of government': 'that in all things appertaining to the Naval Service of this country the final authority is not H.M. Government but the Board of Admiralty', that the Board 'are not the servants but the masters of Government'. The Treasury often hoped that the Board would resign for, as Barstow argued, only thus 'can the Govt. ever hope to control these unruly boys in blue'.[12]

None of the three CIGSs of the 1920s—Henry Wilson (to February 1922), Lord Cavan (February 1922 to February 1926) and George Milne (after February 1926)—were strong or politically skillful departmental spokesmen. Wilson, despite his extraordinary intelligence, made some deadly errors. Cavan scarcely fought at all, although Milne was reasonably effective. None of them ever controlled the War Office as Beatty or Hugh Trenchard did their departments, while the general staff influenced policy less than did the air or naval staffs. There was less central control over policy within the War Office than in the other service departments. The War Office knew that it had political weaknesses, although this may in itself have been a self-fulfilling prophecy. Since the War Office believed that it was politically too weak to defend a strong policy, it rarely attempted to do so, and hence the army declined. Between 1919 and 1922 the other services overcame as many political problems as the army faced. A better political approach might equally have strengthened army policy.

There were two CASs during this period. Frederick Sykes (to

February 1919) was politically unrealistic but professionally able and far seeing. Hugh Trenchard (CAS from February 1919) dominated RAF policy in the 1920s, partly because most senior RAF officers were not particularly competent or forceful. Trenchard controlled the Air Ministry far more than his equivalents did their departments. He is commonly pictured as an inspiring but incoherent prophet, who won his victories through sheer animal energy and the guidance of more astute subordinates or superiors.[13] This view is erroneous. Although Trenchard was anything but articulate, he was a cunning and ruthless bureaucratic infighter. His experiences with political intrigue in 1918 had taught him not to fight unless he either had no choice or the potential rewards were great, but then to strike for the jugular. Trenchard's nose for opportunity led the RAF to grow at the older services' expense.

The need to settle the role of the recently established RAF dominated inter-service relations in the 1920s. Due to the resulting controversies, whenever the services came under pressure they attacked and weakened each other rather than forming a united front. However, the depth of these differences has been exaggerated. It is wrong to argue that the Cabinet and the older services misunderstood the value of airpower and constantly sought to abolish the RAF.[14] They were impressed by airpower. Only once did the politicians really consider abolishing the RAF. Most naval officers wished to end its role in naval aviation and between 1919 and 1922 the army wanted to take over the rest of the RAF, yet the older services just once seriously attempted to eliminate it. Otherwise they sought simply a guarantee that the RAF would meet their aviation requirements and at most demanded the creation of their own separate air units. However Trenchard may have construed these demands, they did not constitute attempts to eliminate the RAF. The abolition of that service was a political possibility only between December 1920 and December 1921. Nor is it correct to argue that Trenchard always refused to cooperate with the older services.[15] He reached some important compromises even with the army, and twice made offers which would have so enhanced the Admiralty's control over naval aviation as to meet virtuually all its legitimate complaints. The Admiralty rejected these offers because it wanted more, and received less, for which Trenchard can scarcely be blamed. The antagonisms between the services were not irreconcilable. However, the opportunities to reach a compromise which could have mitigated them were disregarded.

Several other bodies influenced strategic policy. The Colonial Office and the Indian authorities controlled substantial armed forces and shaped the composition of Imperial garrisons, but they had little effect on grand strategy. Conversely, the Dominions had small armed forces and declined to cooperate regularly in Imperial strategic planning. Yet their views affected the fate of service policies, especially by strengthening the Admiralty against the Treasury. The Dominions (or on their behalf, the Colonial Office) demanded consultation on, or sometimes even a veto over, major initiatives in Imperial foreign policy. Crowe protested that this would prevent Britain from 'moving hard or fast in any matter'. However, the nature of the Dominions role in Imperial strategy was not resolved during this period.[16]

A desire to retain the support of the Dominions shaped strategic policy. Britain realised that the Dominions mistrusted Japan and feared that the United States wanted to persuade them to follow the US lead. A crucial motive behind strategic policy during 1921 was Whitehall's desire to convince the Dominions that Britain alone could defend them against Japan, and thus defeat this American challenge to Britain's hold over the Dominions. The latter's irritation at British policy during the Chanak crisis reminded Whitehall of the need to retain their cooperation. In 1925 a strong official proponent of a British commitment to Europe argued that Britain could undertake a commitment only if it could carry the Dominions with it. 'Let us not forget Chanak. Mr. Lloyd George discovered to his cost what it means to move without the Dominions'.[17] Britain always sought Dominion support for its policy, but was rather less eager to let them shape it. Britain frequently acted on crucial matters without the Dominions' concurrence, as, for example, over the Locarno Pact.

Since most strategic problems were inter-departmental concerns, they could not be handled rationally unless some machinery of government coordinated the departments' policies. This machinery could take two forms. A defence ministry or another inter-departmental arrangement could link the policies of the services, or some variant of the prewar CID could correlate all the departments' policies on strategic issues.

In 1919 the War Office and Churchill, Minister for War and Air, sought a radical strengthening of this machinery. They favoured a defence ministry, while Churchill persuaded the services to establish the 'Inter Departmental Conferences', which were intended to coordinate their policies on a regular basis. During their short life, these conferences rationalised the command structure for the RAF units working with the older services. Under their auspices Trenchard and Wemyss also reached a provisional compromise which offered the Admiralty almost total control over naval aviation.[18] Finally, the general staff, hoping to establish the basis for a 'Joint Naval, Military and Air Staff', convinced the other services and the India Office to prepare a joint Cabinet paper to guide postwar strategic planning. The general staff's memorandum foreshadowed the later Chiefs of Staff Committee (COSC) Reviews.[19]

These proposals offered means to improve the quality of strategic decisions, yet they were rejected because of their links to politics. Churchill and the War Office advocated them in order to strengthen their own power over policy. Other elements in the government opposed them for precisely that reason. The Admiralty and the India Office destroyed the committee working on the strategic memorandum in response to the army's too obvious attempts to dominate their planning. The Admiralty wrecked the 'Inter Departmental Conferences' because Wemyss's subordinates rejected any compromise over naval aviation.[20] Finally, the idea of a defence ministry was particularly controversial. Churchill wished to use such a ministry to establish control over all the services, while he and Wilson believed that it would let them siphon off naval estimates for their own purposes. Lloyd George, while sympathetic, noted that a defence ministry could be established only if the powerful First Lord, Walter Long, was to resign.[21] Wilson regarded this as a hint that Lloyd George wanted to deal with Long so as to establish a defence ministry. Wilson found a means to this end by manipulating the Admiralty's feuding. Beatty, not yet CNS, loathed Long and Wemyss.[22] In an odd combination of political intrigue and naïveté, Beatty told Wilson that he supported the idea of a defence ministry and believed that were the Board to be asked its opinion, only Long and Wemyss would oppose it. Wilson recommended Beatty's 'wise' suggestion to Lloyd George, emphasising its similarity to the latter's procedure in replacing William Robertson by Wilson as CIGS in 1917. In other words, if Lloyd George wished to act, Beatty would back an attack against Long. Beatty, whom Wilson believed was suffering from a 'swollen head', supported a grave challenge to the Admiralty's independence. Ironically, Wilson's own actions threatened the independence of the War Office, for Churchill would have used a defence ministry to strengthen his hold over army policy.[23] However, Lloyd George had his own interests in mind. He may not have wanted to give any minister, let alone Churchill, such power over policy and patronage. He certainly feared a battle with Long. Although Lloyd George recognised the administrative advantages of a defence ministry, he rejected the idea.[24]

The abandonment of these proposals of 1919 was unfortunate. They had offered a practical way to assist in the formulation of a systematic strategic policy. They would have established a different balance of power in that process, which might have strengthened the services. Although various individuals intermittently revived the idea of a defence ministry or of the 'Inter Departmental Conferences', the government never again seriously entertained such radical proposals. Instead, it established its machinery for strategic decision making around the CID.[25]

This development was linked to Maurice Hankey, the secretary to the Cabinet and the CID. Although Hankey is invariably described as a man of influence, his sway over strategic policy during the 1920s cannot be taken for granted.[26] He did influence some decisions, but much less than did the permanent secretaries, the service chiefs or officials like Barstow and Wellesley. Hankey's greatest importance lay in his efforts after 1922 to improve the machinery for the integration of defence policy. Despite his reputation as a friend of the services, he often supported improvements which were integrally related to the Treasury's attacks on the services.[27] Hankey influenced the development of the CID more than any other man during the 1920s, and his predilections also shaped its characteristic failings. He believed that the CID system could develop only at the tempo of inter-departmental concensus, a sure prescription for delay. He held that it could function effectively only if the Prime Minister 'is known to be in charge'. The 'P.M. . . . must always be top dog and keep the rein in his hands'. However, as no Prime Minister of the 1920s wished to become 'top dog' of the CID, this became primarily another body in which the departments pursued their differences. The CID was sometimes a forum for strategic discussions, but never the centre of strategic decisions. Lord Haldane truthfully stated that it was 'confined to what are really masses of detail'.[28]

During the 1920s the CID system was, however, strengthened. By 1920 all the services wanted a committee of their chiefs to advise the CID on strategic issues and, of course, to improve their positions against the government and each other. It was probably for this reason that Lloyd George rejected the idea.[29] A prototype of the COSC first met during the Chanak crisis, when Trenchard and Beatty opposed Cavan's operational assessment, while Lloyd George's policy hinged on the adoption of their views. Hence, the Cabinet ordered the service chiefs to present a collective opinion on Britain's operational position in Turkey.[30] This was a practical necessity, yet Lloyd George's primary concern was to have Beatty and Trenchard overawe Cavan so that the services would offer that advice which the Prime Minister wished to hear. This foreshadowed much of the COSC's own history. In 1923, on the recommendation of the Salisbury Committee, the COSC was formed to provide collective advice on strategic issues. However, until 1926 it remained just another forum for inter-service squabbles. The Salisbury Committee also recommended that the CID should more thoroughly coordinate the departments' strategic policies. By 1926 it began to do so.

Between 1919 and 1925 this machinery of government was not an independent factor in the formulation of strategic policy, nor did it consistently resolve important problems. Although no such machinery can guarantee good decisions, the weaknesses in the CID system contributed to some flawed ones. However, by 1926 the CID and the COSC finally began to analyse strategic policy systematically. By this time the Treasury was able to turn that development to its advantage.

As no central authority regulated the formulation of strategic policy, its evolution followed an unsteady course. A kaleidoscopic range of departmental and political coalitions made specific decisions. These were shaped by the pursuit of individual interests, by misunderstandings of important issues, by the effect of personalities and the mistrust between them. Thus, in 1920 Wilson held that Lloyd George's Russian policy stemmed from the fact that the Prime Minister was a 'traitor'. Conversely, Beatty believed that the army's inability to hold the Caucasus arose from some 'deep laid plot' by Churchill and Wilson, who were 'out to curry favour with some party, Labour I suppose'. Barstow later stated that those members of Baldwin's first Cabinet who were 'not very stupid . . . are mostly knaves'.[31] The government derived a strategic policy from the cumulative effect of a series of uncoordinated decisions. By the nature of the issues at stake a strategic policy would necessarily emerge, but the government formulated it almost by accident rather than by deliberation. It did not adopt what Haldane called a 'first principles' approach, which led to 'a want of grip in our general ideas of strategy'.[32] The government did not start by defining a strategic policy on which to base all its subsequent decisions. It was slow even to form an explicit view of grand strategy. Only in 1924 did Britain really begin to do so, a task which was not completed until 1926.

This occurred because British governments traditionally preferred to deal with problems as they arose, and during the 1920s there were no overriding threats to Britain. Any grand strategy would necessarily be speculative, an approach which Whitehall disliked. In 1920 the Foreign Office sought to avoid departmental responsibility for advising on Britain's strategic responsibilities since these 'depend so entirely upon the future direction of British policy that it would be dangerous for us to make any forecast'.[33] In 1924 Cavan opposed 'wasting' the COSC's time in making 'elaborate plans for war against hypothetical enemies'. Such preparations would be futile

. . .without answers to the following questions:
(1) Who will be our allies?
(2) Who will be allied to our enemy?
We never fight our wars alone and Europe is not even grouped yet; it is too early to decide upon which side we shall be in the next great war.[34]

Moreover, Britain's system for strategic decision making was loaded against the formulation of an explicit grand strategy. Until 1925 no one had both the interest and the influence to draft such a strategy. The Cabinet and the Treasury were not concerned with such questions. The Foreign Office was unwilling to expose its own policy to challenge, which would occur should an inter-departmental strategy be formulated. In any case, it was indifferent to service policies: as Austen Chamberlain said, the less his department knew about their war plans, the better.[35] Further, until 1926 one or another of the services always blocked the formulation of any grand strategy as not being in its own interests. Indeed, every suggestion for this purpose—whether by Trenchard about a study of a war with Afghanistan, by Beatty of one with Japan, or by Cavan regarding the value of a French alliance for Britain's position in the Mediterranean—was intended precisely to further the aims of one against the others. In 1919 the Admiralty destroyed the committee set up to devise a strategic memorandum because the War Office proposed to rule out the United States as a potential threat. In 1924 the War Office hindered the development of inter-service strategic planning while the Air Ministry blocked the only suggestion that the COSC should present an assessment for the government's debate about European security.[36]

These failures led to problems which no one perceived more clearly than Wilson. In 1919 he noted that because:

> we soldiers are not informed of the high policy of the Government nor of how much money we may have our military problem is nearly insoluable [sic]. We have therefore, as we did before the war, taken on ourselves to decide on high policy, and are pegging away at putting ourselves in a military position to ensure and to enforce that policy if need be.[37]

Two years later he argued that the War Office could not

> make plans which will stand the test of war, because it is impossible to consider war in the abstract. We are therefore reduced . . . to having to select our own enemies without even the approval of the Foreign Office, otherwise we shall be making an army fit to fight France and suddenly finding that we were fighting the Afghans, or we shall be making a naval programme fit to fight the Japanese, and suddenly finding that we are at war with America.[38]

Without an agreed grand strategy, each department adopted its own, each emphasising its own interests at the expense of those of the rest. Since the departments did not correlate their ideas they could not coordinate their actions.

In 1922 Wilson delivered a prescient indictment of the government's approach to the formulation of strategic policy. He noted that

> it is the custom of successive Governments to decide on Policy without sufficiently considering whether they possess the power and force to carry it into execution . . . if our great problems are treated in this manner it is not possible . . . to supply . . . an instrument capable of carrying out the Imperial policy.
>
> If . . . High Policy ignores High Strategy and . . . High Strategy is ignorant of High Policy then . . . the lessons and losses of the late war and the present peace will all have been in vain and our terrible experiences will be repeated in the not distant future.[39]

Yet whatever mistakes were made in strategic policy during the 1920s, Britain did have one; it had no other choice. Historians have not fully appreciated this point. One scholar, Anne Orde, has even argued that, excluding East Asia, there was little connection between Britain's service and foreign policies during this period.[40] In fact, only by examining the links between service, financial and foreign policies can one understand the nature of these individual matters. The relationship between them provided the foundation for strategic policy. Historians have misunderstood this relationship because of their mechanistic use of two concepts—'Treasury control' and the 'ten-year rule'.

2 'Treasury Control' and the 'Ten-Year Rule', 1919–24

Historians have agreed that during the 1920s service policies were always dominated by 'Treasury control' and the 'ten-year rule'.[1] They have assumed that the Treasury completely controlled service estimates while the government enforced a two-part formula which prevented the services from preparing for a great war before the end of a ten-year period. Unfortunately, scholars have distorted the nature of these factors and misconstrued the dynamics in strategic policy. These factors were interconnected, since the Treasury's power over the services did depend on the effect of the 'ten-year rule'. Whereas historians have assumed that 'Treasury control' was strong because the 'ten-year rule' was enforced, in fact, between 1919 and 1924 Treasury control was weak because the latter was not applied.

This rule was only one of several principles which Whitehall used to guide its strategic policy. Others included 'balanced budgets', the naval 'one power standard' and the RAF standard of equality in first-line aircraft with the largest 'Independent Striking Force' in Europe. Writers have mistaken the nature and role of these principles by failing to realise that they had variable meanings and effects.[2] These principles were not precise blueprints for action: the one power standard did not define how many battleships Britain needed, nor did balanced budgets indicate any specific level of spending. What these principles did was provide means to calculate requirements like the size of the navy or of expenditure. They did not work in harmony; indeed, these principles often conflicted. The expenditure required to honour the services' standards might wreck balanced budgets: the economies required by the latter might compromise the former. These principles were political tools to further a department's policies. Their meaning was ambiguous and they were interpreted in different ways by the various departments. These were not easy to apply, nor did they command unanimous respect.

Barstow dismissed the services' 'formulae' as being 'merely devices to enable people to dispense with thought', which were always abandoned whenever they became 'inconvenient'. The government should not become 'slaves to a formula', by which Barstow meant the one power standard rather than balanced budgets.[3] The Treasury opposed the services' principles simply because of their political effect. For example, the Admiralty used the one power standard to defend all its proposals, while one of the army's weaknesses was that no such principles bolstered its policies. Since these principles lent support to the aims of one part of the government against the rest, the struggle to establish and interpret them shaped the formulation of strategic policy. The 'ten-year rule' was a more complex subject than historians have appreciated. It was defined in different ways to suit the interests of the various elements in the government. Its meaning was always reinterpreted after the fact whenever that was convenient in order to justify changes in strategic policy which were desired for other reasons. The effect of the 'ten-year rule' differed widely between 1919 and 1931. It was not always a powerful tool, nor even always the Treasury's tool.

In 1919 Warren Fisher summarised opinions which would become the Treasury's view of service policies for the next decade:

> the scale of our defences in personnel and material should be less than before the war; the cost . . . might be somewhat higher . . . owing to improved pay and the rise in prices. The country need not lose the advantage of the naval and military lessons gained in the War, but to ensure that and to keep that experience up to date should be possible for a reasonable outlay; and instead of being bled white we should be safe to re-establish our reserve of wealth to be available if trouble hereafter recurs.[4]

The Treasury denied that British security was under threat. It wanted Britain to have the smallest possible regular forces and to rely on reserves for expansion when that should become necessary. It preferred the most anodyne of principles to calculate military strength: that of comparing the forces needed for defence against 'any *reasonably probable* potential risk' with such forces as 'we can afford'. An example of the imprecision of all such principles is the fact that Admiralty Richmond later stated that the use of a similar formula, 'any reasonably probable risk', would have let the navy fully meet Britain's maritime needs.[5] In spring 1919 the Treasury held that Britain could 'afford' service estimates of only £110 000 000, about 20 per cent less than its real expenditure of 1914. Then, until March 1922, it adopted the Cabinet's figure of £135 000 000. Once service estimates were reduced to £135 000 000, however, the Treasury again sought to cut them to £110 000 000 or, given changes in prices, to about 10 per cent less than those of 1914.

The Treasury demanded much from the services. Its ability to enforce these demands was limited. This hinged on the nature of the two pillars of Treasury control: its administrative and budgetary power. In 1919 the Treasury sought greater administrative control over the civilian elements within the service departments and enhanced power for these elements over the latters' policies. In the end, the Treasury acquired little control over these elements but did increase their power within their departments.[6] This indirectly helped the Treasury since these elements did strive to restrain service spending. However, the core of the Treasury's strength was its position in the formation of budgets and estimates. It was formally entitled to question any department's spending and to delay or refuse authorisation for specific expenditures even after estimates had been approved. These financial means of control would be formidable if the Cabinet backed the Treasury, but not without that help. The Treasury could control the services only if the Cabinet let it do so. Since the Cabinet did not do so between 1919 and 1924, Treasury control over the services was weak.

Between 1919 and 1921 the Treasury did not control any of the services; during 1922 to 1925 it did not control them all. This was because the 'ten-year rule' was not what historians have thought it to be. Indeed, this term did not even come into common usage until after that principle was revoked, and appears to have been used only once before 1933. Between 1919 and 1924 this principle was usually called something like 'the decision of 1919 that the British Empire will not be engaged in any great war during the next ten years', and between 1925 and 1933 the ten-year 'period', 'principle' or 'assumption'.[7] Since the term 'ten-year rule' has acquired a loaded meaning, care must be taken with terminology so as to avoid confusion. Henceforth, this term will refer only to the historiographical concept of that name. The phrase 'August 1919 principles' will indicate the total of the government's strategic decisions of August 1919 while the term 'ten-year period' will mean the various interpretations of the decision of 15 August that 'the British Empire will not be engaged in any great war during the next ten years'. According to this terminology, the 'ten-year rule' is one interpretation of the meaning of the 'ten-year period'. That period was defined in many other ways between 1919 and 1928 and originated as one of the August 1919 principles. These principles were not enforced on the services until March 1922. Moreover, only in 1925 did the ten-year period begin to affect the services in the way which scholars have believed that it always did, and only then did the Treasury begin to control all the services.

In early 1919 the Cabinet declined to establish any service policies until the peace conferences had clarified Britain's strategic position. Although by July many international problems remained, British statesmen assumed that a stable postwar order would soon emerge. The states which might wish to challenge that order, like Germany, would be too weak to do so for many years, while Britain also believed that a formidable coalition would underpin this settlement. Britain was still allied to Japan, the United States appeared to want a special relationship with Britain, while the British and American guarantees of French security could be expected to establish some cooperation between them. The government believed that Britain would remain secure during the foreseeable future.

The services shared these assumptions but demanded exceptionally strong forces to ensure them. The War Office wanted the army to be twice as large as in 1914, with 375 000 men, the RAF favoured 82 squadrons and 55 000 men, while the Admiralty advocated the world's largest navy, which it believed would be possible with a smaller one than in 1914. Until Anglo-American maritime relations were settled, however, the Admiralty demanded forces roughly equal to those of 1914 and larger than that of the United States Navy (USN). The services' proposals would have cost around £170–£190 000 000 per year, or 25 per cent–40 per cent more than real military spending in 1914. No Cabinet could have accepted these unnecessarily heavy demands. Consequently, the question was how Britain would define its postwar service policies. Churchill wanted to do so through a defence ministry, and Hankey through the CID.[8] However, a temporary alliance of convenience between the Prime Minister and the Treasury provided the final answer.

Lloyd George wished to dominate the formulation of all government policy as he had done in 1917–18 through the 'War Cabinet'. In January 1919 he told his Chancellor, Austen Chamberlain, that it would be a 'good thing' if they and their reliable colleagues, Bonar Law and Lord Milner, rather than the Cabinet itself, resolved any 'difficulties' between the Treasury and any department.[9] In

August 1919 this group, formalised in the Finance Committee, replaced the War Cabinet as the central policy making body on all important issues. Only through this means could Lloyd George control spending; the Treasury alone could not do so. In early 1919 the latter re-established its formal control over expenditure but in practice failed to limit that of any department. By July it noted that overspending was leading Britain toward a massive deficit and down the 'road to ruin'.[10] The Treasury sought to make the Cabinet cut all expenditure to fit its proposed 'normal year' budget, in which spending would equal about £740 000 000, with the services receiving £110 000 000.[11] As part of this process, the Treasury defined its own strategic policy.

Barstow gave Chamberlain two memoranda on service policies which he admitted would affect 'matters of high policy outside my province'. Barstow argued that British security would not be threatened for many years. Hence, the services' main concern should be Imperial policing and the maintenance of a framework for expansion against greater and later dangers. Modern weapons should replace more expensive traditional formations. Barstow held that the army needed the same manpower and real estimates as in 1914—184 500 soldiers and £58 000 000. Indian units would cover Britain's increased overseas commitments while aircraft and mechanised units would enable 'a small number of white troops to hold a considerable native population'. Britain was secure at sea although Japan and America might eventually become problems. Thus, economy and the need to avoid arms races should govern naval policy. With reluctance Barstow conceded that Britain required a 'solid block' of battleships. Yet aircraft could replace several kinds of warships whilst battleships were not necessary for duties like suppressing 'riotous niggers' in Jamaica. The navy needed about 66 per cent of the strength of 1914 and the 'Naval problem of the future' would be to establish a reserve manpower and warship system to allow 'the possibility of rapid expansion when danger threatens'.[12] Although Barstow wrote no memorandum specifically on the RAF and no doubt rejected its proposals, he emphasised the value of airpower. His desired level of service estimates cannot be determined, but probably exceeded £110 000 000. Thus, the service policies favoured by the Supply Service Branch may well have been more expensive than the 'normal' service estimates advocated by the Finance Branch. Barstow's analysis was an intelligent one and the Treasury retained it until 1932. His opinions also influenced the strategic decisions of summer 1919, as the Cabinet, the Treasury and Lloyd George combined to press the services in the same direction, towards reductions in their proposals.

In July Austen Chamberlain told the Cabinet that Lloyd George regarded £150 000 000 as being 'far too large' a sum for normal service estimates. This warning to the services was reinforced on 5 August, when the Cabinet correlated all its policies. After defining internal reform and reconstruction as the priorities, Lloyd George stated that if Britain's postwar military strength exceeded that of 1913 'people would say, either that the War had been a failure', or that Britain was 'preparing to fight an imaginary foe'.

> The Government must be prepared to take risks, just as the soldier had to take risks; and they must decide what risks they could best afford to take . . . the War Cabinet had to decide . . . not a matter of Naval or Military policy, but rather a question of foreign policy, or statecraft. That is, what provision in respect of our armed forces we must make for say, the next five to ten years. It was for the Government to say to their Military Advisors: "These are the risks which you have to provide against" and "This is the basis on which you must act" . . . In five or ten years it would be necessary to review the situation, but so far as external forces were concerned, he felt that risks could be taken.

The Cabinet in effect adopted several strategic axioms: that 'there would be no great European war for the next five to ten years', when Britain's chief concern would be Imperial policing; that service strengths approximating those of 1914, together with the RAF, would meet these needs; and that 'scientific weapons' should replace manpower in Imperial policing.

The Cabinet then considered how to define its actual service policies. Long and Churchill argued that these should be made only after the services had told the Cabinet how 'best and most economically' they could meet their obligations. Lloyd George retorted that the Cabinet or the War Cabinet, assisted by the CID, could define these policies 'It was not a question of deciding upon a policy for the next twenty years; perhaps for not as long as ten years; possibly only for five years'. Chamberlain suggested that the Finance Committee should present its 'considered opinion' on Britain's financial position. Churchill, scenting danger, demanded that this committee should consider only major issues, leaving each minister free to use his estimates as he saw fit. While Chamberlain and Lloyd George soothed his fears they offered no such guarantees. The Cabinet ordered the Admiralty, the War and the India Offices to prepare assessments of strategic developments during the next five to ten years. The Finance Committee meanwhile would examine questions involving 'large financial expenditure': that is, every question.[13]

Long and Churchill agreed that the services could assume that no great war would arise during the next five to ten years. Churchill had originated this formula and already enforced it on the RAF. Trenchard and Wilson favoured it because this would let them ignore the costly need to maintain forces simply for an imminent European war. Instead, they could concentrate on meeting immediate threats to Britain's Imperial position and to developing modern forces for the long term.[14] Long and Churchill also insisted that strategic requirements should govern service estimates: that Britain should first decide what the services must do and then give them enough money for the purpose. Under the pressure of these Cabinet discussions, the services radically readjusted their policies.[15] They assumed, however, that these would be settled only after the Cabinet had defined the nature of the services' duties over a lengthy period of peace.

Instead, Lloyd George took the lead in determining strategic policy and for three reasons. First, he learned that President Wilson's emmisary, Colonel Edward House, had proposed a means to resolve the fundamental problem in Anglo-American relations, their naval policies. Lloyd George accepted the core of these proposals, that the two powers would not treat the other's fleet as a threat, with one vital provision: that America would abandon its naval construction programmes.[16] Lloyd George wished to close quickly with this offer. He was unwilling to await the result of a lengthy Cabinet debate about strategic policy, especially since any discussion about naval issues would be divisive. Second, Lloyd George wanted immediate economies, particularly given growing criticisms in Parliament on that point.[17] Above all, he wanted to dominate any important decisions himself.

On 11 August, the first working day after the receipt of House's proposals, the Finance Committee decided that it alone could cut spending. It took drastic steps in that direction. It agreed that while the army's overseas commitments had risen since 1914, an expeditionary force was less necessary. The army should not prepare for war against Russia on the northwest frontier of India nor the navy against the US. Since 'serious' problems would arise with British public opinion should the USN be larger than the Royal Navy, London should approach Washington for a naval limitation agreement. The committee defined service estimates which, taking account of inflation and increased personnel costs, almost precisely equalled those of 1914: £60 000 000 for naval estimates and £75 000 000 for army and RAF estimates together. It ordered the services to make fresh estimates on some such lines as the following:

(1). . .that no great war is to be anticipated within the next ten years, although provision should be made for the possible expansion of trained units in case of an emergency arising.

(2). . .that their principal responsibility is the provision of sufficient forces to keep order in the United Kingdom, India and all British (other than self-governing) territory.

(3). . .in fulfilling these responsibilities the utmost should be made of air-power and other mechanical devices in order to save man power.[18]

On 15 August the Cabinet approved these recommendations with four amendments. It stated that £135 000 000 was a 'maximum figure' for service estimates. It emphasised that 'mechanical contrivances' should replace manpower for reasons of economy. It approved a variant of the ten-year proposal: 'It should be assumed, for forming revised Estimates, that the British Empire will not be engaged in any great war during the next ten years, and that no Expeditionary Force is required for that purpose'. Finally, the Cabinet said nothing about naval limitation but stated that 'No alteration should be made, without Cabinet authority, in the pre-war standard governing the size of the Navy'. This 160 per cent standard against the next largest fleet excluding the USN could, if interpreted strictly, leave the Royal Navy smaller than the USN. The Cabinet did not want that but equally did not wish the Admiralty to use the USN as a means to measure its own strength. Long and Churchill agreed to examine the problem on this basis.[19] Hankey claimed that Long accepted these principles while Churchill found 'cutting expenditure distasteful' and disliked being a 'War Minister without a war in prospect'. In fact, Churchill pressed these principles upon his services while Long rejected them as compromising maritime security.[20]

Scholars have regarded this as the central moment for service policies between 1919 and 1931. However, some have considered the Finance Committee's edict and others the Cabinet's decision to be the real 'ten-year rule'. Only J.K. MacDonald has noted that these bodies approved different principles.[21] Nonetheless, both defined the same general clauses: the ten-year period, the decisions that Britain's naval standard would not take account of the USN, that Imperial policing would be the services' primary role, the substitution of modern weapons for manpower and the £135 000 000 limit. Historians have, moreover, misunderstood the origins of these decisions. Only Roskill and MacDonald have sought to explain the issue. They have argued that in order to control naval policy, Lloyd George formulated a general strategic policy on the basis of a memorandum by Hankey. In fact, while naval issues were a main factor in these decisions, Lloyd George and the Treasury were also concerned with army and RAF ones. Hankey's memorandum said nothing about a ten-year period, a specific financial limit for the services or substitution, and his analysis was commonplace. Barstow and Churchill made equally influential recommendations which resembled the August 1919 principles more than did those of Hankey. Indeed, Sykes had earlier made proposals which were strikingly similar to the ten-year period.[22] The origin of these principles lay in Lloyd George's desire to control overall strategic policy, which he did by adopting a concensus which had emerged among decision makers.

Writers have assumed that these principles provided an unambiguous and authoritative basis for all service policies until 1932. Yet they have analysed neither the intentions behind nor the meaning of these principles. Brian Bond has noted that confusion later emerged around these points, but has not discussed what this indicates. Roskill has provided the standard explanation for the effect of these principles: that they automatically and immediately gave the Treasury 'the whiphand' over the services' policies. The evolution of strategic policy between 1919 and 1931 cannot be understood without a more careful analysis of these issues. Lloyd George and the Treasury had won the struggle to determine strategic policy. The government adopted views similar to those of the Treasury about service policies, although leaving them larger estimates than suited the 'normal year' budget. The Finance Committee had replaced the War Cabinet as the central policy making authority. Yet this committee's decisions were not intentionally controversial; rather, they were based on the Cabinet's views of 5

August and embodied Whitehall's strategic concensus. Nor did they define specific service policies. Instead, they simply offered guidelines to govern their formulation.

According to these decisions the Cabinet would have to authorise new service policies incorporating these principles. The services were to emphasise peacetime duties while retaining reserve elements for insurance purposes. The three services were to live on financial limits which had sustained but two in 1914. Even were that level maintained, the army, the navy or both would receive less than in 1914 or the RAF would disappear. On the basis of a figure of £60 000 000 the navy had already lost the equivalent of most of its prewar construction expenditure. Army and RAF estimates were not precisely defined, leaving Churchill to allocate as he chose £75 000 000 between them. These principles did not constitute a strategic policy but simply the basis for one. They were neither definite nor definitive, and controversy soon arose concerning their original purpose. Hankey stated in 1923 that the 'Cabinet's supposed decision that there would be no great war for ten years' had been intended only to guide the services in preparing their 1920–21 estimates but subsequently had 'been interpreted rather more widely than intended'. As Bond has noted, these principles were intended to have a wider effect than this.[23]

Yet the effect of these principles remained uncertain because they contained ambiguities around which debate swirled until 1926. This was particularly so because the ten-year period, the intellectual core of these principles, arose from an 'empirical' rather than a 'scientific' assessment.[24] The supposition of ten years of security was simply a guess, being, as Austen Chamberlain said of the 'rolling ten year rule' in 1928, 'merely a hypothesis for framing estimates'.[25] Subsequent circumstances might alter the period of time in which Britain believed that it could anticipate security. Moreover, if the services could not plan for a great war occurring before 1929, they were not forbidden to prepare either for a smaller war or to match the strength of other powers. Indeed, as W.S. Chalmers has noted, the services could exploit a 'loophole' in this formula, which every department interpreted in a legalistic fashion.[26] This could mean that each must be fully ready for major war in 1929—or that none could even begin such preparations until 1929, or until the Cabinet instructed it to do so.

By one definition the services could justify programmes for a small war or to match other powers before 1929, or for a great one in 1929. By the other they could do none of this until the Cabinet specifically authorised them to do so. Nor had any term been set to the duration of the ten-year period. This formula could even be defined to mean that the end of that period should always be ten years away, as the CID did in 1928. Virtually any programmes could be, and were, justified on that formula. The ten-year period ruled out only immediate and full-scale preparations for another great war before 1929, which no service intended to make. The only principle which could regulate the choice between these alternatives was the £135 000 000 limit. Yet that arbitrary figure might itself be amended up or down as a result of strategic or financial imperatives. The meaning of the August 1919 principles was open to debate; their effect would depend entirely on future developments. For these principles were based on several assumptions: that the peace conferences had established the world order, that 'peace reigned', that the empire was already secure and that an acceptable naval limitation agreement could be reached with Washington. Britain recognised that a gap existed between its intended military strength and that which might be needed to suppport its policies.[27] It did not regard this gap as important. The August 1919 principles were individually ambiguous. They were established on the foundations of an overly optimistic strategic assessment and a momentary turn in the balance of power within the government. Changes in Whitehall or the world could alter the interpretation and the application of these principles. Such changes quickly occurred.

In autumn 1919 the Finance Committee and the Treasury together pressed for service economies. The Treasury, seeking above all else to enforce its normal year budget, implied that even £135 000 000 was too much for service expenditure.[28] However, its resurgence in power hinged on the politicians' support. This power was broken in November 1919, when the Finance Committee rejected the 'normal year' budget because that would force Britain to abandon any social reform programmes. Consequently, Chamberlain publically stated that the 'normal year' budget could not be enforced until 1922. The Treasury increased that budget by £290 000 000 to £1 029 000 000 and doubled the level of its proposed 1920–21 budget.[29] This decline in financial pressure strengthened the services against the Treasury which, to its dismay, failed to affect their 1920–21 estimates.

Further, the assumptions underlying the August 1919 principles proved unrealistic. The US refused to enter naval negotiations, the world remained unstable and Britain faced extraordinary operational problems in Ireland and the Middle East. Britain discovered the size of the gap between its strength and its commitments. The services could scarcely be cut to normal levels when conditions were abnormal. These circumstances brought the August 1919 principles into question. Trenchard wanted the services to 'force' the Cabinet to redefine 'the Imperial policy which is the basis of our preparations'.[30] The other services ignored this suggestion for that policy had become academic; the government did not enforce it. The August 1919 principles created no greater changes in service policies than the Cabinet's earlier discussions had already caused, and the services interpreted these principles to suit their own interests. The RAF alone accepted them all, precisely because they did so. The army denied that 'mechanical devices' could replace manpower. The navy refused to reduce its strength until Anglo-American relations were settled, while the announcement of the one power standard turned the USN into the guide for British naval strength. Every service opposed the £135 000 000 limit. The Admiralty declined to accept less than £75 000 000 per year (that is, claiming its prewar construction expenditure) unless the Cabinet would publically accept naval inferiority to the US. The Cabinet approved 'normal' army and RAF estimates of £62 000 000 and £15 000 000, which exceeded their August 1919 level by £2 000 000.[31]

The services refused to subordinate their needs to those of the Treasury. Wilson, for example, accepted the August 1919 principles in abstract, but doubted that 'the allotments of an arbitrary sum' could support his service's requirements. The 'cart was before the horse all through' the August 1919 decisions: until Britain defined what the services should do, it could not very well determine their estimates.[32] However, in 1920–21 neither the August 1919 principles nor any guidelines at all were enforced on the services. In particular, the government remained uncertain about the ten-year period. Chamberlain and the Finance Committee used the 'five to ten years' formula while Long adopted the term 'prolonged peace' rather than 'ten years peace'.[33] The vaguer or smaller this period, the less it would affect the services. The latter also exploited the ambiguities in this principle. As Barstow noted, they interpreted the decision 'that they need not expect a great War for the next ten years as an announcement that a War *will* take place in ten years time'.[34] Until

1922 Treasury control and the ten-year period remained negligible factors in strategic policy.

During 1921 this situation began to change. The Treasury pressed the services to live on £135 000 000 in 1922–23 and again cooperated with Lloyd George against their spending.[35] Meanwhile, the preconditions for the August 1919 principles became established. Operational commitments declined while the international situation appeared to improve. The RAF's control of Iraq embodied substitution by 'mechanical devices' and a naval limitation agreement was achieved. Finally, the ten-year period resurfaced in two forms. The Treasury and its political allies argued that this period should let Britain defer for years to come considerable expenditure on service programmes against major threats. Trenchard and Beatty retorted that this period justified current spending on such programmes. Arthur Balfour managed to maintain both these interpretations at the same time.

In March 1922 the Cabinet established a new strategic policy and finally brought the August 1919 principles into effect by defining specific policies for the services. The Cabinet again assumed that Britain would be secure in a stable world during the foreseeable future. In these circumstances, its strategic views were identical to those of August 1919. Although all the August 1919 principles had been imposed on the services, however, ambiguities remained at the heart of strategic policy. The ten-year period, which was intended to govern the services' long term programmes, was still open to conflicting interpretations. Moreover, these decisions of 1922 sparked off two trends in strategic policy, one which supported the Treasury and one which crippled it. This conflict was not resolved until 1925.

The Treasury was involved in but did not determine the decisions of 1922, which were dominated by the politicians. However, these decisions reduced service estimates to £135 000 000, achieving the Treasury's basic aim. In 1922 it finally began to assert its control over service spending and sought to curb their policies. It completely controlled army estimates and cut global service spending. Yet this was a limited victory. Most of these cuts did not affect real service spending and all the real reductions came from the army. Between 1922 and 1925 RAF estimates continually and dramatically increased while the real funds available to support naval policy rose notably. This occurred because the Treasury was losing the decisive battle in strategic policy. It could not control the programmes of two services. In 1921–22 Lloyd George's government approved three major rearmament programmes against other powers: the Home Defence Air Force (HDAF) programme against France, the Singapore base and the oil-fuel ones against Japan. Baldwin's first government approved current expenditures on these programmes and on a naval replacement one directed against Japan. MacDonald's Cabinet retained them all except the Singapore base, which Baldwin's second government restored in November 1924. These programmes were not overly expensive between 1923 and 1925 but at their approved rate and scale they would cause service estimates to rise by £30 000 000 per year after 1925.

The Treasury could not block these programmes because they were determined by internal and international developments beyond its control. Three governments held office between November 1922 and November 1924. After the Chanak and Ruhr crises they believed that Britain's future security could not simply be assumed and they regarded other powers as potential threats. Consequently, the government challenged the ten-year formula. In November 1922 Beatty reminded the CID that despite that assumption, Britain had barely avoided a war with Turkey, while Crowe stated that the Foreign Office could not predict whether Britain would be secure after 1925.[36] The CID thereafter supported the navy's programmes against the Treasury. In 1923 Beatty complained to the Salisbury Committee that 'everything we asked for which involved money . . . which we could do without in the next ten years was to be avoided'. Salisbury, who had never before heard of that ruling, replied significantly, 'But we are rather shortening that now'.[37]

During 1923–24 the ten-year period was a minor influence in strategic policy. A small factor in the army's decline was that Cavan agreed it should not even begin to prepare until 1929 for a major war. Conversely, Beatty and Trenchard used this principle as one weapon against the Treasury and not the other way round. They denied that this ruling should govern their programmes: Beatty for example noted that it was 'in a sense incompatible' with the one power standard.[38] While willing to reduce spending on ancillary programmes to suit the ten-year period, these services believed that their standards should override it on any major issues. Indeed, they used that period to govern the rate of completion for the programmes they were authorised to undertake against other powers. 1929 was a good target for that purpose, since by 1923 that date was but six years away. The closer and more definite that target, the more they could spend on these programmes. Between December 1922 and

December 1924 the Admiralty and the Air Ministry turned the ten-year period against the Treasury. The artificial deadline of 1929 had originally been selected to curb service spending; by 1923, to the Treasury's horror, this deadline began to encourage it.

The Treasury sought to alter this situation by increasing its means of financial control over the services. None of these attempts were successful because they could not redress the Treasury's real weakness: that so long as the Cabinet allowed these services to rearm, the Treasury could not control their estimates. The Treasury needed another means to establish its control over them. Barstow grasped a crucial point: that it could do so by forcing a reinterpretation of the ten-year period. In 1919 Lloyd George had stated that this period should be reconsidered periodically. Between 1921 and 1924 Barstow resurrected this view, arguing that it would be 'a good plan to revise the Cabinet decision of 1919 from time to time' and to rule 'that a Great War is no nearer now than it was in 1919, i.e. still 10 years off'. Then he raised the decisive point: 'But could such a decision be given?'[39] This question was not posed to the Cabinet until November 1924. Only when it was answered in the affirmitive could the Treasury finally begin to use the ten-year rule to control the services.

During the 1920s Britain needed some means to select its financial priorities, some principles to guide its strategic policy and some department to regulate its aims and means *'as a whole'*.[40] Treasury control over the services ultimately went to extremes but in principle it was necessary. Indeed, service policies became expensive and inefficient whenever that control did not exist. Moreover, the August 1919 principles in themselves could have led to an excellent strategic policy. The idea of completing military programmes over the course of ten years was eminently reasonable: no government could let the services prepare as though Britain was under imminent threat. Neither Treasury control nor the ten-year period was wrong in principle and they need not have created a poor strategic policy. The problem lay with their use in practice. Treasury control and the ten-year rule ultimately hampered the services, but simply because this suited the Cabinet's ends.

However, in 1919–24 neither of these factors had much effect on strategic policy. The Treasury did not control the services. The August 1919 principles shaped strategic policy but the ten-year period did not. For that matter, even between 1928 and 1931 the ten-year rule was no more important an element in the Treasury's arguments than were international developments such as the Geneva Disarmament Conference and internal ones like Britain's financial predicament.[41] Treasury control and the ten-year rule were not enforced on army policy until 1922–23 and on RAF and naval policies until 1925–26. Since historians have misunderstood these matters, they have misinterpreted those which did decide the evolution of strategic policy during the 1920s.

3 The Elements of Strategic Policy, 1919–26

The purpose of strategic policy was to use Britain's military, diplomatic and economic power in order to preserve the British Empire. Although some statesmen had a premonition of Imperial decline, the psychological basis for strategic policy was an unshaken confidence that Britain could preserve the Empire.[1] Nor, even considering the nature and the consequences of Britain's decline in power, were statesmen wrong to believe this. Of course, the economic effects of the great war and trends like rising nationalism in its colonies, were eroding the foundations of Britain's strength. Nonetheless it remained among the greatest economic and industrial nations on earth, while its military and diplomatic power countered every immediate threat to its existence. Despite the potential gap between its strength and commitments, Britain remained a formidable power. Britain's dilemma of the 1930s, of a single-handed war against several states, does not demonstrate that its relative strength had fallen so far that it could no longer defend its empire. This situation would have threatened Britain even at the peak of its power; it had always faced grave perils whenever it fought several states by itself. The dilemma of the 1930s stemmed not so much from the decline of British power as from the failure of its diplomacy to forestall the rise of a specific international environment. This deadly predicament need not have arisen and different strategic decisions could have countered the effects of Britain's decline. During the 1920s Britain's absolute power gave it a real chance to preserve the British Empire for a far longer period than it actually did survive.

The formulation of strategic policy was complicated by an unstable relationship between the imperatives of foreign, financial and service policies. Service estimates and programmes depended, respectively, on financial and foreign policies. Financial policy had a constant and foreign policy a variable effect on the services. The makers of financial policy always opposed costly service programmes while those who determined foreign policy might demand more or less military strength than existed at any particular moment. The imperatives of foreign and financial policies were as likely to conflict as to coincide over service ones. Foreign policy might require rearmament programmes which financial policy would oppose, or foreign and financial policy makers might combine against such programmes.

Britain wanted armed forces which could maintain its security and support its diplomacy. It believed that military spending or the maintenance of forces beyond the minimum necessary would harm the economy and alarm other powers, thus causing developments which might lead to another great war. Britain thought that its security could be threatened if its armed forces were too large or too small. There were two margins in strategic policy: one which regulated the maximum armed force which Britain could maintain and one which determined the minimum force which Britain should maintain. Financial policy dictated the level of the upper and foreign policy that of the lower margin. During the 1920s the debate in strategic policy was over this lower margin. Financial policy makers demanded the minimum service spending but the exigencies of foreign policy alone defined Britain's minimum military needs. Whenever the imperatives of foreign policy supported those of financial policy, then service policies declined. Whenever these imperatives supported service policies, then the fortunes of the latter rose. Foreign policy determined the answer to the question of strategic policy: how to balance the forces which Britain seemed to need with those which it appeared able to afford.

Many writers have assumed that during the 1920s financial consider-ations above all else shaped strategic policy.[2] This view is simplistic. Financial restraints obviously affected the services: the question is, to what degree. This did have some unfortunate consequences. In order to gain larger estimates the RAF had little choice but to try to replace elements of the older services, contributing to inter-service conflicts; Milne abandoned a progressive armoured policy because that could be financed only by sacrificing existing forces. Throughout much of the 1920s, however, the services had a great deal of money at their disposal while the Treasury found it hard to achieve its central aims: to have orthodox financial policy dominate all government concerns and, in particular, to balance all budgets. Although the Treasury's views have been disparaged, they stemmed from classical economic theory and were supported by the best contemporary economists. Thus, most economists favoured the 'tight money' policy of 1920 while John Keynes wanted it to be even tighter.[3] Until the late 1920s everyone accepted in principle the Treasury's central argument: that so as to spur Britain's recovery from the postwar recession, the burden of taxation on industry should be reduced by retrenching government spending.

Although the government purported to favour rigorous economy, it did not automatically adopt the Treasury's policy. It often wished to reduce unemployment by increasing the manufacture of military material. Although the Treasury disliked such proposals, Barstow conceded that during the current recession they would harm the economy no more than the dole. In 1922 several ministers, including Churchill, even favoured the ultimate heresy in the Treasury's eyes, the principle of a deficit budget. In practice these suggestions were close to the economic proposals of Keynes and others after 1927. Indeed, by 1925 William Bridgeman and Hankey justified such actions with a primitive variant of the idea of 'priming the pump': that increased orders for munitions would invigorate the arms industry and indirectly stimulate Britain's staple industries.[4] Yet the Treasury overcame these challenges and re-established its financial policy. Between 1919 and 1922 its main concern was to reduce government spending to fit the 'normal year' budget. It did so by 1922–23 and from 1924–25 to 1930 budgets were only marginally reduced each year. In 1923, just before Britain reached budgetary stability, Barstow reported that Neimayer was 'rather alarmed at the prospect of a Budget surplus which he will do his best to avoid!', because any surplus would encourage further extravagance.[5]

Throughout the 1920s real government spending was always more than twice that of 1914. The problem lay in the allocation of these revenues. Since 1914 two factors had gained weight in the budgetary balance: the heightened emphasis on social reform programmes and the need to carry the burden of war debts. The Cabinet and the Treasury respectively regarded social reform and the repayment of debts as having the first call on its funds. They disagreed over these priorities but neither could be achieved unless service estimates were restrained. Accounting for increased costs in wages and weapons, about £135 000 000 would have been needed to equal the services' real 1913–14 estimates. Their estimates ultimately fell about 20 per cent below this level and Britain spent far more on social reform and debt redemption than in 1914, relative to total expenditure. A fundamental trend in financial policy was to sacrifice service estimates to these priorities.

Statesmen thought that this step would actually strengthen Britain's strategic position. Their views were similar to the later doctrine that finance was the fourth arm of defence, although this argument was not explicitly adopted until 1926. The government regarded finance as a more important element of power than armed force. According to the Treasury, the great war had demonstrated the 'supreme importance of financial power as the basis of economic power, and of economic power as the base of military power'. Britain's victory had stemmed directly from six aspects of its prewar financial policy:

1. A substantial sinking fund.
2. Moderate taxation.
3 A sound currency.
4. Large private savings.
5. Highly organised financial markets.
6. Large foreign investments.

The markets and the foreign investments were the result of savings. The savings were increased by the sinking fund, and were not encroached upon by taxation because taxation was moderate. A sound currency was made possible by a sound budget and was a prerequisite condition for everything.

The Treasury conceded that the war had hampered this position but still argued that 'expenditure on armaments in excess of what is absolutely necessary would be highly injudicious', that it would wreck 'the financial recovery necessary before we can face another war'.[6] In accepting these arguments, decision makers misunderstood the relationship between economic strength and military power. They were also living in the past. If Britain's financial sector was the key to its position in the world economic order before 1914, the war had crippled the former and the latter alike. Nor had Britain's economy been a completely satisfactory base of power during the great war. Blood and iron had been essential components of its strength, which hinged more on the shape of the services than of sterling. The Treasury also exaggerated the role of gold relative to steel in economic strength and thus distorted the importance of financial compared to military factors in power as a whole. Above all else, decision makers overrated the strategic value of Britain's economy, assuming that whenever necessary this could sustain whatever rearmament its security might require. Only when Britain began to rearm did it learn the truth in this matter and also discover that this process depended as much on the existing strength of its armament industries and services as of its finances.

The size of their estimates shaped the services' abilities to pursue their policies. Insofar as they have measured this issue at all, historians have relied on one crude indicator, the face value of the services' net estimates. Yet to know that a service received £X is meaningless without examining those factors which determined how much of that money could be used for what purposes. Thus, a service's ability to fund new projects hinged on the level of its disposable income. Fixed costs absorbed almost all army estimates by 1923 and RAF and naval ones after 1928, but until these dates the services could finance major expansion programmes. Conversely, they wasted much money due to the poor selection between or the mismanagement of their programmes. The scale of this factor, however, defies precise calculation. Nor is it easy to determine how changes in prices affected their purchasing power. General price levels doubled between 1914 and 1919 and fell about 20 per cent by 1922, then remaining constant until 1929. The services' estimates moved in direct accordance with general price changes, which did not normally affect their purchasing power. However, some of the reduction in service estimates in 1923–24 was a delayed reaction to the earlier fall in prices and did not actually affect their purchasing power. Conversely, the costs of specialist military equipment increased above general price levels while the services' pay scales of 1919–25 more than doubled those of 1914. Across the board, these increases in wages and weapons probably raised real service costs by about 10 per cent above those of 1914.

Accounting conventions determined the realities behind the face value of the services' estimates. These were measured in two ways. Gross estimates indicated the total funds passing through a service's hands, including those allocated to or received from other departments as 'grants in aid'. Net estimates were those funds actually available for a department's use, excluding grants. Although net estimates basically represented a service's finances, that position was modified by gross ones. India always paid the maintenance costs of about 20 per cent of the British army and 10–20 per cent of the RAF, indirectly subsidising their net estimates to the same degree. In 1922–23 and 1925–26 similar transfer payments from the Colonial Office and the Admiralty respectively began to maintain another

25–30 per cent of the RAF's squadrons, again boosting net RAF estimates. Conversely, from 1925–26 naval estimates carried a charge of £700 000–£1 000 000 which RAF ones had hitherto borne.

Service estimates were divided into 'effective' and 'non-effective' spending. After 1922–23 the latter, the deadweight of matters like pensions which did not support current policies, absorbed 10–20 per cent of army and naval estimates but only a tiny fraction of RAF ones. Finally, the services did not use all the funds which they received. At the end of a financial year any unspent part normally reverted to the Treasury. Due to delays caused by strikes, the Treasury, and mismanagement by firms or the services themselves, the services often failed to spend up to 10 per cent of their net estimates. Moreover, in 1924–25 a system of 'shadow cuts' was inaugurated, whereby some funds which the services believed they would be able to spend were not included formally in their net estimates. The services would receive these in addition to their net estimates only if they could in fact be spent; otherwise they would revert to the Treasury. This paper transaction did not alter service spending. The 'shadow cuts' affected only that part of their estimates which they could not have used in any case.

The services' real financial capacity was their net estimates plus part of their gross ones, minus non-effective spending and any money which they did not use. The single best guide to this issue (modified by matters like transfer payments) are their 'current effective' estimates, from which two points become clear.[7] At a basic level the navy had less to spend on policy, the army roughly the same and the RAF far more than their formal estimates indicate. However, between 1922–23 and 1925–26 only the army really lost any of the money allocated for this purpose. The funds available to support naval and RAF policy swelled significantly.

During the 1920s Britain always had the funds to maintain far larger service estimates than it actually did. This level was determined not by necessity but by choice. The government always wanted to minimise service estimates and in doing so reduced its military strength and its margin for error. Britain allocated less money to the services than was desirable, yet not necessarily less than was required. Indeed, in each year during the 1920s Britain spent absolutely at least as much money on its armed forces as did any other state. Of course, other nations may have spent more than they admitted, while conscription and variations in wages, prices and rates of exchange caused the purchasing power of military expenditure to vary between states. Nonetheless, not until 1922 and 1926 did cuts even begin to damage the army, and the navy and the RAF respectively. Nor was it inevitable that service estimates would be so reduced. The imperatives of financial policy were but one factor in strategic policy. Britain intended to spend enough money to maintain the forces which it seemed to need to ensure Imperial security.

In November 1918 Britain possessed incomparably the strongest navy on earth and one of the largest armies and air forces. Down to 1926 it led the world in the development of naval aviation and strategic bombing forces. The navy remained larger than the USN and equalled any other two fleets combined. Only France had a significantly larger air force while the British and Indian armies fielded 400 000 regular soldiers. The Dominions and overseas paramilitary units (which garrisoned most of the empire) and the Territorial Army (TA) provided another 400 000 men. Although by 1931 the relative level of Britain's services had fallen, its aggregate military strength and expertise remained formidable.

It has been argued that during the 1920s the services misunderstood the value of the modern arms which were to be so crucial in war.[8] In fact, there was room for a debate about these matters. It was not self-evident that battleships were nearing obsolescence or that strategic bombing, naval aviation and armoured forces were on the wave of the future. None of these arms had reached maturity during the great war and each had technical limitations which were not overcome until after 1935. During the 1920s the services made many errors regarding these issues. The army overestimated the value of cavalry and underestimated that of armoured forces, as the navy did regarding battleships and naval aviation. The RAF exaggerated the importance of strategic bombing and minimised that of ground and sea support. However, the services did want to prepare for the future and their attitude toward new *matériel* like helicopters was progressive.[9] They recognised that modern arms were important and would significantly affect the nature of operations. They overemphasised material aspects when considering these issues and misunderstood the full effect of these modern arms. Still, their theoretical and practical attitudes towards them were no worse than those of any other of the world's armed forces.   The fate of service policies hinged on the government's view of Imperial security. This could be endangered should any power control certain seas or threaten Britain and its possessions with land or air attack. Whitehall expected the services to meet three needs: 'Imperial policing', to overcome minor internal and external problems; 'deterrence', to convince other powers not to risk an attack on vital British interests; and 'insurance', to defend these interests should deterrence fail, and also to mobilise Britain's strategic resources. The army was maintained only for the purposes of Imperial policing and insurance but the navy and the RAF met all three of these needs, especially deterrence. The government regarded airpower as the basis for home defence and deemed seapower the foundation for Imperial security. However, there were differences over the nature of Britain's maritime needs. Beatty stated that any country's 'authority . . . in the councils of the world depends primarily on her naval strength', and the Admiralty wanted to retain Britain's traditional maritime supremacy.[10] Conversely, many politicians and the Treasury wished only to defend Imperial 'home waters' against likely threats.

Decision makers often drew analogies to commercial insurance when considering Britain's strategic needs. Warren Fisher argued that 'We cannot ensure against everything whether as a country or as private individuals, not merely because we cannot afford it, but also because that would not be "insurance"'. Conversely, Bridgeman held that

> When a man ensures his house or his car, he endeavours to secure for himself the value of either in the event of their destruction, and the premium he pays is one which the Company regards as sufficient to provide that sum. If his car is worth £1000, he does not say 'I do not think my car is likely to be smashed, and therefore I will only ensure for £500'. He pays his premium in order to recover the full amount of his loss. In our case we have to secure ourselves against a defeat ruinous to our Nation and Empire which cannot be computed in £.s.d. or a costly war in which we may ultimately succeed but which might cost us in actual expenses of war and resultant loss of trade perhaps £6 000 000.
>
> As against such risks a premium of about 1% in the former case and a great deal less in the former, does not seem excessive.[11]

Britain could determine its needs for strategic insurance in two ways. The services and some politicians held that Britain should not live on the 'sufferance' of other powers, and must always be able to defend its vital interests against any state, even if none were perceived as a threat. Thus, in 1925 Balfour defended the HDAF programme by agreeing that

> a war with France is a most improbable eventuality . . . but the consideration is wholly irrelevant. Personally I do not believe that there will be any first-class war in the lifetime of the youngest member of the Cabinet. But we do not frame our naval and air policy on prophecies of this character nor ought we to do so.[12]

This view would lead Britain to fund programmes which might never be needed, thus hampering the economy or setting off an arms race.

Conversely, the Treasury and some politicians wanted to prepare only against likely threats and to 'take the risk of not protecting' certain interests, like Canada or Hong Kong. Barstow claimed that the 'sufferance' argument

> means in effect that the only way a nation can be sure of not being attacked or deprived of its possessions, is to be stronger than its neighbours or at least as strong. Every nation must therefore be as strong as every other nation and a country with scattered possessions must be as strong everywhere as any of its neighbours anywhere! Even then it will not be as strong as any two of its neighbours who may combine to attack it. The whole argument seems to me a reductio ad absurdem of politics . . . Despite the inequalities of strength all over the world, the nations continue to exist on sufferance of one another just as individuals do.[13]

If this approach was adopted, Britain might be unable to defend the vital interests on which the survival of the empire depended.

Britain's main areas of strategic concern were the high seas, the western Pacific, the Middle East and western Europe. The balance between the British and US navies affected both the symbol and the basis of British power, its maritime strength, and also indirectly shaped Britain's position in the Pacific. Britain wanted to secure its interests there through agreements with Japan or the US and hoped to retain its overall maritime supremacy. Instead, by 1922 Britain had made major sacrifices in both these areas; it had to rely on its power alone for security in the western Pacific and to concede equality with the US in the central elements of seapower. In 1919 Britain intended to keep all the great powers out of the Middle East and to establish hegemony there, in order to control its resources and to defend India. By 1923 these ambitions had miscarried and the Middle East became a theatre of secondary strategic concern.

Many statesmen believed that by withdrawing into Imperial isolation, Britain could survive any dangers arising from Europe.[14] Yet they also appreciated that developments on the continent could threaten British security. To further stability and balance in western Europe, they often considered commitments to that region. They rejected any responsibilities in eastern Europe, although they recognised that events there could not be divorced from those in the west, especially given Poland's relations with France, Germany and Russia. Britain held that Europe could only become stable when Germany regained its territorial *irredenta* from Poland, particularly the Danzig corridor. It hoped that this would occur peacefully, but many decision makers doubted that Poland would survive and agreed that Germany would expand to the east.[15] They believed that this need not threaten the stability of western Europe.

Although secondary states like Turkey affected strategic policy, Britain's main concern lay with the great powers. Between 1919 and 1926 it did not treat Italy as being one. Britain disliked Soviet Russia because it was Soviet and Russian, compounding a traditional fear of Russia with a new loathing of bolshevism. Austen Chamberlain regarded it as 'a nightmare of Tsarist Russia'.[16] The government always feared that Russia would become the centre of any axis of powers opposed to Britain; its own nightmare was that Russia would ally with Japan, Germany and Turkey. Whitehall expected Russia to challenge British interests wherever it could, although Britain feared a direct Russian threat only in 1920 and 1925–27.

Britain disliked the policies of France and Germany alike. It feared that their mutual animosity might lead to another great war, perhaps, given France's alliances in eastern Europe, sparked by Germano-Polish troubles.[17] Statesmen also regarded French military programmes as threats to Britain. They wanted Germany to be powerful enough to restrain to some extent the current French hegemony in Europe. At the Paris Peace Conference Britain wished Germany to retain an army and air force exceeding that which Britain actually maintained during the 1920s, of 250 000 soldiers and 625 aircraft. Even Henry Wilson wanted Germany to be 'sufficiently strong to be no temptation to the French!'.[18] However, Whitehall believed that Germany would eventually dominate Europe and perhaps endanger Britain. Even Imperial isolationists like

Hankey conceded that Britain must join with France should Germany threaten the low countries. Men who exaggerated the French menace to Britain, like Balfour, agreed that French power was essential to European stability. Others, such as Wilson, held that only an alliance with France could assure British security against Germany. Britain wanted France to remain sufficiently strong to counter to some extent Germany's eventual power. In all, Britain sought to alter the Treaty of Versailles and the French security system in Europe. It hoped that this delicate and gradual policy would lead Germany to accept the postwar order. Equally, these actions increased the risks involved should Germany challenge that order.

Britain's strategic policy making élite regarded the United States as the most powerful nation on earth and exhibited greater sentimental predilections towards it than any other country.[19] The only state with which Britain deemed war to be 'unthinkable' was the US, although it did in fact think about this.[20] Some decision makers nursed hopes for a special strategic relationship with the US while during 1919–20 opinion favoured an Anglo-American *entente* and some common 'Anglo-Saxon' policy. Yet even then statesmen recognised that British and US interests clashed. They favoured such ties simply because they calculated that these would best support British interests, for their attitude towards the United States was hard-headed. Britain wished to avoid provoking America needlessly but not at the price of compromising British interests. Whitehall was as much hostile as friendly towards the US. Few politicians regarded Japan as a threat and for sentimental and strategic reasons wanted close ties with it. However, both the Foreign Office and the Admiralty, the departments most concerned with strategic policy in the Pacific, mistrusted Japan.

There were certain irrational elements in the government's strategic assessments. Sentimental attitudes towards other powers marked but did not seriously distort these perceptions. The necessarily narrow perspective of each department did do so, however. For example, the Foreign Office, preoccupied with immediate diplomatic needs, underrated the strategic consequences of its proposals. Moreover, racialist suppositions shaped Whitehall's view of the characteristics of other peoples. The Air Ministry stated that the 'Japanese are not apt pilots probably for the same reason that keeps them indifferent horsemen'. When considering British air defence against France Lloyd George questioned the wisdom of relying in so large a measure on the superiority of our race . . . whereas we are naturally sailors and an amphibious race, we could not count on these qualities to give us marked superiority in the air. The French, on the other hand, are naturally soldiers. They are daring and have mechanical genius. They have qualities of dash and recklessness which . . . would give them great value as airmen.[21]

Finally, especially in 1919–21, the government clung to a 'conspiracy theory' view. Many decision makers held that Japan and Asian nationalists were intriguing against Britain and feared the 'Yellow Peril'. Wellesley argued that Japanese control over China 'may not only lead to the ejection of the British from Asia and Australia, but ultimately to the destruction of Europe by Asiatic invasion'. Beatty claimed that Soviet domination of east Asia would make 'the Yellow Peril very real' while if Japan adopted bolshevism then 'the Prophecies of the Pyramids would come true, that the Races of the North and East would join hands and sweep across Europe'.[22] Others regarded 'Pan Islamism' and bolshevism as similar conspiracies, while Hankey perceived the Turkish nationalists as being a front for the prewar 'Committee of Union and Progress' (CUP) and that 'whole Crypto-Judaic Neo-Turk gang'. Decision makers frequently referred to the presence of Jews among these occult elements. Some tied all these conspiracies into a great one. In 1920 Churchill and Edwin Montagu regarded the CUP leader, Enver Pasha, as the hidden link between Pan Islamism, Turkish nationalism, bolshevism and German revisionism. In 1922 the general staff referred to 'a world-wide conspiracy fomented by all the elements most hostile to British interests—Sinn Fein and Socialists at our own doors, Russian Bolshevists, Turkish and Egyptian Nationalists and Indian Seditionists . . . working with the connivance–if not under the active direction of—the German Foreign Office'.[23]

These concepts distorted Britain's perceptions of some issues but were not completely misleading. These racialist ideas did not lead it to misconstrue the strategic potential of any state except Japan. The concern with issues like Pan Islamism was largely a response to the rise of nationalism in the colonised world, as the government recognised in 1922.[24] Conspiratorial groups were indeed intriguing against Britain, and there were secret connections between Germany, Russia and Turkey. These misconceptions did not prevent Britain from rationally assessing its strategic position and its aims and means in foreign policy.

From 1926 to 1931 the Foreign Office consistently told the COSC that Britain's aims in foreign policy were: '(1) to seek peace and ensure it; (2) to preserve the status quo; and (3) to protect and develop British interests in foreign countries.' These interests could be affected by 'almost any dispute that arises' anywhere on earth, but Britain had

> no territorial ambitions nor desire for aggrandizement. We have got all that we want—perhaps more. Our sole object is to keep what we have and live in peace. Many foreign countries are playing for a definite stake and their policy is shaped accordingly. It is not so in our case. To the casual observer our foreign policy may seem to lack consistency and continuity, but both are there. We keep our hands free in order to throw our weight into the scale on behalf of peace. The maintenance of the balance of power and the preservation of the status quo have been our guiding lights for many decades and will so continue.[25]

Many historians have argued that in the 1920s Britain was a status quo power which wished to avoid another great war and to ensure that the world order changed only through gradual evolution. This view is roughly accurate, although given Britain's territorial ambitions in 1919–20, it truly became a status quo power only after 1922. Yet peace can be preserved in many ways, including war, and in attempting to maintain a general status quo any power may pursue radical changes in parts of it. The Foreign Office noted in 1920 that Britain's methods of foreign policy had traditionally been 'inductive, intuitive and quite deliberately opportunist'.[26] Such an attitude could foster many forms of diplomatic behaviour. The questions are whether (and, if so, why) Britain systematically favoured or rejected specific ones. Many historians have argued that it disliked aggressive actions which might threaten other powers or lead to war and preferred peaceful reconciliation with other states. They have suggested that these attitudes arose from the debate between two schools of thought, which might be called 'liberals' and 'realists'.[27] Each school offered a different theory about the causes of international conflict and favoured different means to overcome them.

'Realists' believed that clashes between the interests of states caused such conflicts, dangers which could be minimised through an accommodation of interests and the maintenance of the 'balance of power'. At best this might lead to a 'concert of the powers' but any state should match the worst case through alliances and strong armed forces. Whereas 'realists' regarded conflicts of interest and war as natural components of international relations, 'liberals' believed that these were unnatural, disasters which no peoples wanted. 'Liberals' feared that the worst case prescriptions of 'realists' would start a vicious circle which could lead only to war. They preferred to resolve conflicts through mutual security, arms limitation, international reconciliation, the development of moral authority and reliance on international public opinion.

Historians have used these concepts in a curious way. Their evidence for the nature of 'liberal' views comes mostly from the opinions of public pressure groups. Writers have assumed that these ideas represented those of decision makers, who were swung by public pressure towards 'liberal' behaviour. In fact, the government believed that public opinion simultaneously supported many conflicting things, such as service economies and RAF and naval rearmament. Public opinion did not drive Britain in one direction alone or determine its policies, nor did pressure groups represent the views of statesmen: indeed, what they were striving to do was to change the latter. Moreover, historians have not considered whether the terms 'liberals' and 'realists' actually describe the views of decision makers. Barnett has deemed Curzon a 'liberal' because of one statement the latter made about Britain's moral authority. One might just as well consider MacDonald a realist because he once used the term 'balance of power'.[28] Many scholars have assumed that most decision makers were 'liberals'. Yet a system of categorisation which cannot distinguish the views of Eyre Crowe from those of Robert Cecil is useless.

Historians have argued that Britain's diplomatic behaviour was that of one of these schools, the 'liberal' group, that these schools embraced all decision makers and that these views were mutually exclusive. Thus, 'liberals' entirely rejected the theory and practice of 'realists' and vice versa; if one held that clashes of interests caused conficts, one could not believe that arms races did so. These assumptions have led scholars to misconstrue Britain's modes of analysis of international relations and its forms of diplomatic behaviour.

Few decision makers clearly belonged to either the 'liberal' or 'realist' schools. Still, with reservations one can describe men like Cecil and most of MacDonald's Cabinet as 'liberals' and Crowe, the service chiefs and politicians like Leo Amery as 'realists'. Members of these schools sometimes clashed. In 1924 MacDonald refused to

> draw these false distinctions between idealism and practical*ism*. The one thing that matters is psychology. All the sage materialists and self-styled realists will never be able to produce anything but wars. That is their natural offspring. Unless we change the qualities of our minds we had better arm to the teeth.

Crowe, never a materialist but always a realist, retorted that 'it is not sufficient to change our minds—supposing that they need changing. What is necessary is to change the minds of other people, notably the possible peace-breakers. Unless we succeed in doing that, we cannot afford to ignore realistic views'.[29] Yet such clashes between 'liberals' and 'realists' were not the cause of fundamental disagreements in foreign policy between 1919 and 1926.

The differences between the views of these schools was not reflected in those of individual 'liberals' and 'realists'. Members of one school often clashed over various issues while adherents of different ones agreed about the same matters. Thus, in 1924 MacDonald and Amery opposed and Cecil and the general staff favoured British commitments to Europe. Nor did 'liberals' and 'realists' always act as expected. Indeed, their modes of analysis and means of action were not dissimilar while decision makers did not treat them as mutually exclusive. Members of both schools believed that arms races, hostile alliance systems, 'militarism and economic imperialism' had helped to cause the great war.[30] The 'liberal' idea of reconciliation and the 'realist' one of accommodation of interest were not far different, while many statesmen merged the concepts of mutual security and alliances by favouring regional security pacts under the League of Nations. From a 'liberal' framework of analysis one could advocate 'realist' solutions to certain problems and vice versa. So to maintain British security 'realists' often favoured arms limitation and 'liberals' accepted rearmament.

The concepts of 'liberals' and 'realists' have a limited value as an analytical tool. They can categorise certain types of thinking and action. They cannot explain the actions or thoughts of statesmen. The differences between these schools affected foreign policy less than did matters like the split between those who wanted Britain actively to maintain mutual security or the balance of power; and those who favoured strategic isolationism, in which Britain would defend its own interests through its own power and eschew any involvements outside the Empire. Virtually everyone unified the modes of analysis and means of action of these schools into a wide spectrum of opinion which might be called 'liberal realism'. Statesmen believed that clashes of interest or arms races could cause conflicts. They were willing to resolve these through arms limitation or rearmament, the creation of a moral position or the maintenance of the balance of power, through reconciliation or alliances with other states.

In a perfect world decision makers would no doubt have preferred 'liberal' means but in the world as it was they accepted the value of 'realist' ones. Britain did not systematically favour or reject 'liberal' or 'realist' means. It adopted whatever ones it thought would best achieve its aims in specific circumstances. Unfortunately, no one type of diplomatic behaviour would necessarily achieve all its ends simultaneously. Thus, to preserve its security, Britain might have to rearm, which it feared might lead to arms races. Arms limitation might avoid that danger yet hamper security. Whitehall drifted uneasily between these options. It disliked the potential consequences of them all yet had to choose between them.

Britain wished to establish a system of relationships between the powers which would regulate the status quo and, where necessary, adjust it in detail so as to preserve the whole. The idea of doing so through a 'concert of the powers' on the model of the European settlement after 1815 marked Britain's entire policy in 1919, Lloyd George's system of conference diplomacy in 1920–22 and the Foreign Office's approach to Europe during 1925.[31] The League also became important in foreign policy by 1924 because statesmen believed that it could serve as a clearing house to help regulate the international system. However, given the obvious limitations to these means, Britain had to consider others to achieve its ends.

Everyone agreed that force was one of these means. MacDonald refused 'to throw to the four winds all our experiences of how little defence we really get from military developments. At best they are some sort of security that when war comes we shall not be beaten'. Yet 'liberals' often supported rearmament programmes. In 1919 Cecil stated that Britain should spend its 'last shilling' to maintain its maritime security against the US. During 1925 he was almost the only minister to support the navy's cruiser programme.[32] In 1924 MacDonald's Cabinet regarded the continuation of the HDAF programme as a strategic necessity and also began 25 per cent of the cruisers laid down between 1919 and 1930. So as to maintain security between 1921 and 1925 every government approved large rearmament programmes. However, they also held that too much military strength would be unnecessary or counterproductive. Hence, 'realists' and 'liberals' alike favoured mutual arms limitation. Some, like Barstow and Cecil, treated this almost as a universal panacea while others, such as Crowe, argued that 'agreements for the limitation of armaments will always be "dodged' by some of the participants'.[33] Yet even Hankey and Beatty believed that arms limitation could suit some British interests. No government before 1929 tolerated unilateral disarmament for its own sake, but Britain only turned to rearmament when arms limitation seemed impracticable.

Britain could also further some aims by sacrificing others. This approach should be described through a careful use of language. 'Appeasement' has been increasingly seen not as a unique character-istic of British policy in the 1930s but as a traditional one.[34] It is correct to note a continuum within British foreign policy between 1816 and 1939. Equally, it is dangerous to analyse that continuum through the use of a term which has acquired the meaning of paying the danegeld as one's sole means to achieve the single end of avoiding war. Used in this sense, that term does not fit British policy in the 1930s, let alone of any other era. If this word must be used, it should be treated as one of many forms of international reconciliation or accommodation of interest; not as a euphemism for these entire classes of behaviour.

As had been the case for centuries, a pragmatic willingness to accommodate the interests of or to reconcile other states marked British foreign policy in the 1920s. However, no government was eager to sacrifice British interests to make what Curzon called a *'beau geste'* nor, given their confidence in British power, did they see any overriding need to do so.[35] In only one such case, its approach to naval disarmament and Anglo–US relations in 1929–30, did Britain not strike the hardest bargain which its material resources would allow and, indeed, further its interests in the process. Otherwise it only sacrificed assets which, as with its informal empire in Afghanistan, China and Turkey, it could not hope to hold; or, as when it abandoned the Anglo-Japanese alliance, it had to choose between two evils—not between alienating Japan or the US, but between Tokyo and Ottawa. Britain recognised that some interests might have to be sacrificed to preserve international stability. As ever, it preferred that these be made by other powers, most notably France. Whenever between 1919 and 1926 Britain felt that its vital interests were under challenge, it took strong measures to defend them.

An important means by which to take such stands was by making commitments to other powers. Some decision makers argued that commitments would strengthen Britain's position: that an alliance with France would enable London to influence French policy and further British security against Germany. Others claimed that commitments would have the opposite effect: that an alliance with Japan would antagonise Washington without securing influence in Tokyo. No one wanted to send soldiers to Europe, not even the War Office, the one department which consistently regarded commitments there as strategically essential. Statesmen preferred loose pledges rather than definite promises to take specific steps in certain circumstances. Yet Britain was willing to undertake meaningful commitments. In 1919 it accepted one to defend France; between 1920 and 1925 many decision makers were willing to do so again. In 1919–20 most statesmen wanted an Anglo–US alliance, in 1921 the Cabinet wished to retain that with Japan and in 1923–24 several ministers and officials advocated British commitments to mutual security in Europe.

Barnett has supposed that 'liberal' means were inherently foolish and necessarily led to strategic failure. Actually, in cases like the Washington naval treaty, 'liberal' means were Britain's best solution to specific problems. The only alternative there, for example, was to extend an arms race with the United States, and for no particular reason to provoke a more powerful nation which was offering to throw away a sizable lead in that potential competition. Until 1929 no 'liberal' actions weakened Britain's strategic position. In any case, it always selected its diplomatic means after making a hard-headed calculation of which of them would best suit its interests.

Between 1919 and 1924 there were 'liberal' aspects to British foreign policy. However, British policy was basically 'realist' because 'liberal' means seemed inadequate to achieve its ends. The world was unstable and British security seemed to be under threat. So to maintain its interests Britain pursued traditional accommodations with the other victor powers. So as to maintain its security it rearmed and favoured alliances with other states. Conversely, between 1926 and 1931 the government accepted some 'realist' means. Nonetheless, 'liberal' solutions dominated British foreign policy because 'realist' ones seemed unable to achieve its aims. By 1926 Britain held that the foundation had been laid for a stable world, but it also saw dangers which could hamper this development. It thought that the adoption of 'realist' means could only exacerbate this possibility. It feared that British military preparations would so frighten Japan or Russia that they would seek to overturn the world order, that naval construction would spark an arms race with the United States, that international arms limitation alone could prevent Germany from rearming. So to avoid these problems and thus precisely to maintain British security, it favoured the smallest possible service strengths. This solution to one set of strategic problems, however, reduced Britain's ability to deal with a subsequent one.

During the 1920s Britain considered many forms of diplomatic behaviour. It simultaneously followed 'liberal' and 'realist' paths, although at any time it favoured one above the other. Such changes in preference about means did not indicate a change regarding ends. Britain simply adopted different solutions to different problems. All these forms of behaviour were intended to further aims shared by every decision maker: to create a stable world in which Britain would be secure.

Historians have come to believe that during the interwar era trends in the terms of power were inexorably driving Britain from the status of a great power to that of a secondary one. Paul Kennedy has argued that the imminent end of the British Empire was almost inevitable. Scholars have also discerned a change in the very nature of the attitudes and behaviour of British statesmen. Barnett has assumed that between the times of Lords Castlereagh and Palmerston and those of Grey and Halifax, generations of cold-eyed realists decayed into soft-brained sentimentalists.[36] These views are fallacious.

Even at the peak of its relative strength Britain had never been a superpower, as the United States is alleged to have been in the 1950s. Britain was simply one of the greatest of the great ones. Moreover, the real beginning of the end of this status can be dated no earlier than 1940, for even in 1939 Britain remained among the greatest of great powers. If its relative strength had declined since 1860, this was no less powerful than it had been in 1816. During the interwar years Britain's power was limited: it always had been. Still, its absolute strength provided a powerful hand for British statesmen, which they perceived and played exactly as had their forebears. Indeed, when reaching their decisions of the 1920s statesmen ranging from Austen Chamberlain to Ramsay MacDonald conciously reflected on those of their predecessors, particularly of Castlereagh and George Canning in 1816–24. Lloyd George's attitudes towards economy and foreign policy in 1920 were even influenced by a misreading of the history of Lord Liverpool's administration after 1816.[37]

There are fundamental parallels between the strategic attitudes of all British decision makers between 1816 and 1939. In 1816, for example, Castlereagh stated that the 'System' of British foreign policy would be

> founded upon no separate view of Interest or Ambition:—There is no longer any Object which the Prince Regent can desire to acquire for the British Empire, either of Possession or of Fame—beyond which Providence has already blessed it with.
>
> —His only desire is, and must be, to employ all his Influence to preserve the Peace, which in concert with His Allies he has won. To this great End you may declare that all His Highness's Efforts will be directed;—to this purpose all minor Considerations will be made subordinate. Wherever His Voice can be heard it will be raised to discourage the pursuit of all Secondary and separate Interests at the Hazard of that general Peace and goodwill, which after so long a period of Suffering it should be the object of all the Sovereigns of Europe to preserve to their people. . .
>
> The language of such a Power as Great Britain is calculated in itself to do much; But when its views and Principles are understood, when it is distinctly known to be leagued with no particular Court, to the oppression of Another; that it's only Object is the Peace of the World; and that it is determined to use all it's Means to combine the Powers of Europe against that State whose perverted policy or criminal Ambition shall first menace the Repose in which we all have a common Interest; I am sanguine in my Hopes that the most salutary results may be expected from such a line of Policy.[38]

The style of British state papers changed between 1816 and 1926. The principles which guided its foreign policy did not, the emphasis being on the maintenance of peace and the preservation of the status quo; nor did its strategic actions.

This century of statesmen were always both lions and foxes, depending on the nature of the competition and the state of the prey. The material limits to their power prevented them from precluding certain undesired developments, whether it be the Russian expansion in central Asia of the 1870s or the Soviet revival there of 1920–25. In particular, every statesman since the days of Canning was reluctant to commit Britain to the use of force on mainland Europe. At the relative peak of its power, Britain had often sacrificed peripheral interests, in order to accommodate states which were stronger in those regions, and could not enforce its will on critical matters in the heartlands of Europe, Asia or elsewhere. Yet all these statesmen refused to tolerate threats to vital British interests or live on the sufferance of other states. Britain acted identically against France in the 1860s, France and Russia in the 1890s, Germany in the 1900s, France and Japan in the 1920s and Germany, Italy and Japan in the 1930s. British statesmen of the 1920s attacked fewer non-European peoples than had their forebears, but then the map was running short of areas which were not already painted red. Even so, they managed to suppress many internal risings and took over much of the Middle East.

Britain's approach to strategy between 1816 and 1939 changed only in degree and not in kind. British decision makers of the 1920s had generally come to intellectual maturity between 1870 and 1914. They were true children of Palmerston, Lord Salisbury's sons, cynical, calculating, determined as ever to use every means at hand to hold what they held. However, not only were these means weaker than they had been in 1870, but they were also smaller than statesmen of the 1920s realised. Their problem was not that they had forgotten too much of the attitudes of their predecessors; rather, they had forgotten too little. Decision makers did not see British power as it was but as it had been. They overestimated Britain's relative power and the stability of the world order. They failed to recognise that only an active commitment to the maintenance of that order could preserve British security. In A.J.P. Taylor's words,

English people got the Balance of Power theory wrong. They came to think that it worked automatically, like the law of supply and demand or any of the famous economic 'laws' that the Victorians imagined they had discovered. In international affairs, as in economic affairs, you only had to look after your own interests and everything would be perfect. . .[39]

Britain assumed that its economic strength would meet its strategic needs, that its security would not be threatened for years and then only after a lengthy warning period. Consequently, the government believed that Britain required only the minimum possible armed forces which could protect its interests during a long period of peace and which could subsequently be expanded as necessary. This was Britain's traditional strategic policy, but that had worked solely because its economy had been relatively so powerful. By the 1920s this was no longer the case. The government retained a strategic policy which was feasible only if this condition still held true.

By acting on the assumption that Britain was strategically better off than it was, the government took decisions which actually weakened its long-term position. Yet throughout the 1920s Britain followed several different approaches to strategic policy. Statesmen always recognised that Britain could be seriously threatened, particularly by a coalition of powers, and frequently denied that international stability would continue during the foreseeable future. They often identified dangers to British security and sought to deal with them by such means as rearmament, which might have strengthened Britain's relative power. At four different times, each separated by a three-year period, the government instituted radical changes in strategic policy: in 1919, 1922, 1925 and 1928. Only after seven years of development did the imperatives of foreign and financial policies definitively converge against those of the services.

4 Strategic Principles and Service Policies, 1919–20

By December 1918 Britain had emerged a victor from the great war as had the coalition government from the coupon election. This government had a unique opportunity to strengthen Britain's position in the world and to formulate an effective strategic policy. It failed to do so because of overconfidence and adverse circumstances. Lloyd George dominated the Cabinet, supported by Bonar Law, the Conservative Party leader and Lord Privy Seal, while the Finance Committee composed the inner Cabinet. By 1920 its members were Lloyd George, Bonar Law, and the ministers for the departments involved in strategic policy: Curzon, Long, Churchill, Austen Chamberlain, Montagu, the India Secretary and Milner, the Colonial Secretary. This government had great ambitions: to establish British hegemony over the Middle East, a stable balance of power in Europe and the Pacific, and close ties with several victor powers. On the assumption that Britain would be secure during the forseeable future, while the world would become stable, it intended to use the August 1919 principles to govern service policies.

Contrary to these expectations the world remained unstable and Britain's relations with the powers became uncertain. Diplomacy could not achieve its full strategic aims while British military strength barely met its minimum ones. Driven by the political imperative for demobilisation, the government drastically reduced the size of the armed forces, creating extraordinary difficulties for the army and the RAF. By summer 1920, with five divisions committed to the troubles in Ireland and Iraq, the empire had few reserves available. This decline in armed force prevented Britain from retaining the hegemony which it desired over Persia, the Caucasus, Afghanistan and Turkey. Britain's services were too weak to support its foreign policy yet too expensive to suit its financial one. Britain failed to balance its aims and means, and could not follow the strategic policy of August 1919. When the preconditions that Britain would be

53

secure in a stable world did not emerge, these principles could not be enforced.

Consequently, Britain had to refashion this policy and resolve its operational and diplomatic problems. It was swamped by immediate issues and did not formulate a long-term policy. It left each department free to pursue its own aims and allowed foreign, service and financial policies to drift apart. The Cabinet did not control service policies nor, without its support, could the Treasury do so. Hence, the services gained all the estimates they requested and formulated ambitious postwar policies, the fate of which hinged on whether the Cabinet would adopt them when it finally did re-establish a strategic policy. Although its decisions on these issues occurred only in 1922, their foundation was laid in 1919–20, and was linked to the August 1919 principles.

These principles had little effect on service policies during 1919–20 but in 1921–22 they became the basis for them. The services' ability to defend their policies then turned on how well these were reconciled with those principles. A debate over the £135 000 000 limit and the ten-year period affected service policies in 1921–22, but far less than did the other clauses of the August 1919 principles. The politicians would judge naval policy by the principle of Britain's standard of naval strength relative to the USN; and the policies of the army and the RAF by that of the substitution of 'mechanical devices' for manpower in Imperial policing. The services could safeguard their policies only by tailoring them to suit these principles or by altering the latter to suit the former. The development of service policies in 1919–20 set the stage for the Cabinet's decisions on strategic policy in 1921–22.

During 1919–20 Britain decided that it needed neither more nor less than a one power standard in battleships and battlecruisers with the United States. This decision involved matters of naval policy, maritime diplomacy and grand strategy. The historians who have addressed these issues, Stephen Roskill, Arthur Marder and J.K. McDonald, have overlooked key pieces of evidence, like Britain's flirtation with the idea of taking over the German fleet to counter US pressure. They have also misconstrued the political process by which Britain reached these decisions.[1] Only by examining the relationship between strategic principles and these maritime matters can one understand the origins of postwar British naval policy.

In 1919 Britain did not fear the lesser naval powers or even Japan, although it recognised the strength of the Imperial Japanese Navy (IJN) and its '8–8' construction programme (eight battleships and eight battlecruisers).[2] Instead, one of Britain's central strategic problems was to preserve its maritime security against the world's strongest nation. The US was challenging the traditional basis of Imperial security, British maritime supremacy. In pursuit of naval equality at least with Britain, its leaders approved the '1916' and '1918' programmes, each consisting of 16 battleships and battlecruisers, which would outclass most British vessels.[3] The Admiralty warned that danger lay ahead unless the US abandoned these programmes or Britain matched them. By 1925 the '1916' programme would create Anglo-American naval equality. Any further construction would make the USN the world's strongest fleet.

The questions are why Britain preferred to overcome this challenge through diplomacy and why it sacrificed its maritime supremacy in the process. Barnett and Kennedy have suggested that underlying these decisions was a sentimental belief in Anglo-American friendship, which made British statesmen willing to 'appease' the United States by compromising Britain's real needs.[4] They have also argued that since its industry could not match the USN's potential growth, Britain could only hope to limit that through diplomacy. There is some truth in these arguments. Britain ultimately abandoned maritime supremacy because it did not regard the US as a threat, an attitude shaped by its perceptions of the United States, while statesmen and sailors agreed that the US could potentially build a greater fleet than Britain. Lloyd George, for example, feared that a naval race would lead Britain to 'bankruptcy or war'.[5]

Statesmen further recognised a link between British war debts and Anglo-American naval rivalry. As Churchill wrote, Washington might insist that Britain pay at least the interest on its debts, if 'you don't agree to leave off shipbuilding, i.e. to accept the second place, and quit your objectionable association with Japan'.[6] Roberta Dayer has even argued that this issue alone determined British policy towards the Japanese alliance and naval limitation alike. In fact, it did have a minor influence on these policies in late 1921, but nothing suggests that it did so during the critical period of their formulation in 1919–21.[7]

These arguments of sentiment and weakness explain why Britain was willing to compromise on certain issues. They do not explain why it refused to do so on others. In fact, Whitehall intended to preserve British maritime security against all threats and knew that Britain had formidable resources with which to do so. Decision makers were very hostile toward US ambitions in 1919–21. At this stage they did regard the United States as a potential menace and did consider responding through naval construction, by taking over the interned German fleet or by renewing the Japanese alliance. Statesmen and sailors believed that Britain had a strong bargaining position against the US and could defend its security. Britain had by far the world's strongest and best fleet and the shipbuilding and financial capacity to match any US programmes short of full economic mobilisation for naval competition. Even then, Britain could have put up a hard fight. Britain knew that so long as the United States was not provoked, such mobilisation would be unthinkable, for American public opinion would not accept the enormous costs required to achieve maritime supremacy.

Neither sentimental attachments to the United States nor fears of weakness dominated Britain's maritime decisions. Instead, it made a hard-headed attempt to resolve a complex problem, with which the dangers involved in failure were so high that Britain preferred not to overplay its hand. It hoped to maintain its maritime supremacy, to avoid a naval race with the US and to form an *entente* with the latter, but above all it needed to avoid two worst-case situations. If the United States achieved maritime supremacy, Britain would become strategically dependent on it, while an arousal of Anglo-American hostility could have incalculable consequences. Britain preferred maritime diplomacy because this was the best and safest means to avoid these worst-case possibilities and to attain its other aims. Britain also knew that if diplomacy failed, it would have to find other means to further these ends.

Britain's fundamental need was to prevent the United States from even attempting to establish maritime supremacy, for that would automatically drive Britain into these worst cast situations. Its actions, therefore, depended on those of the US. Since Britain pursued so many different goals, it would inevitably have to sacrifice some to achieve others. The obvious compromise was that Britain and the US should establish the principle of maritime equality: that Britain would abandon its existing and the United States forego its potential maritime supremacy. Should this position have ever become possible, Britain would have been foolish to refuse it. The principle of maritime supremacy was of symbolic importance yet in practice Britain simply needed to maintain its maritime security against threats. If the US was not a threat, then that principle could be sacrificed as part of a bargain, so long as Britain maintained the practical conditions for naval security against real dangers. Britain could abandon a word to secure a reality.

The imperatives of grand strategy led Britain to maritime diplomacy. The exigencies of the latter moved towards naval equality, which in turn gave rise to the one power standard. However, the progression of these events was complicated by confusion over maritime matters in London and Washington. Even more than usual, US naval policy was incoherent and its diplomatic signals ambiguous. Whitehall misinterpreted the latter because it misunderstood the former. In 1919 the Admiralty overstated the likelihood of an American threat and underestimated its naval demands, while Lloyd George trusted too much in Colonel House. Decision makers exaggerated the prospects of Anglo-American strategic cooperation and also differed over British maritime policy.

Statesmen and sailors favoured different diplomatic approaches towards the US, the Admiralty demanding the toughest possible stand while Lloyd George was more cautious. The Admiralty regarded security and supremacy at sea as inseparable. By August 1919 Whitehall held that naval equality could provide British security although it still preferred supremacy and hoped that underneath the principle of parity Britain would retain a stronger fleet. The Admiralty wanted a navy which could maintain security regardless of expense, while the government demanded major cuts in naval spending. The Admiralty held that battleships were the measure of seapower and that Britain had to match any American construction of such vessels. The government questioned these beliefs. The fate of naval policy turned on the resolution of these differences.

These disagreements most affected naval policy between November 1918 and August 1919, during a covert struggle in which each party pursued its aims without revealing them to the other. Lloyd George kept a loose rein on maritime developments, waiting for an opportunity to secure the largest relative naval position he could at the smallest absolute cost. He was caught between the dangerous combination of America and the Admiralty. The latter demanded that Britain should retain maritime supremacy without compromise, assuming that Washington would abandon its naval challenge and that Britain would treat supremacy at sea as its overriding aim, regardless of the financial or strategic price. Initially, the Admiralty expected the price to be small.

In 1918 it established a committee to examine postwar naval policy, on the assumptions that Britain would be secure at sea and that naval estimates would approximate those of 1914. This committee recommended a fleet with fewer battleships, battlecruisers and cruisers than in 1914 and with more submarines, aircraft carriers and destroyers.[8] Immediately after the armistice the naval staff favoured major increases in this strength to provide the 'Decided Superiority' required over both the USN (the only 'potential rival, and consequently menace' to Britain) and the IJN. The Board, however, believing that the navy could be some 20 per cent smaller than in 1914, approved the bulk of the committee's proposals for a postwar fleet. It assumed that this strength would preserve supremacy at sea. By March 1919, after US decisions on naval construction had invalidated this assumption, the covert struggle intensified. Long hinted to the Cabinet that Britain must begin construction unless the United States abandoned its own. He demanded that Lloyd George force the US to concede British maritime supremacy.[9]

Yet in March–April 1919 a formidable faction of naval figures flirted with ideas which would have wrecked any diplomatic settlement. Beatty, Admiral Madden, the commander of the Atlantic Fleet and the naval staff branch at the Paris peace conference, believed that the US wished to subvert the British Empire. They wanted the Royal Navy to respond by taking over the modern elements of the German fleet. This, they argued, would secure maritime supremacy and lead to sound Anglo-American relations by forcing Washington to realise that it could never match Britain at sea.[10] Long expressed similar ideas to the Board: that while Britain must match American construction, public opinion would oppose large spending for that purpose should, as was intended, the German fleet be scuttled. Instead, it 'might become necessary' to divide that fleet among the victors, with Britain taking the lion's share.[11] Long's logic led in a vicious circle. Britain would need construction if diplomacy faltered, which would be politically possible only if it took over the German fleet, which would have antagonised the US and caused diplomacy to fail.

These ideas reveal the strength of naval feelings, but they were soon abandoned. The naval staff noted that the German vessels would not solve the real problem at hand, the potential US superiority in post-Jutland warships by 1925. Wemyss conceded that the German fleet should not be destroyed until America provided 'some sort of assurance' regarding its naval intentions, for the disposition of these warships was 'a pawn in the game'.[12] Yet he demonstrated that British maritime supremacy could be threatened only if other powers completed their construction programmes, and he foresaw economies on the horizon. Were the peace conference successful, the 'question will not be what ships shall we build but how shall we man those that are already built'. Thus, for strategic and political reasons the Admiralty should work with Whitehall to defeat the US challenge through diplomacy.[13] Wemyss converted Long, who finally realised that the government would not authorise any construction in 1919–20. However, Long raised the vital question of what standard of naval strength Britain could accept. Although Britain might eventually 'have to fight' Japan or the United States, he apparently favoured a 'Two Power Standard' of France and America.[14]

The Admiralty dropped its most illogical ideas, but its policy could be tenable only if diplomacy was successful or if Britain abandoned all other strategic aims *vis-à-vis* America for the sake of maritime supremacy. Partly due to Long's pressure, in April 1919 Lloyd George took a firm stand with the United States.[15] The latter did not clearly define its aims, but by abandoning the '1918' programme demonstrated a willingness to forego maritime supremacy. Similarly, by refusing to cancel the '1916' programme or recognise in principle Britain's 'special' position at sea, it showed a determination to pursue parity. Sailors and statesmen drew different lessons from these events. The Admiralty took them to prove that another strong diplomatic stand could force the US to accept British supremacy at sea. Britain could then reduce its naval strength below that of 1914, although in the interim it must maintain equality in numbers of commissioned battleships and battlecruisers (21) with the USN, and far more in reserve.[16] If such a settlement did not occur, the Admiralty's demands would clearly force a confrontation with the US. Conversely, Whitehall was becoming willing to accept the principle of parity. It wished to avoid naval rivalry and, given the delicate situation, favoured a conciliatory approach. Hankey and Barstow urged that Britain should ignore US naval strength. Churchill even suggested that Britain should offer the German fleet to Washington in return for cancellation of the '1916' programme.[17]

Above all, Lloyd George moved to dominate naval policy. House led him to believe that America wanted a strategic *entente* with Britain, founded on an agreement that neither would regard the other as a threat. Such an *entente* would have been valuable in itself, while such a loose naval limitation agreement would have left Britain free to meet its needs against third powers. This might have avoided the crippling of British seapower between 1929 and 1936 caused by rigorously specific ratios of naval strength. However, Britain accepted House's proposals as a more serious indication of American desires than was justified, for it did not appreciate that he was no longer his master's voice. Moreover, House implied that Britain must leave the United States a free hand with Japan, and, in certain circumstances, let the US establish a larger fleet. Lloyd George carefully did not mention these implications, but he offered to accept the rest of House's proposals if both nations would cease naval construction: if Washington would abandon the '1916' programmes and leave Britain stronger at sea. Whether Lloyd George expected the US to accept this condition or used it as a negotiating gambit is uncertain. However, he probably hoped to retain maritime supremacy but was willing to accept parity in principle if that was necessary to secure a satisfactory settlement.

In order to clinch this bargain, Lloyd George had to control naval policy. He did so through the August 1919 principles, which stated that until the Cabinet ruled otherwise, Britain would ignore the USN when calculating its maritime needs. This ideally suited Lloyd George's interests. It allowed him to open negotiations on the basis of House's proposals and prevented the Admiralty from justifying large estimates by reference to the USN. Yet this decision was ambiguous. Taken literally it left Britain determining its naval strength by comparison with that of an ally, Japan, and might mean that Britain's navy would be smaller than the USN. The Cabinet had not reached a definitive decision about naval policy but was indeed trying to avoid doing so. The shape of British seapower rested on the course of Anglo-American negotiations.

Yet the Admiralty's policy had been rejected and in autumn 1919 it reached one of the two nadirs of its interwar power in Whitehall. The Finance Committee rejected its proposals and flirted with Barstow's policy, while Long dared raise no major issue 'until the general naval policy of the future is settled. It wd. only confuse Cabinet'.[18] However, the Admiralty simultaneously formulated a new policy which challenged the August 1919 principles. It approved a smaller fleet of 20 commissioned battleships and battlecruisers. Although it favoured maritime supremacy, its minimum demand became 'mere' equality with the USN. Since the government would not support supremacy, the Admiralty preferred parity rather than no defined standard with the USN.[19] It also noted that the ten-year period would defer the beginning of any warship programme until 1925, thus (accounting for lead times in construction) interpreting this principle to mean that the navy should be fully ready for war by 1929. The Admiralty believed that Britain must remain prepared against possible naval threats. It could not ignore the USN and must match any US construction, which could require a large and immediate rearmament programme.

The dispute between the Admiralty and the government centred on whether naval policy should ignore the USN. Diplomatic developments let the Admiralty win this dispute and alter the meaning of the August 1919 principles. The Finance Committee had recognised that its policy could succeed only if the US continued maritime diplomacy. During autumn 1919 Britain sought to convince Washington that it had adopted House's proposals.[20] However, the US government, paralysed, would not discuss these issues while its naval policy became uncertain. The '1916' programme fell behind schedule but the USN wanted to establish American maritime supremacy. When the US Senate refused to consent to the Treaty of Versailles, any possibility of Anglo-American strategic cooperation vanished, however much Whitehall might have yearned for it. Since diplomacy had failed, Britain needed a new means to forestall a US attempt to establish supremacy at sea, without provoking Washington. Long and Beatty used this opportunity to score a decisive victory for the Admiralty.

When Beatty became CNS he wished to rebuild the Admiralty's political position. He held that the politicians misunderstood

> the meaning of Sea Power. They are all military mad and fed by the War Office have come to consider the Navy as an Appendage to Military Forces and only exists for the purpose of carrying the Army and keeping the road open for them and we are in their eyes no longer the Spear Head of Great Britain which we have been for over a hundred years. Well they will have to be educated thats all and I must see that the Education is thorough. [sic.]

In pursuit of his pedagogical aims, Beatty gave Lloyd George a biography of Drake.[21] Beatty also wanted the Cabinet to define a 'General Naval Strength' which would match US and Japanese 'Naval Expansion'. He preferred an 'Alliance or an Entente' with the United States, based on 'Equality in Naval Material', but failing this Britain would have to match all US construction. In January 1920 the Board demanded that Britain should maintain 'at least' naval equality with the United States, through a 'One Power Standard'.[22]

Long told the Cabinet that he planned to inform Parliament that this standard would govern naval policy. However, in order not to compromise any negotiations with America, in 1920 the navy would not maintain more commissioned battleships and battlecruisers than the USN nor would it begin new naval construction. Long made no promises about 1921. After a bitter fight over naval estimates, during which Long denounced the Cabinet for 'risking sea supremacy' and for trying to reduce 'this great Service to a subordinate position', he gained a curious victory. His estimates were approved 'on the understanding' that the size of the fleet would soon be 'reviewed'. Later Long simply refused to tolerate such a review. He also told Parliament, using precisely the terms which he had outlined for the Cabinet, that the fundamental principle in naval policy was that the navy 'should not be inferior in strength to the Navy of any other Power', specifically including the USN. The navy's 'strength and standard of efficiency' must 'enable it to do its duty by the Empire'.[23]

Although the Cabinet had not formally authorised this statement, Long could not have made it without ministerial approval. Lloyd George probably regarded Long's declaration as a clear but not a provocative warning to America which did not commit Britain to specific actions. In fact, Long had reversed the August 1919 decision about naval policy. The Cabinet could not easily abandon the one power standard and the Admiralty could defend virtually any proposals by using this vague concept. Indeed, Long's statement could actually justify the navy being larger or smaller than the USN, depending on the meaning of 'strength' and 'duty'. The Admiralty soon provided a costly definition of maritime equality.

It took the one power standard to mean numerical equality in battleships and battlecruisers with the USN. However, Britain did not require equal numbers of post-Jutland warships providing that its vessels matched US ones—by the Admiralty's judgement—in terms of their total fighting power. The Admiralty also wanted superiority in virtually all other classes of warships. The Board believed that Britain must respond to the American and Japanese programmes so as not to become the third strongest naval power. Between May and October 1920 it decided that Britain should do so by constructing between 1922 and 1926 four aircraft carriers and eight battleships and battlecruisers, each of 51 900 tons, mounting 18-inch guns. These would render obsolete the vessels in the '1916' programme. Long asked the Cabinet to approve this £84 000 000 programme and so maintain the one power standard.[24]

Based as it was on political rather than on strategic calculations, this standard might prove to be either larger or smaller than that needed for British security. Although the declaration of that standard had clarified naval policy, it had not assured Britain's maritime position. By December 1920 Britain faced worse problems in this regard than it had before. The US President elect publically advocated American maritime supremacy while the USN wanted to complete the '1916' programme and an entirely new one by 1926. Britain had to find other means to prevent America from seeking to establish maritime supremacy. The Admiralty's reinterpretation of the August 1919 principles had opened the gates to an ambitious naval policy. It was uncertain whether the latter could maintain maritime security.

As with the navy, in 1919–21 one strategic principle ruled the fate of army and RAF policies, and it was embodied in an emphemeral issue. The principle was 'substitution'; the issue was the means by which Britain would control Iraq and Palestine. Historians have misunderstood the relationship between this issue, that principle and these two services policies. Most historians of the RAF, like H. Montgomery Hyde, have argued that its main aim always was to establish strategic bombing forces for major wars, although they have agreed that a secondary cause for its success was that it alone could economically substitute modern forces for elements of the older services.[25] Students of the army, such as Basil Liddell Hart, have argued that it should have been modernised to enable it to fight major wars and that it was not because its leaders were reactionary. Recent scholars like Bond have partly accepted these views but have emphasised that the army could have been modernized only if it had been authorised to prepare for a major war. Since the politicians let it prepare for nothing more than Imperial policing, which required small numbers of old fashioned units, the army became the 'Cinderella service', without large or modern forces.[26]

Bond's argument holds true for army policy after 1922. However, in 1919–21 the RAF did not emphasise strategic bombing while the army did strive to modernise and did have an opportunity to do so through the role of Imperial policing. Moreover, the reasons why the RAF did and the army did not achieve their aims were linked: their policies conflicted and the army failed because the RAF succeeded. Both hoped to maintain large and modern forces but had been assigned the same central role, to emphasise Imperial policing and to save money in that task by substituting 'mechanical devices', aircraft or mechanised ground forces, for cavalry and infantry. The future of their policies regarding strategic bombing and mechanisation turned on which controlled this role of substitution. The army's loss of this struggle crippled its chances to pursue a progressive policy. Only because the RAF won was it able to develop strategic bombing forces.

During 1919–21 Britain placed itself in a position in which it could develop either strategic bombing or mechanised forces, but not both. The army and the RAF could defend their long-term aims only by demonstrating their immediate relevance to Imperial policing. They competed for the same strategic niche. As the government would not finance both their aims, one service alone could succeed. It would gain greater estimates and the chance to establish its aims at the other's expense. Thus, by controlling the role of substitution in Iraq, the RAF expanded its relative share of service estimates, which let it live to prepare strategic bombing forces. Conversely, this development led the politicians to reduce both the army's estimates and its size. Moreover, armoured car operations in Iraq provided useful and otherwise hard to find lessons in mechanised warfare.[27] The loss of the role of substitution in those possessions where it could best be established deprived the army of a chance to gain experience in mechanised operations and reduced the likelihood that it would modernise. Mechanised units were less necessary for its other Imperial policing duties, and could be built only by reducing conventional units which were essential for these tasks.

In effect, Britain chose to develop strategic bombing rather than mechanised forces and did so because the RAF won the struggle over substitution. However, these developments were anything but inevitable, for the politicians simply wished to save money through substitution. They favoured the army's mechanised elements and did not want it to be the 'Cinderella service'. They wanted aircraft for the purpose of substitution but evinced no interest in strategic bombing. Moreover, two departments which later hampered the development of mechanised forces did not do so in 1919–21. The Treasury disliked expenditure on new mechanised equipment but approved most of the army's requests for that purpose, and certainly favoured substitution.[28] The Indian army wanted many mechanised units, in part to replace conventional forces in India.[29] In 1919-21 the War Office had its greatest opportunity of the 1920s to establish a progressive policy of mechanisation. Not only could it have modernised through substitution, but this approach alone could have led the politicians to support a progressive policy. Above all, the army could easily have defeated the RAF in the struggle over substitution.

In 1919–21 neither service was ready to establish substitution but both were able to do so by 1922, the army no less than the RAF. The RAF's system in Iraq depended as much on mechanised, conventional and paramilitary forces as on aircraft, and mechanised units could have replaced aircraft as the central element in this system. These units were disorganised, their equipment was not designed for Imperial policing, and they could not operate easily in parts of Iraq.[30] The RAF, however, had even greater problems. Trenchard admitted that until late 1922 the RAF would not even be able to meet 'normal requirements without experiencing difficulties and delays'; that the RAF could establish substitution in Iraq only when it was reorganised, if an air route system was built to allow rapid redeployment of RAF units and when it directly controlled many RAF squadrons overseas. These conditions were not met until autumn 1922.[31]

The RAF established this system only because the army refused to do so. Churchill wanted a modern army to gradually substitute mechanised units for traditional ones, especially cavalry. This approach would have had limitations. Mechanised units could have replaced many conventional ones but could not have fulfilled all Imperial policing requirements; indeed, a few cavalry units would have been needed for certain tasks. Still, the army could have modernised only by following Churchill's approach to mechanisation through substitution. Although his proposals would not have guaranteed a sustained policy of mechanisation, they would have removed many obstacles which blocked its development. The army missed this chance.

Churchill held that it did so because its reactionary leaders misjudged the value of modern arms.[32] Actually, in 1919–21 almost all generals overseas favoured a large measure of immediate substitution. Wilson, however, wrote: 'Do not put too much faith in mechanical devices taking the place of good stout English boys.

One of these days some fool may invent a machine-gun which will go off by itself, but until this is done keep as many Englishmen as you can to pull the trigger'. Despite a progressive attitude towards mechanisation, the general staff believed that such units could not replace many conventional ones. It underestimated the value of modern weapons in Imperial policing, but not because of a reactionary intellectual stance. It correctly warned that aircraft and mechanised forces alone could not surmount widespread colonial disorders, as Britain discovered in Palestine during 1929 and 1936–38. Moreover, given the organisational problems of the army and the RAF, much time was needed to establish a policy of substitution. Wilson was more honest than Trenchard and more realistic than Churchill regarding Britain's immediate ability to do so.[33]

Even so, the War Office did not reject the idea of substitution, which it was willing to enact in the future. This, however, was the flaw in its position. The key to the struggle over substitution was not the services' ability to establish it but their willingness to promise to do so. In 1920–21 the RAF gained because of its proposals for substitution, although it could not create that system until autumn 1922. Conversely, the army opposed the politicians' demands for immediate substitution, because of its grand strategic views.

Wilson feared the rise of a military alliance in the Middle East between Russia, Turkey and other states, which might attack British possessions. His solution was to make a generous peace with Turkey and to leave friendly buffer states between British and Soviet territories by withdrawing from Persia, the Caucasus, Constantinople and all Iraq except Basra.[34] As ever, aspects of Wilson's assessment were questionable. His warnings of an imminent apocalypse were absurd; he overstated the likelihood and the dangers of such an alliance. However, with the important exception of Iraq, by 1923 Britain had adopted his Middle Eastern perimeter rather than those of Lloyd George or Curzon. Wilson's central arguments were absolutely correct: that Britain was strategically overextended, that its aims must not exceed its means and that it must alter its Middle Eastern policy. Nonetheless, these views hampered army policy in one way: they caused the general staff to reject immediate substitution. It opposed any reductions in its already strained conventional forces until the possibility of a military threat in the Middle East vanished. The army sought to defend Iraq against Turkey when its real enemy was the RAF. By surrendering the principle of substitution, Wilson inadvertently ensured the defeat of his entire policy. Although he wished to destroy the RAF, his miscalculations alone allowed it to survive. Only the success of Trenchard's substitution campaign saved the RAF from elimination in 1921 when, instead, a progressive army policy was jettisoned.

These developments arose from the relationship between Churchill, Trenchard and Wilson. Unlike the CIGS, the CAS understood what was at stake in substitution while long-term policy, above all else his claim for substitution, was Trenchard's primary concern. He pursued this carefully, moving only when he had political support, especially from Churchill. Conversely, Wilson, following many disparate aims, did not consistently pursue long-term policy because he was overwhelmed with immediate matters. His entire policy hinged on his grand strategic views, for unless the Cabinet accepted the latter they would reject the former. Wilson fought virtually all of Whitehall, making more enemies than he could afford. His diplomatic proposals irritated Lloyd George and the Foreign Office, his bureaucratic aggrandisement angered the other services while his rejection of immediate substitution antagonised the Cabinet, the Treasury and Churchill. The War Office could not defeat all these opponents. The most dangerous of its foes was Trenchard and the most unnecessary of its defeats was over substitution. Wilson alone caused Churchill to support Trenchard's substitution campaign, and only Churchill's support allowed the latter to win it.

In 1919–22 Churchill dominated army and RAF policies. Despite his usual cavalier disregard for consistency, he provided an admirable blueprint for reform. He wished to govern all three services and preferred to control the navy and the RAF because 'though aeroplanes will never be a substitute for armies, they will be a substitute for many classes of warship'.[35] Ultimately, Churchill could apply his ideas only to the RAF and the army. In early 1919 he stressed the value of modern units and favoured large forces: an RAF of 102 squadrons and an army of 375 000 men.[36] By summer, recognising that his services' estimates would be smaller than anticipated, Churchill revised his proposals.

The best indication of his priorities was Churchill's allocation of his £75 000 000 between these services. He gave the army £62 000 000, exactly its real estimates of 1913–14, and left the RAF just what remained.[37] He intended to establish his first priority, a modern army with its 1914 strength, at the expense of the RAF, a service which he did not even treat as completely independent. This decision hinged on Churchill's views about substitution. He believed that this should be established through the army, supported by the RAF. He regarded aircraft as just one element in modern garrisons, along with mechanised and conventional units. Only when the army refused to cooperate did Churchill treat the RAF as the primary element in substitution. Wilson drove him to support the RAF at the army's expense, entirely contrary to Churchill's instinct.

The Air Ministry's original postwar policy was ambitious. As CAS, Sykes advocated an RAF of 348 squadrons, 50 per cent larger than its peak wartime strength while the Air Council favoured 154 squadrons and 110 000 men.[38] However, Churchill demanded major alterations in RAF policy and appointed Trenchard CAS so to further this aim. Historians have argued that Trenchard favoured a small élite RAF, proposals which Churchill accepted after some debate.[39] In fact, Trenchard's initial ideas for the RAF's size were unrealistically large and similar to the last ones of Sykes. Trenchard and Churchill had different RAF policies over which they fought bitterly, for Churchill wanted the RAF to be a far smaller élite than did the CAS. Churchill allowed Trenchard to pursue his detailed policies only after halving the latter's proposed scale for the RAF.

By summer 1919 Trenchard wanted 82 squadrons, including 42 cadre ones, and 55 000 men, costing £23–£25 000 000. This would be 'a solid groundwork on which to begin. Any smaller basis would . . . be useless'. Churchill demanded a smaller basis. He offered £13 000 000 for RAF estimates and ignored the central elements in Trenchard's case: separate RAF administrative services, complete Air Ministry control over all RAF units and an independent role in Imperial policing. Churchill preferred a policy in which '(1) unit efficiency, (2) theoretical and practical mastery of air warfare and (3) mechanical leadership through experience' would take precedence over '(a) passive defence in all its forms, (b) mere numbers of men and machines and (c) multiplication of stations and dispersal of effort. We have to aim at quality and progress rather than quantity and immediate war power during the next ten years.'[40] Indeed, he was less sympathetic to Trenchard's plight than was the Treasury.[41]

However, by September Churchill and Trenchard had reached a compromise. Trenchard accepted Churchill's limits on the RAF's size while Churchill agreed that it must be independent and authorised Trenchard to present his detailed proposals to the Finance Committee.[42] Trenchard gave that committee three options: 'A', for major strategic requirements, repeated his 82 squadrons and £23 000 000 scheme; 'B', for Imperial policing with a small reserve, required 55 squadrons (including 21 cadre ones) at £17 000 000; 'C', for Imperial policing purposes alone, required 45 squadrons (including 18 cadre ones) at £15 000 000. Trenchard presented 'B' as a happy medium between two extremes. Lloyd George overcame this manoeuvre by authorising estimates of £15 000 000 within which Trenchard could incorporate the 'essential parts' of scheme 'B'[43] The government was well disposed towards Trenchard but its decisions were far from the RAF's hopes. The Air Council had expected the RAF to be treated as Britain's 'first line of defence'.[44] That idea had been fallacious and the RAF needed to find an independent role to justify its existence.

Most historians have stated that during the 1920s Trenchard always saw strategic bombing as the RAF's main role. Conversely, Malcolm Smith has argued that substitution was the RAF's overriding concern, with preparations for strategic bombing in the 'back seat'.[45] These interpretations are both misleading. Contrary to the orthodox view, the RAF usually emphasised substitution above strategic bombing. Until 1921 Trenchard never once argued that Britain should begin to develop strategic bombing forces: indeed, he stated in 1919 that no 'Independent Force in which the Air predominates will act in Europe during the next 20 or 30 years'.[46] Contrary to Smith, however, in 1922–25 the RAF sought above all else to develop strategic bombing forces, while the alacrity with which Trenchard leapt to establish this aim as soon as it became politically possible indicates that he was interested in this even in 1919–20. Yet for political reasons Trenchard pursued this aim through an indirect approach. He saw substitution and strategic bombing as complementary policies, his emphasis on them at any moment varying with the degree to which they could further his fundamental objective, to preserve a strong and independent RAF. In 1919–20 he realised that strategic bombing could not achieve this end until the politicians regarded the creation of such forces as an immediate necessity. He could most easily have impressed them by arguing that the RAF could significantly replace both the older services. However, until 1921 Trenchard dared not systematically advance this claim, which would have forced a battle with both the older services at once.[47] Instead, Trenchard concentrated on the policy which he had the best chance to achieve, to replace the army in Imperial policing. This caught army policy on a vulnerable flank.

Historians have argued that the army's policies failed because its desire to 'return to real soldiering' led it to oppose reforms, while the government also rejected a progressive policy. In fact, in 1919–21 the army's policy was intelligent and the government favoured it no less than those of the other services. The Treasury and the Cabinet, including even radical Liberals like H.A.L. Fisher, favoured a large and modern army.[48] The War Office wanted one at least as large and relatively as modern as in 1914. It maintained a Territorial Army (TA) of 14 divisions and hoped to maintain an expeditionary force of 6 divisions and to restore the Cardwell system, which in theory retained numerical equality between army units at home and abroad. It initially wanted 375 000 men but by late 1919 favoured 300 000 men, or 177 battalions: about 50 000 larger than in 1914. Wilson's immediate aim was to establish 158 battalions and an 'Interim' expeditionary force of two infantry divisions and one cavalry brigade.[49]

The army also wished to modernise its forces, which essentially meant mechanising them. Historians have emphasised the doctrinal debate of the 1920s about mechanisation but have paid little attention to the army's policy regarding it in 1919–21. Several key figures, including Churchill and the Master General of Ordnance, General Furze, then believed that mechanised forces would dominate warfare. The general staff's opinion was less radical but still progressive. It wished to assimilate armoured forces '*into* the Army', where they would augment conventional units rather than create a new mode of warfare.[50] Despite its flaws, this view was no more fallacious than J.F.C. Fuller's belief that armoured forces were already the only useful elements in war.

The War Office favoured the development of an 'Independent Tank Force for exploiting or forcing a success' plus armoured units for 'close cooperation' with infantry. It authorised a 3000-man Tank Corps and planned to form 2–3 infantry tank battalions for an 'experimental brigade' in 1920.[51] By late 1920 it had eight mechanised companies with men and material for many more, while the general staff and Churchill wished to allocate £625 000–£1 000 000 to create three tank battalions in 1921.[52] The Deputy CIGS, General Chetwode, noted that the army was 'trying desperately' to form an experimental brigade for 1921. Wilson termed this 'looking round the corner': to learn how modern weapons would affect warfare five to eight years ahead, a date which coincided with the end of the ten-year period.[53]

The War Office made many errors regarding mechanisation in 1919–21. It failed to use much of the money allocated for armoured equipment while its experts spent most of the rest on the abortive Medium 'D' tank.[54] Due to operational requirements the 1920 experimental brigade manoeuvres were cancelled. The mechanised units were disorganised and, in Wilson's words, received a 'rotten time'.[55] Yet some such problems were inevitable. The general staff devoted attention and money to armoured forces and planned to investigate how these had affected war. Whatever its failings, this was a promising start for mechanisation.

The army's policy was progressive but it pursued many expensive proposals to meet the requirements of Imperial policing and major war. Unless the army received very large estimates it would face a dilemma in which any of its policies could be maintained only at the cost of others. For example, the TA was essential for major war but useless for anything else, and was budgeted at £8 000 000 per year, about 15 per cent of normal army estimates, at the expense of the regular army. To avoid this problem the general staff often tried to abolish the TA, a suggestion which the government always rejected.[56] Nonetheless, the War Office was trying to do too much. It could have justified its policies to the politicians only through a careful selection of priorities between them or through effective politics. Since the War Office did neither, it could not prevent the politicians from imposing their own priorities on the army.

The War Office made costly political errors in 1919–20. Unlike the other services it neither gained nor sought the Cabinet's authorisation for its policies. The Finance Committee simply approved a statement by Churchill that although normal army estimates would be £62 000 000, for some years the army would require only £55 000 000 by living off stocks.[57] Yet the War Office's policies would cost well above £62 000 000. It also failed to reconcile its policies with the Cabinet's strategic principles. Whereas the prewar army had two roles, Imperial policing and insurance against major threats, the August 1919 principles specifically forbade it to prepare forces solely for great wars. Although Wilson accepted this principle, he wanted larger forces for this purpose than did the politicians, for he saw immediate threats and declined to ignore major requirements. He wished to maintain a strong and modern army for Imperial policing, which would incidentally be effective for large wars in Europe or elsewhere.

This was a reasonable interpretation of the August 1919 principles and a good army policy. Unfortunately the politicians had not approved this definition while the army followed precisely the approach they most disliked. It wanted mechanised units without immediate substitution, large and modern forces and support services for Imperial policing. Wilson's army policy was far sighted; his politics were not. His failure to tailor his policy to suit Whitehall left the army vulnerable to the RAF. When Trenchard established his claim for substitution, army estimates were slashed, wrecking any hopes to further its proposals. A policy of substitution under its own control would have cost the army some conventional units but increased its mechanised ones. Instead, it lost the former without gaining the latter because of Wilson's greatest mistake: his rejection of Churchill's ideas for substitution.

Churchill argued that overseas garrisons needed only to maintain internal security, while Imperial reserves would withstand external aggression. He favoured an Iraq garrison of 5000 British and 15 000 native troops with the 'requisite aeroplanes, armoured cars, etc'. Only 10 RAF squadrons and 50 000 British soldiers should be stationed in India, about 10 000 less than in 1914. All cavalry regiments and most artillery units should be mechanised. One tank battalion could replace six or more cavalry regiments and at least 50–60 per cent of Britain's 28 cavalry regiments should be abolished. Churchill sought to hasten this process by increasing expenditure on armoured equipment, realising that until this was ready the army's 'general problem' would be insoluble. 'We cannot do without the manpower until the mechanical devices are in existence'.[58]

By early 1920 Churchill reduced the forces in the Middle East but told the Cabinet that further economies would require substitution there; thus, a garrison of 6000 white and 16 000 native soldiers designed to maintain internal security would reduce Iraq's defence costs from £22 500 000 to £5 500 000. The Finance Committee supported these proposals.[59] Churchill still wanted the army to establish these garrisons, which he believed that no RAF officer would command until the 'distant future' The commander in Iraq, General Haldane, reported that Churchill

> wants me to cut down expenditure in Mesopotamia . . . Defences to be organised differently . . . There would be certain risks in reducing, and if I felt they were too great I must represent the fact. Garrison must be reduced; have fort at Bagdad, flying columns, air force, river gunboats, native levies, steel pepper-

boxes, road cantonments. If there was a Bolshevist invasion, that would be a different matter and would require other action.[60]

However, the general staff rejected Churchill's proposals until the Middle East became more stable.[61] Trenchard used this opportunity to show Churchill that there was another way to establish substitution.

In 1919 the RAF had proved useful in Iraq and Afghanistan, but the decisive demonstration of its value came in Somaliland.[62] Writers have differed about that campaign. Leo Amery and Andrew Boyle have argued that seven aircraft alone won it, a task for which the army allegedly demanded three or four divisions, while Lord Ismay has claimed that the RAF was useless in these operations.[63] In fact, during 1918 the Colonial Office decided to destroy the power of Sayyid Hassan, the so-called 'Mad Mullah'. The War Office stated that 35 aircraft and one division would be needed for this purpose, but offered no forces for it. The Colonial Office decided to mount the campaign anyway, with two paramilitary battalions and 'plenty of aeroplanes'. Trenchard, sensing a chance to further his claims for substitution, recommended an 'Independent' RAF campaign without any ground forces. The Colonial Office insisted on a combined operation.

The campaign aimed to kill or capture Hassan, crush his forces and capture his livestock and fortresses, the pillars of his power. Seven aircraft killed important Mahdist leaders, narrowly missed Hassan and scattered his forces and livestock, a rout completed by the RAF and paramilitary forces. The RAF failed to damage his main stronghold but paramilitary forces easily captured it and almost caught Hassan. His power was shattered.[64] Although paramilitary forces alone might have crushed his fragile position, in the actual campaign ground forces and aircraft were both essential, while the RAF was the decisive element. These operations demonstrated that some combination of 'mechanical devices' and conventional units magnified the power of Imperial policing forces, a fact grasped better by the Colonial Office than either service. The War Office had exaggerated the forces required while the Air Ministry had overestimated the effect of airpower. However, the RAF had demonstrated that it could establish substitution exactly when the general staff elected to oppose it in Iraq.

Before February 1920 Churchill only intermittently advocated the use of aircraft overseas. Still, he demanded substitution in Iraq and when the army declined to cooperate he immediately approached that service which would. This marked the turning point for army and RAF policies in the 1920s. Churchill offered Trenchard an extra £5–£6 000 000 for the RAF if it would take over Iraq in the immediate future. As before, aircraft were just one element in Churchill's proposals. In place of this scheme, Trenchard substituted his own, in which 10 RAF squadrons would dominate all other elements.[65] In practice, the RAF could not replace any conventional units anywhere, but its mere claim to do so strengthened its policy, for the Finance Committee approved an increase of five squadrons, specifically for Iraq. This, the first postwar increment in any service's strength, bolstered another RAF aim. Trenchard favoured a 'policy of concentration', in which squadrons 'in general reserve . . . could perform the double role of reinforcements for Naval as well as Military requirements'. The Air Ministry turned these five squadrons into such a reserve, under its direct control.[66] This gave Trenchard the means to pursue a general campaign of substitution against the older services. In 1921 the RAF survived only through claiming the ability to do so, while the army declined because it had lost the struggle over substitution.

By December 1920 each service had a postwar policy which it wanted the government to adopt. The fate of these policies hinged on their relationship with the August 1919 principles. The Admiralty had altered the latter to suit the former; the Air Ministry had tailored its policy to suit these principles; while the War Office had pursued neither alternative. Their policies soon came under pressure, for the government began to coordinate a strategic policy just as a powerful axis arose against the services. The Treasury sought to increase its role in strategic policy, to cut expenditure and to alter service policies. Barstow wanted the Cabinet to rule that 'the interests of finance must now be regarded as preeminent and superior to all other national interests beyond the actual security of the Empire from hostile attack'. Although Lloyd George considered Chamberlain and his officials alike to be 'hopeless', political necessity drove him to cut spending and thus to cooperate with the Treasury.[67]

In 1919–20 Lloyd George had dominated the Cabinet through his prestige in the country and his influence over the Conservative leadership. By December 1920 that position had changed. His prestige was declining while a public campaign was attacking government 'squandermania'. In Whitehall, Hankey observed 'a sign that often precedes the collapse of a Government' — that the

Cabinet increasingly could not resolve debates over policy. The Prime Minister 'is very keen on drastic economy. He has been reading history and finds that after the Napoleanic Wars a strong Government like his was knocked out by Parliament on expenditures'.[68] This inaccurate reading of history spurred Lloyd George to action. If he intended to avoid that fate, he could no longer let strategic policy drift. That had become bound up in his political survival.

5 Service Policies and Financial Policy, 1921

Throughout 1921 Lloyd George sought to rebuild his political position, to resolve Britain's strategic difficulties and to cut service spending. It was politically difficult to do so. In spring 1921 three Conservative ministers resigned, Long, Milner and Bonar Law, which weakened Lloyd George's hold over the Cabinet and necessitated its reorganisation. He made Churchill Colonial Secretary, Robert Horne Chancellor, Laming Worthington Evans War Minister and Lord Lee the First Lord. Frederick Guest became Air Minister but as that was not a Cabinet post, Churchill represented the RAF's interests there. Austen Chamberlain, the Conservative Party leader, became Lord Privy Seal while Balfour, the Lord President, became responsible for the CID. These appointments altered the politics of strategic policy. Churchill and Balfour gained influence over service policies as a whole, while the services' power declined. Their new ministers fought ably but none of them was politically strong. Lloyd George had selected them precisely for that reason, to ease the cutting of their estimates. This indirectly strengthened the Treasury, although not enough for its purposes.

In 1921 the government began again to correlate its foreign, service and financial policies. The imperatives of defence and economy clashed and those of diplomacy held the balance. Instead of making unrelated service decisions, the government sought to coordinate them and to link them to the August 1919 principles, most important of which were substitution and Britain's naval standard, although statesmen increasingly tried to use the ten-year period and the £135 000 000 limit to govern service policies. These principles were enforced on the services after a year-long struggle over strategic policy.

The first round of this struggle occurred between November 1920 and March 1921. The Treasury warned that the 1921–22 budget would equal £1 319 000 000, with service estimates of £255 000 000, figures which should be cut to the 'normal year' level. The Finance

76

Committee ordered the Treasury to propose 'drastic' reductions, including 'at least' £100 000 000 on the services. The politicians wished to make a public statement of their proposed economies so as to conciliate the 'squandermania' campaign, but this declaration challenged the services' policies. The Cabinet pledged to reduce service spending to the minimum necessary to maintain 'our Imperial obligations and national safety'. It would examine the RAF's 'position' relative to the older services, which hinted that the RAF would either be abolished or take over roles from its fellows. The Cabinet promised to reduce Britain's Middle Eastern garrisons and to delay the navy's construction programme.[1]

The Finance Committee complained that the services wanted 'the best of everything', to be 'doubly or even trebly ensured against every conceivable . . . risk'. It demanded radical alterations in their policies: to make the army adopt substitution, the navy accept Barstow's policy and to eliminate the RAF's independent administrative services. It argued that instead of first determining and then funding Britain's strategic requirements, Britain should determine levels for service estimates and leave the services to meet these needs within those limits. However, the Finance Committee lost its battle against the services. It wanted service estimates of £174 000 000 while the services demanded £207 879 000: army and RAF £125 000 000 and navy, £82 879 000. They received £206 400 000: navy £82 500 000, RAF £18 411 000 and army £106 500 000.[2]

Yet economies remained politically necessary for Lloyd George while the Treasury needed them to balance the coming budget. In May 1921 Horne warned that revenues would fall sharply in 1922–23 to £950 000 000 while debt charges would approach their first peak, of £465 000 000. As just £485 000 000 would remain for departmental expenditures, £118 000 000 less than in 1921–22, all departments should reduce their spending by 20 per cent for 1922–23. The Cabinet authorised this proposal but reserved its control over 'any alterations in policy'.[3] That is, it might support any department which rejected such a cut on the grounds that this would compromise its policies. This did not suit Lloyd George and Chamberlain who, along with their allies Horne and Eric Geddes, intended to cut expenditure. Geddes warned that administrative economies would only scratch 'the problem with a pin, whereas we want to get on it with an axe'.[4]

Thus began the second round in the struggle for strategic policy. The services could surmount this threat only by standing on the issues which defined their requirements, strategic principles and grand strategy. Wilson recognised the army's dilemma:

> . . . the War Office is never given a standard up to which to work . . . we are greatly handicapped as compared to the Navy who have always had either a 2-power standard, a 1-power and 60% standard or a 1–power standard. Soldiers have no standard but not only that we have got a voluntary Army and no voluntary Army has any relation whatever to war . . . therefore the unfortunate War Office is given an instrument which has no relation to any known or unknown war, has no standard up to which to work and then is asked to make plans.[5]

The general staff accepted the principles which underlay the other services' policies, the need for maritime security and the role of strategic bombing.[6] It did not try to establish principles of its own, while the politicians rejected its grand strategy, problems which compromised army policy during 1921. Conversely, the RAF strengthened its policy through the arguments for substitution and the need for home defence against air attack, which became linked to Britain's attitudes towards France. The navy did so through Britain's relations with Japan and the US and the one power standard.

In December 1920 the Cabinet made the anodyne announcement that Britain would maintain a naval 'standard of strength which shall adequately secure the safety of the Empire and its maritime communications'.[7] Although the CID agreed that the one power standard would govern naval policy, the meaning of that standard was obscure. As Barstow noted, it

> has never been authoritatively interpreted and in one very important sense it is far from clear. Does it mean that the British Fleet is to be equal to that of any other Power in British Waters? or in the selected area of operations of the rival Powers? or finally, is it to be equal on paper?

Bonar Law commented that the standard 'might mean much more' than its name; equally, it could mean less.[8] It was used to justify a fleet larger and smaller than the USN. The Admiralty interpreted it to mean that 'the Navy should be maintained at sufficient strength to ensure the safety of the British Empire and its sea communications as against any other Naval Power'. As it refused to accept a 'defensive strategy', it claimed in principle that the standard required equality to the USN in American waters: or a fleet larger than the USN and, incidentally, than any other two navies. Conversely, the Geddes Committee noted that 'the translation of that standard into £.s.d. in the Estimates admits of wide variation', while Lloyd George and the Treasury wanted to meet it just on paper.[9] It was a symbol of power. It did not define British naval needs.

The foundations of Britain's maritime position were undergoing change. Since the naval powers were spread across the globe, it could no longer 'command' every sea simply by dominating European ones. As no state could easily concentrate its strength in another's waters, maritime power was becoming regionalised, while submarines and aircraft were altering the exercise of the functions of seapower. The value of seapower for Britain was shrinking while its relative industrial decline reduced its ability to meet eventualities such as war with several naval powers. This posed problems for an empire founded on seapower, but not insurmountable ones. Britain had always had difficulties in fighting several naval powers. In 1921 no state threatened Britain, which retained the world's largest fleet and shipbuilding resources and had the time necessary to safeguard its position at sea.

Nor did Britain face simply a naval problem; rather, a grand strategic one. That could be resolved by gaining allies and cutting commitments as well as through naval means. Richmond later argued that during the interwar period Britain forgot its traditional principle 'that the navy should be capable of meeting the combined attack of any reasonably probable coalition, in the several seas in which vital British interests lay'. Yet in 1921 he conceded that diplomacy alone could meet dangers such as a single-handed war against the US and France.[10] That is, Britain's maritime needs could only be gauged according to reasonably probable threats and naval means alone could not meet every possible one.

However necessary for prestige, the one power standard did not measure Britain's maritime needs. War with the US was unlikely and if one occurred even this standard could not necessarily sustain a British victory. The real criterion for maritime security was a two power standard excluding the USN, the ability at Britain's average moment to deter and to surmount an attack from the IJN and any European navy at their selected moment. Britain could have legitimately relied on diplomacy to avert still worse circumstances, such as arose by 1936. It had the resources to support this standard.

Yet to reach rational decisions on naval policy Britain had to understand the nature of its maritime requirements. At the heart of naval policy in 1921 was a controversy over these issues.

In 1920 Beatty synthesised the Admiralty's ideas on Britain's maritime imperatives: that it must match foreign 'Naval Expansion', develop the infrastructure necessary to maintain the fleet in its likely areas of operations, and recentre that fleet in the Mediterranean Sea, the 'hub of the Wheel of British Sea Power'.[11] The naval staff turned these ideas into a policy. The Admiralty decided that battleships and battlecruisers would dominate seapower during the foreseeable future, as, in fact, they did. Its designs would have provided the world's best such warships while Britain was extending its lead in naval aviation. The naval staff realised that a base at Singapore was needed to let the fleet operate in the Pacific. Finally, the Cabinet authorised the gradual accumulation of a one-year reserve of oil fuel for the fleet. The Admiralty initially planned to concentrate this reserve in the Atlantic, but extended it to Singapore to allow operations in the Pacific.

By 1921 the Board approved a construction programme, the 'eastern route' fuel reserve and the Singapore base, while the first plans were made to redistribute the fleet.[12] These proposals were necessary responses to specific problems but they would be dauntingly expensive between 1922 and 1926, costing £4 900 000 for Singapore, £84 000 000 for construction and £6 000 000 for fuel.[13] As usual, the navy's cost projections no doubt understated the real expense. Further, its policy contained a paradoxical flaw: the politicians were unlikely to complete these programmes according to their proposed rate and scale, yet even if fully completed, they could not meet the navy's strategic aims.

In case of war the navy planned to strike immediately at American and Japanese waters, annihilate their fleets and win through blockade. It stated that by 1930 such operations would require 29 battleships and battlecruisers and 202 other vessels.[14] This planning did not account for the changed nature and balance of seapower. Although Britain could have had this absolute strength by 1930, that would not necessarily have been enough to pursue such operations. Moreover, Britain's foes need not have fought immediate engagements, which in any case might not have produced decisive victories, or British ones. The naval staff appreciated the possibility of war against more than one power, but believed that Britain could only deal with this danger by concentrating its naval strength to quickly crush one enemy and then redeploying it against the others. The 'Mobility of the Fleet must . . . be the keystone of British Naval strategy'.[15]

Although the naval staff recognised that British naval strength was limited, its plans could not have worked unless that power had exceeded even its demands. In reality, any maritime war would have lasted for years, leaving the navy engaged in distant operations and Britain meanwhile vulnerable to other states. Britain would have found it difficult to fight two or more naval powers. The Admiralty failed to appreciate these facts because it had not analysed the nature of seapower, Britain's maritime requirements or its grand strategic situation. It simply assumed that every naval power was a threat which Britain must counter without considering whether Britain needed to, or could, counter them all. The Admiralty's programmes would provide the naval strength needed to maintain Britain's real maritime needs, but not to let the navy do what it believed that it must do.

Despite its flawed understanding of Britain's maritime position, the Admiralty's proposals were better than the alternative. Lloyd George and Barstow believed that the Admiralty's demands were larger and costlier than necessary. They raised far-sighted questions about the value of battleships while Barstow perceptively challenged the practicability of the navy's war plans, arguing that any naval war would be agonisingly slow and long.[16] Above all, both men held that since the terms of maritime power had altered, Britain could no longer 'command' all the world's seas and must readjust its position to ensure at least the security of its 'home waters'. Lloyd George argued that Britain should offer the US 'unchallenged superiority' in its 'special seas' while retaining the same in Britain's own.[17] Barstow asked whether it was

> reasonable to ask [Japan and America] [*sic*] to accept . . . a modest claim on our part that the British Fleet is always to be supreme *everywhere*? and if not, are we to be content with a weaker fleet in the rival Power's waters? and if a weaker fleet, does it matter very much how much weaker so long as we are strong in our own?

He argued that in determining Britain's maritime requirements

> the true criterion surely is that the Fleet is to be of *such a strength as will protect the vital national interests.* Not all the interests which are desirable are vital just as not all the risks which are

theoretically possible have the remotest probability. If we find that the protection of certain interests is beyond our power, we may have to take the risk of not protecting them.[18]

While entirely correct in principle, these arguments rested on fallacious foundations in practice. Britain could only have divorced its 'special seas' from those of other powers if it reached a secure maritime arrangement with the latter or wrote off its ability to defend part of the empire. However desirable these options might have been, the government did not establish the former or pursue the latter; thus, other powers could endanger Britain's maritime interests. Barstow and Lloyd George assumed that during the foreseeable future Britain would not be threatened at sea. However attractive this situation might be, it could not simply be wished into reality. By opposing all the navy's programmes they would have left Britain unprepared against unexpected dangers.

Despite Beatty's fears that 'The Politician has his knife into the Navy and the Navy is going to suffer', the Admiralty overcame these challenges.[19] In December 1920 Lloyd George established the Bonar Law Committee to examine the naval programme and, he hoped, to recommend that battleships were obsolete and their construction unnecessary.[20] This committee failed to achieve these aims or, indeed, any majority verdict. Three of its members, Bonar Law, Geddes and Horne (following the opinion of Richmond) argued that battleships were not outmoded but that no programme was needed, since war with the US was unlikely, while that expense would hamper Britain's strategic priority, the strengthening of its economy. The other members, Long, Beatty and Churchill, retorted that the programme was essential to maintain the one power standard.[21] Lloyd George then turned to another political manipulation to achieve his maritime aims. He offered to make Lee First Lord only if Lee would act as an 'Economy Minister' and tell the admirals 'to go to hell'.[22] Lee did cut the navy's 1921–22 estimates but, supported by Churchill and Balfour, he pursued its programmes.[23] By July 1921 the Cabinet approved these programmes in order to support Britain's diplomatic needs regarding Japan, the US and the Dominions.

This was to approve a policy which could maintain British maritime security. However, naval policy would soon face heightened financial pressure while these programmes had been approved only to support a temporary diplomatic purpose. They might be abandoned once they had done so. Since Britain did not understand the nature of its maritime requirements and was divided over how to meet them, there was no guarantee that it would continue to take the grand strategic actions which alone would preserve its maritime security.

Throughout 1921 an inter-service struggle dominated RAF policy. During 1919 most naval personnel had wished to control naval aviation while the army wished to govern the rest of the RAF. Since neither service pressed these ambitions decisively, most specific disputes were temporarily settled, leaving open the question of their relations in the future. The Air Ministry informed the older services that it could not meet all their air requirements during 1920. To gain their cooperation in this difficult period Trenchard pledged that their air 'cooperation squadrons' would eventually become 'an arm of the older Services'. Moreover, he promised Beatty that naval aviation would become a 'branch' of the navy, for which the latter would control policy while the RAF would provide personnel and material. Beatty, accepting this offer, agreed not to challenge the RAF's independence in 1920 if it would meet the navy's air requirements.[24] Although this condition patently could not be met, that problem was immaterial; the basis of this agreement was political, for a compromise over this issue would free Trenchard and Beatty to pursue others. This agreement affected only a small part of the RAF. As 75 per cent of its squadrons were in overseas garrisons, similar concessions to Wilson would leave the RAF subject to the army, precisely what the latter wanted. Wilson, disdaining Trenchard's 'vast ambitions', declined to make any promise of forebearance to the RAF. Ultimately, Churchill empowered the Air Ministry to determine the RAF's 'general strategic distribution' and to propose independent operations directly to the civil authorities overseas. However, he left the army operational control over all RAF squadrons in military garrisons.[25]

The RAF became quasi-independent, a status it would completely escape only in 1922, a supplying agency to the navy but basically separate from the army. The older services regarded as definitive Trenchard's pledge to give them their own air arms. Yet this agreement left ambiguous the practical relations regarding these squadrons and did not settle the real power of the services over the RAF. Throughout 1920 every service questioned this settlement. However, the older ones did not threaten the RAF's existence until Trenchard drove them to do so, by attacking them in order to overcome dangerous political pressures. In December 1920, for the only time in the 1920s, important politicians and officials seriously considered abolishing the RAF, believing that it would remain a luxury unless it could economically replace the older services. The Finance Committee also criticised the latter for extravagance because they declined to reduce their forces to account for the value of airpower.[26] Trenchard, facing a stark choice between the abolition of his own service or an attack upon the others, naturally chose to hunt with the pack. This achieved his main aim, for although the Finance Committee and the Treasury initially criticised Trenchard's 1921–22 estimates, they conceded more money than he had first requested once he began to challenge his colleagues.[27]

In January 1921 Trenchard prepared a memorandum which argued that the RAF could solve all British defence problems. It should control national defence against air or sea attack; could police overseas possessions, especially Iraq; could fulfill every function of seapower and soon sink even battleships.[28] Realising that these claims would force an inter-service battle, Trenchard moved only where he had political support. In order not to overplay his hand, he did not reveal beliefs such as that the RAF should control the older services' cooperation squadrons.[29] In early 1921 Trenchard struck at the army when he had Churchill's support, yet his main target was a more high-profile one, the naval programme.[30] Despite warnings from his advisors that the argument was untenable, Trenchard officially claimed that the RAF would soon decide naval operations. He reminded the Bonar Law Committee that no major war was supposed to occur before 1929. By then, if the RAF received some of the money from the naval programme, land-based aircraft would dominate the seas and battleships become 'an insurance for which we cannot afford to pay the premium'.[31]

Although this claim impressed Geddes, Bonar Law and Horne, Trenchard had to abandon it. He wanted Churchill to issue the doctrinal memorandum under his own name, which Churchill did only after bowdlerising it so as to claim that the RAF could simply fulfill subsidiary maritime functions.[32] This alteration shaped the inter-service struggle. Both the older services opposed Trenchard's doctrinal claims and feared that the RAF's increasing independence would sap their control over their air cooperation squadrons. The War Office wished to subordinate the RAF to the older services, along which lines naval and general staff officers were 'concerting' a joint operation.[33] The Admiralty might have supported this move had Trenchard continued to attack it. Since Churchill's amendments reduced this threat, the Admiralty declined to combine against the RAF until autumn 1921. By this time Trenchard had strengthened his position through two crucial victories.

He published his doctrinal memorandum and decided that the time was right to disclose his ideas about strategic bombing. He told the CID that civilian morale, the decisive target in war, could only be attacked directly by strategic bombing, which could be countered solely by responding in kind.[34] Trenchard did not claim that such a threat existed nor that Britain should begin to develop strategic bombing forces, but rather that this danger was possible and could only be met by creating such forces. Trenchard was not trying to make strategic bombing the RAF's main role; his case still centred on substitution. However, he laid the foundation to justify the establishment of such forces whensoever a European air threat should materialise, and used these arguments as another means to demonstrate the importance of an independent RAF. Balfour, acting for the Cabinet, accepted this case and gave the RAF primary responsibility for home defence.[35] This victory impressed the government, but, to ensure its survival, the RAF had to show that it could force defence economies. It did so in Iraq because of Churchill, the one politician willing to gamble on Trenchard's scheme for substitution.

In 1920 the RAF gained from its claims for substitution, but during the Iraq revolt the scheme itself became 'academic' and by autumn its future was uncertain. Trenchard and Churchill alone wholeheartedly favoured the idea, but they remained silent for the moment. While accepting the economic advantages of Trenchard's case, Whitehall evinced serious and reasonable reservations about its morality and efficacy. Despite pressure from the Somaliland government, the Colonial Office did not build its garrison around aircraft. The Indian authorities denied that the RAF could replace any army units on the northwest frontier, while the War Office opposed the Iraq scheme on the grounds that controlling a possession through 'baby-bombing' was immoral and impracticable. General Haldane regarded the RAF as an auxiliary arm, for 'the man with a rifle impresses the Arab where a mechanic does not'. The Iraq administration, which had advocated substitution in 1919, became more cautious about it in mid-1920, while the departments which controlled Iraq disliked Trenchard's scheme. Crowe termed the proposal 'rather mad', Curzon denounced the idea that junior officers should 'regulate' policy through 'well detonated bombs' while the India Office feared that reliance on a *'deus ex machina'* would hamper administration. Hankey and Montagu believed that aircraft could replace some internal security forces in Iraq but wanted to test this system before extending it wholesale.[36]

Substitution and the fate of RAF policy were at an impasse, for Britain demanded defence economies in Iraq, criticised the RAF for failing to replace the army but questioned Trenchard's scheme for Iraq. Churchill broke this impasse in December 1920. He first gave Wilson's proposals to the Cabinet: that Britain could hold all Iraq with three divisions, costing £25 000 000 per year, or withdraw to Basra, requiring one division and £8 000 000.[37] The Cabinet rejected these alternatives, wishing to retain all Iraq but more cheaply. It gave the Colonial Office control over Iraq and Palestine and the means to defend them. As Colonial Secretary Churchill adopted the RAF system. The Cabinet agreed that the RAF would control Iraq at £5–£6 000 000 per year, with its garrison falling from three divisions to eight Indian battalions, four British armoured car companies and eight RAF squadrons by spring 1922. At that strength RAF control would begin in October 1922. The Cabinet also approved the first air route, from Cairo to Bagdad.[38] Trenchard's proposals for Iraq had paid dividends, for this indication that the RAF could lead to defence economies profoundly impressed the government. In 1922–23 the RAF received most of the Colonial Office grant for Middle Eastern defence, which alone prevented reductions in its strength. Conversely, this decision crippled army policy.

The War Office had continually urged that British commitments should be cut to match its strength. It wanted Britain to make these cuts by abandoning Persia, Constantinople and Iraq and by concentrating for a final offensive in Ireland.[39] Although Britain evacuated Persia, it elected to hold Constantinople, enter negotiations in Ireland and control Iraq through the RAF. This new balance between strength and commitments had one devastating result. Whereas in 1920 the army had too little strength to meet its commitments, in 1921 it had too few commitments to justify its strength. By early 1921 Chetwode noted that the army might have to cut the expeditionary force by one division in 1922 unless the Treasury were to be 'a little bit more liberal with us'.[40] That was to ask the unlikely and by summer 1921 the situation had worsened. The decision about Persia and Iraq rendered a division surplus to requirements in 1922–23; that on Ireland would eliminate the 'normal' Irish garrison of one division, which was included in the expeditionary force. That force and overseas garrisons alike would have a spare division. Given the financial situation, the obvious solution under the Cardwell system was to eliminate them both.

The War Office recognised this danger. It opposed any reductions in fighting units although it believed that, if necessary, support services and the TA could be halved.[41] However, Wilson disliked this prospect and knew that much of the army's problem stemmed from the scheme to control Iraq through 'Hot Air, Aeroplanes and Arabs'.[42] He held that this could not defend Iraq against attack from Turkey or Russia. Britain could do so only by reinforcing Iraq, yet as any troops removed from there might be eliminated, no reinforcements would exist and débacle would be certain. However, the army had the surplus strength to garrison Iraq and, by doing so, could reduce the scope for cuts. Thus in July Wilson demanded that Iraq either be evacuated except for Basra or garrisoned with 22 battalions, including at least seven British ones.[43]

The Cabinet rejected these ideas but the War Office tried to alter this decision by attempting to wreck the RAF's system in Iraq. It refused to provide any forces for that system including armoured car units, without which it would have been unworkable.[44] Wilson thus alienated friendly officials, increased Churchill's hostility to army policy and yet gained nothing. Trenchard prepared to control Iraq without the army, particularly by forming armoured car units under the RAF, while Churchill also gave the RAF control over Palestine. The Iraq garrison for 1922–23 was increased only marginally, to two British and seven Indian battalions instead of just eight Indian ones.[45]

The army's cuts of 1922 stemmed from these decisions about Iraq and Ireland. The army could not have altered the latter decision, except by winning the Irish war, but with a different policy in 1919–20 it could certainly have established its own substitution system in Iraq. The Irish decision would have forced reductions but these were magnified by the army's concurrent loss of Iraq, of a role and the funds which had justified and financed a British division. Under the Cardwell system every unit left in Iraq could have saved itself and another from elimination. Had the army created its own substitution scheme it would have lost some conventional units but not so many. It might have preserved 33 per cent of the strength cut in 1922 (losing only those units wholly recruited from southern

Ireland) and in turn would have increased its mechanised forces.

Instead the RAF fed at the expense of the army's conventional and mechanised units. By 1921 the army reorganised its mechanised forces, developed reliable equipment and decided to replace four cavalry regiments with four tank battalions between 1922 and 1924. Wilson recognised that modern weapons would soon cause 'something of a revolution in (the army's) preparations for war, and other things being equal, that army will win which has most surprises in store for the enemy'. He wanted experimental brigade manoeuvres to 'peep into the future so far as money will allow us'. Although these manoeuvres were not overly progressive, they still studied the role of tanks, anti-tank weapons and aircraft.[46]

By autumn 1921 the general staff adopted an approach to mechanisation similar to Churchill's proposals of 1919; to downplay the role of armoured forces for European conflicts but to develop them for Imperial policing. As Chetwode wrote, 'our first business was to make ourselves as invincible as possible in India or the Near East or in any of the small affairs in which the British Empire is constantly engaged. For these purposes tanks, even the ones we had at the end of the war, would probably prove decisive'.[47] This policy, the best the army could have followed in the 1920s, was formulated too late. By 1921 the government refused to finance new armoured units unless they could immediately save money by substitution. Yet the army had lost the best areas in which to do so and the surplus conventional units to exchange for mechanised ones. Since the army had opposed immediate substitution the government regarded it as reactionary, and consequently wrecked the army's progressive proposals for mechanisation.

By late 1921 politics, strategic principles and diplomatic developments had strengthened naval and RAF policies but not those of the army. The future of their policies hinged on their 1922–23 estimates, which Warren Fisher told them should be £40 000 000 less than in 1921–22, excluding savings from the Middle East, or around £165 000 000. The services' sketch estimates equalled £171 058 600, including £12 720 000 for Middle Eastern defence. The Admiralty demanded £81 200 000, the Air Ministry £12 957 000 (excluding a Colonial Office grant of £1 720 000) and the War Office £64 198 000, with another £11 000 000 for the Middle East. In formal terms the navy offered a 2 per cent cut on 1921–22, the RAF 20 per cent and the army 35 per cent. Reckoning for matters like changes in accounting procedures and the fall in prices, however, the reality was different. For example, the army reduction of £30 000 000 was a real cut of only £3 500 000. In effect the RAF and the army offered only to defer some ancillary spending; the navy demanded estimates about 10 per cent larger than in 1921–22.[48]

Although these proposals approached the Treasury's initial demands, this pressure soon increased. On 2 August Horne asked the Cabinet to empower an independent committee of businessmen under Geddes to propose cuts in government spending but not to 'criticise' policies. Since many ministers opposed this idea, the Cabinet gave this body only advisory and not 'executive functions'. Chamberlain and Horne wished to reduce even these powers but Geddes insisted that Lloyd George's allies had agreed that his committee must challenge policies. Lloyd George supported Geddes and forced the Cabinet to let this committee recommend changes in policies, and to propose a £100 000 000 cut in the draft budget.[49]

Even Lloyd George's allies misunderstood his intentions. The Geddes Committee was his means to cut certain types of spending, pre-eminently of the services. Notably, its proposed cuts fell most heavily not on social but on military expenditure. Lloyd George and the Treasury hoped that this committee would secure their aims against the services. The latter played into their hands. By autumn 1921 they realised that economies were inevitable, which the older services wanted the RAF to absorb while it returned the favour. The older services resented Trenchard's 'usual exaggerated. . . "if", "may' and "possibly"' claims that they should be cut today because the RAF might replace them tomorrow. Following Trenchard's example Beatty and Wilson chose to preserve their services by attacking another. For the only time in the 1920s the older services jointly sought to abolish the RAF.

The services used the Geddes Committee to further their internecine aims. The Admiralty and the War Office claimed that eliminating the RAF would provide economies, while the Air Ministry claimed that it could force the same on them.[50] By accusing each other of extravagance, they placed this committee of businessmen in a familiar environment, a buyers' market in strategy. This weakened them all against the Treasury. The latter raised objections to their policies identical to those which it had made since 1919, but this time with some effect. The Treasury believed that Britain would be secure during the foreseeable future and that service expenditures could safely fall below £135 000 000. It challenged the services' use of strategic principles, particularly the ten-year period. Barstow argued that the Admiralty planned to 'be ready for a major war in 10 years (from 1919)' but, 'if as the years go on the prospect of war continues to recede, there is no reason why the programme of accumulation even if maintained at the total previously contemplated should not be slowed down'.[51]

The Treasury demanded the elimination of every army unit which was not required simply for Imperial policing. It favoured some cuts in, but not the abolition of, the RAF because Britain 'is vulnerable from the Air' while the RAF had already 'undercut' the army and might 'render all battleships obsolete'. The Treasury entirely rejected naval policy. It opposed the Singapore base and the fuel programme, demanded sweeping reductions in personnel and warships and wanted naval estimates to be less than £60 000 000. It denied that Japan or the US were threats and believed that any British construction might spark an arms race which alone could cause them to become so.[52]

The Geddes Committee adopted these views. In December 1921 it criticised the services for demanding 'nothing short of perfection'. It recommended that the ten-year period should be enforced on the services, which should be told 'how much money they can have and . . . frame their principles accordingly'. The services absorbed £59 700 000 of the proposed £100 000 000 cut: navy £21 000 000, army £20 200 000 and RAF £5 500 000 with another £13 000 000 of unspecified economies from the older services. The committee recommended that 35 000 naval and 55 800 army personnel and many commissioned warships should be cut. It supported the independent RAF and proposed primarily the reductions which Trenchard had offered, the elimination of $8\frac{1}{2}$ of the $9\frac{1}{2}$ army and naval cooperation squadrons.[53] Trenchard turned the committee to where it would least harm the RAF and most damage the older services.

The third round in the struggle over strategic policy occurred between December 1921 and March 1922. The stakes hinging on the Geddes Committee's proposals included Lloyd George's political future and the policies of the services and the Treasury. The economisers, believing that the services wanted more than necessary for defence, demanded changes in their policies. Although they criticised the army they most challenged the navy, while Trenchard had gained their support for the RAF's survival. The Geddes Committee's proposals would further the ends of Lloyd George and the Treasury but would leave the navy weaker than the USN and the army and the RAF scarcely fit for minor operations. The question was whether Britain dared take these risks. The answer turned on the nature of its foreign policy.

6 Strategic Policy and Diplomacy, 1919–22

After the armistice Britain wanted to dominate the Middle East, maintain its maritime security and establish a new balance of power in Europe and the Pacific. In the belief that Britain would continue to be secure and achieve its diplomatic aims during the foreseeable future, the government formulated its strategic policy of 1919. When these assumptions proved unrealistic, strategic policy had to be altered. Even in the best circumstances Britain would have had to curb some of its ambitions in order to secure the remainder through an accommodation with other powers. The need for such alterations arose when unexpected events, like the US withdrawal into isolationism, hampered British policy. Since the government overestimated the strength of its diplomatic position, however, it declined the compromises needed to accommodate other states. Consequently Britain found it increasingly difficult to further its foreign policy and came to believe that other nations were challenging its vital interests, while the balance of power which Britain had hoped would underwrite its security did not emerge. The prospect of strategic cooperation with the United States receded, which caused Britain to reconsider the wisdom of its commitments to France and Japan. Simultaneously, statesmen came to think that many nations, especially a coalition centred on Russia, could threaten Britain.

Historians have seen the concepts of such matters as a Russo-German-Japanese alliance as being, in Professor Nish's words, a 'will-o'-the-wisp'.[1] Yet these ideas did not refer to immediate but rather to eventual dangers. Britain was right to consider the nature of future threats and the desire to forestall them did influence its foreign policy in 1920–22. Proponents of an Anglo-French alliance, like Crowe and Henry Wilson, and supporters of more lenient terms to Germany, such as Lloyd George and the general staff, referred to the need to prevent a Russo-German alignment. Churchill and Montagu argued that only generous terms to Turkey could prevent a Russo-Turkish-German combination. The wish to avoid a Russo-

German-Japanese axis shaped the debate over the Anglo-Japanese alliance while fear of potential French, Japanese and US threats also affected British policy.[2]

Underlying British foreign policy in 1920–21 were debates over two fundamental issues: which interests should be sacrificed to further what others and whether strategic isolationism or commitments would best suit its aims. Statesmen disagreed over these questions and their answers were dominated by Lloyd George and Curzon, supported by the Conservative Party leaders. Although most ministers differed from these men on certain matters, and Churchill on virtually them all, the Prime Minister and the Foreign Secretary could be overridden only when they disagreed between themselves, as over the Turkish peace treaty on 6 January 1920. Lloyd George and Curzon shared strategic views and often compromised on diplomatic ones so to dominate the Cabinet. Thus in 1920 Curzon supported Lloyd George's Russian policy while the latter backed Curzon's Middle Eastern one, though each disliked the other's approach.[3]

By 1921 statesmen realised that Britain could not achieve all its postwar ambitions. So to further as many of these as possible, they finally steeled themselves to painful actions such as sacrificing certain interests, accepting commitments with foreign powers or approving service programmes. Britain's decisions on strategic policy of 1922 turned on its success in adjusting these ambitions.

In 1919–21 Britain's policies towards the United States and Japan were interrelated, as it sought to prevent the US from striving for maritime supremacy and to bolster its strategic and diplomatic position in the western Pacific and east Asia. Since historians have misjudged the connections between Britain's decisions on the Japanese alliance, naval construction and the Singapore base, they have misunderstood the nature of each of these decisions. Thus, Roskill has not examined how foreign policy shaped naval policy. James Neidpath has argued that since the Singapore base was intended simply to ensure British maritime communications, therefore its development was unaffected by strategic views of Japan or the Japanese alliance. In fact, since Britain held that Japan alone could threaten these communications, its decisions on this base always hinged on its attitude towards Japan and especially the alliance. Conversely, Nish has misconstrued the strategic background to Britain's decisions about the alliance, for example, its fears that

Japan might join a revisionist coalition. MacDonald has argued that fears of naval rivalry with the US led Britain to abandon the alliance, without explaining why in mid-1921 the Cabinet wished to renew it.[4]

Britain's decisions on these matters were shaped by its perceptions of Japan and the United States. Barnett has argued that Amcricophile attitudes led statesmen to sacrifice British interests in pursuit of an illusory Anglo-American friendship. In fact, Britain's approach towards Washington was calculating, with any sentimental predilections for or against it being balanced by similar ones towards Japan. Professor Watt has defined four groups of viewpoints towards America in Whitehall: the 'nationalists', 'Americophiles', 'neo-imperialists' and those 'in search of a possible America', which would support British aims.[5] However, this system does not adequately categorise the actions or explain the motivations of decision makers. One can rarely determine which of them belonged to what group at any time, particularly as they all pursued a 'possible America'. Watt himself has found it hard to place individuals within these groups, assigning, for example, Churchill to all four of them at various times, which could equally well be done with others like Beatty and Wellesley, chief of the Foreign Office's Far Eastern Department. Nor did members of these groups behave as might be anticipated from their names. One would expect 'nationalists' to defend British interests more firmly than 'Americophiles'. Yet 'nationalists' like Bonar Law opposed naval construction as a means to maintain maritime equality because they feared that this would spark an arms race while, despite this risk, 'Americophiles' such as Lee favoured construction. One can understand how Britain's attitudes towards the United States affected its decisions only by placing these views within the context of Britain's perceptions of Japan.

A feeling of kinship with the United States and of suspicion of Japan affected British decisions. Beatty referred to America as being 'allied to us in blood, in language and in literature, and with whom we share the mutual aspiration of maintaining the peace and progress of the world'. More realistic decision makers like the general staff agreed that Britain should clash with the US only on the most vital of issues, while fears of the 'Yellow Peril' shaped Britain's perceptions of Japan. The CID held that 'the most likely war for some time to come would be one between the white and yellow races whose interests lay in the Pacific'. Wellesley agreed that Japan was pursuing 'the ultimate supremacy of the yellow races under Japanese leadership', which could threaten 'the future of civilisation'. Churchill feared that Japan was dominated by 'Jingoes' who wished to attack America; notably, after the Washington Conference, when these 'Jingoes' appeared to have lost their influence, he altered his views regarding the Japanese danger to Britain. Many Foreign Office officials believed that since Japan desired to dominate China, Britain and the US shared diplomatic interests while Britain and Japan did not.[6]

These perceptions led a few politicians and many officials to exaggerate Britain's differences with Tokyo and underrate those with Washington. Yet decision makers supported cooperation with America only on terms which suited British interests and recognised the advantages of liaison with Japan. Lloyd George and Chamberlain regarded Japan as a 'scrupulous and faithful' ally while, to Curzon, Japanese statesmen might drive 'hard bargains ... yet they attempt to play the game'.[7] Whitehall had progressively less faith that US ones would do the same, or even knew the rules of play. Britain did have more to gain from cooperation with Washington than Tokyo but, whereas it assumed that Japan would happily remain an ally, it could never be assured of support from America. Britain also appreciated that both Japan and the United States could become threats, Japan by attacking British possessions, America by subverting British maritime security or the loyalty of the Dominions. Hankey alone wanted to rely solely on Imperial strength for security in the Pacific.[8] Other decision makers favoured strategic cooperation with Japan, the United States or both.

Only an Anglo-Japanese-American *entente* could have achieved all Britain's vital interests. Since American attitudes prevented Britain from retaining both the Japanese alliance and good Anglo-American relations, it had to choose between these powers: to renew the alliance or to abandon it and pursue close ties with Washington. Either choice could dangerously antagonise one of these states. Since, despite its advantages, an Anglo-American *entente* could not be established, Britain's best choice was to retain Japan as an ally and still to seek tolerable relations with Washington. Admittedly, this policy could have alienated America while Japan might have accepted nothing less than strategic support against the United States.[9] Although the cancellation of the alliance did weaken Britain's position, the only alternative might have been equally dangerous.

In any case Britain did not sacrifice its vital interests to 'appease' America, but sought to defend them against the latter. British officials initially preferred not to renew the alliance because they hoped to establish an *entente* with the US. When that hope vanished and the United States appeared to be threatening British interests, the Cabinet wished to renew the alliance regardless of its repercussions in Washington. Since the latter offered nothing to Britain, London refused to sacrifice anything in return; indeed, by showing Washington the power of its hand, Britain hoped to persuade America to abandon its challenge at sea. Some decision makers wished to renew the alliance precisely to strengthen Britain's strategic position against America. Madden and Wilson noted that the alliance could support Britain during conflicts with the United States. Whereas Churchill perceived 'no more fatal policy' than to rely on Japan against the United States, Lloyd George saw 'one more fatal policy'; to remain at America's 'mercy'.[10]

In 1917–19 Whitehall rejected House's proposals that a condition for an Anglo-American *entente* would be Britain's abandonment of Japan.[11] It seemingly wished to have both the alliance and an *entente*. By 1920 this arrangement was not feasible and the question became whether cooperation with Japan or America would best further Britain's interests. The Foreign Office posed this question to the Admiralty and the War Office, asking them to consider whether Britain should renew the alliance in 1921. Only the War Office wholeheartedly wanted to do so, because, unlike other departments, it recognised the impossibility of an *entente* with America. The Admiralty wished to abandon the alliance although it admitted that Britain could not pursue a 'strong policy involving the possible coercion of Japan'. It anticipated Anglo-American cooperation and expected Britain to strengthen its naval position in the Pacific. The Foreign Office believed that renewing the alliance would antagonise Washington but increase British influence in Tokyo, and feared that if the alliance were abandoned Japan might eventually ally with Russia, Germany or France. Curzon wanted to renew the alliance but his officials, excluding Crowe, who denied any possibility of 'co-operation' with the United States, strongly favoured an Anglo-American *entente* directed against Japan. They wanted to renew the alliance only if America declined any cooperation whatsoever with Britain.[12]

The departments believed that an Anglo-American *entente* would eliminate any American challenge to Britain and allow them together to control Japanese policy. By spring 1921, however, these officials had no influence on Britain's decisions while the government simultaneously recognised that such an *entente* was out of reach and that Britain must counter US naval policy. Contrary to Nish's account, Britain did not choose to renew the alliance at a moment when it believed that Washington favoured a naval limitation agreement. Britain chose to do so because it believed precisely the opposite. Britain's ambassador to Washington, who had earlier argued that renewing the alliance would wreck Anglo-American relations, claimed by 1921 that nothing could be lost by renewing it, since America would remain hostile to Britain while nothing but informal naval limitation agreements could ever be possible. The Foreign Office expected the USN to complete at least the '1916' programme and doubted the significance of the pressure for naval limitation in the US Congress, led by Senator Borah. Tyrrell who regarded Borah's actions as a 'very dishonest and despicable political move', held that 'nothing will stop the execution of the 1916 programme'.[13] Although the politicians wanted naval limitation, they did not regard this as immediately possible. Everyone, including 'Americophiles', intended to meet this challenge.

However, Britain was defending not one but two vital interests: its strategic position relative to both America and Japan. No single means could achieve both simultaneously; indeed, any solution to one would complicate the other. Unless Britain matched US construction, its maritime security would suffer; but this might produce an arms race. Abandoning the alliance might please Washington but anger Japan; renewing it would do the opposite. The government saw but two solutions to this dilemma, to renew the alliance or to begin a naval programme. It treated them as mutually exclusive, assuming that to adopt neither would compromise Britain's position and that to adopt both would antagonise Washington too dangerously.

Churchill, Lee and Balfour wished to abandon the alliance and maintain security against America through naval construction or limitation and against Japan by completing the Singapore base. Conversely, Lloyd George, Curzon and Austen Chamberlain hoped for arms limitation but agreed that if Washington would not agree, it would be threatening British interests. If so, Britain should respond by renewing not construction but the alliance. This would secure Japanese support and also influence US policy towards Britain, by which Lloyd George and Curzon apparently meant its naval policy. In the Cabinet on 30 May 1921 they and Chamberlain argued that the Japanese 'stand by those who stand by them'. Curzon noted that if Japan were not allied to Britain, it must become 'decidedly hostile', which Britain could not risk. For

> although Russia and Germany had for the moment ceased to be Great Powers which had to be taken into account, there was no certainty that in a few years' time we should not have a regenerated Russia; and whatever the form of the Russian Government might then be, the dangers of the past would be renewed. Moreover, with a resuscitated Russia and a renewed Germany . . . in ten years' time we might be faced with a combination of these Powers in the Far East, and to meet such a situation the Alliance with Japan would be a natural guarantee.

Lloyd George, who had 'for some time past thought a Russo-German combination to be a future possibility', argued that if Britain abandoned Japan, it might become 'easy prey for Russo-German advances'. The Cabinet agreed that Britain should renew the alliance and then ask the US to call a conference to address the disputes in the Pacific.[14] By retaining the alliance, the Cabinet hoped to bolster British strategy; by renewing this before the Pacific conference, it sought to strengthen Britain's maritime bargaining position with the US. The Dominions, however, mistrusted Japan. The need to gain their support for British policy shaped the Cabinet's decisions on the Singapore base. In June it favoured the construction of that base not for defence against Japan but against the Dominions. It 'strongly emphasised' the

> great importance of being in a position to tell the Dominion Governments that we had a Naval Policy . . . the United States were continually suggesting that the American Navy was available for the protection of civilisation and the white races of the world. But the main point was that we must be in a position to say that we had a practical plan. This was even more important than actually commencing the work of beginning Singapore at the present.

As the Cabinet forbade 'considerable expenditure' on the base before 1924, this would have little value for many years.[15] The base was approved simply to show that Britain could protect the Dominions against Japan, in order to gain their support for Whitehall's strategy against America. At the Imperial Conference, however, the Dominions rejected this policy. Despite their division over the alliance, they all favoured cooperation with the United States and wanted the Pacific Conference to occur before, not after, any decision about the alliance. Nor did the Australasian Dominions agree that the Singapore base could defend them against Japan. Dspite Lloyd George's protests, in response to these objections and particularly to ensure that Canada would stay in the empire, the Cabinet postponed any decision on the alliance. It elected first to pursue political and naval agreements with Tokyo and Washington.[16]

These decisions compromised British policy in the Pacific. Britain would enter the Pacific Conference with few bargaining chips against America and little influence over Japan unless it could renew the alliance. Washington had, in effect, a veto over this move. Instead of being an accomplished fact, the alliance became a topic for negotiation and Whitehall rarely referred to the possibility of renewing it. Britain would be simultaneously pursuing US concessions at sea and Japanese ones in Asia, with few strong cards of its own and with neither power committed to supporting any British interests. This turn of events crippled Brtain's chances of securing all of its aims.

In July the Cabinet, seeking to surmount these problems, adopted all the navy's programmes, not for strategic reasons but for diplomatic ones. Beatty was instructed to show the Dominions that the US could not defend them against Japan while Britain could do so through the Singapore base. The Cabinet also authorised the navy to build four battlecruisers. Whereas the Admiralty intended to complete this programme, the Cabinet regarded it as a 'bargaining factor' to gain US maritime concessions.[17] However, these steps rebuilt only part of Britain's position. In autumn 1921 at the Washington Conference, Britain sought to defend its interests at sea, in the Pacific and in Asia. Its bargaining position was too weak to secure them all and also fostered a flaw in British policy. Its naval proposals would let Japan dominate the western Pacific, which contradicted Britain's diplomatic and strategic aims.

The Foreign Office's concerns were the questions of Japan's policy in China and of 'the mastery of the Pacific'. Wellesley argued that Japan wanted a 'strong defensive' position in that ocean so as to dominate China, whereas Britain and America wished to 'rehabilitate' China and prevent 'any one nation' from dominating the Pacific.[18] Britain believed that its diplomatic interests in Asia coincided with those of America against which, however, its naval proposals were directed. It also wished to finish the Singapore base while preventing the development of any bases between Singapore, Pearl Harbor and the Japanese islands.[19] This proposal would cripple US naval strength in the western Pacific and leave Japan dominant there.

For Britain the Washington Conference produced surprisingly satisfactory immediate effects but potentially dangerous long-term ones.[20] The Washington naval treaty maintained as favourable a balance in main warships between Britain, America and Japan as Britain could have retained through continued construction, at a lower level of absolute strength. It did not in the least alter their existing areas of maritime dominance. The incipient naval race ended with Britain scrapping only obsolete warships while America and Japan sacrificed modern ones. This bargain suited Britain, for had an open-ended arms race continued, it would have had to spend a fortune to maintain its existing position, all the while haunted by the possibilities that it might fail to do so or provoke the hostility of a more powerful state. Britain could have gained one thing only from a continuation of naval construction: more modern and perhaps larger numbers of battleships and battlecruisers for the 1930s. However, its real problems in this regard stemmed not from the decisions of 1921–22 but of 1929–30.

The Washington naval treaty maintained the one power standard and in effect a two power one at their selected moment against Japan and any European state. It established a 5–3–1.75 ratio in the total tonnages of battleships, battlecruisers and aircraft carriers between Britain and America, Japan, and France and Italy. After the signatories completed their approved programmes, Britain would have 20 battleships and battlecruisers of 580 450 tons; the United States, 18 of 525 850; Japan, 10 of 301 320; France, 10 of 221 170; and Italy, 10 of 185 500. Between 1933 and 1945 the signatories would replace these vessels. All new battleships and battlecruisers, including two British battleships to be laid down in 1922–23, were limited to 35 000 tons and 16-inch guns. Britain and America could maintain an aircraft carrier strength of 135 000 tons; Japan, of 81 000; and France and Italy, of 60 000 each.[21]

This treaty left Britain the greatest power at sea. It had a decided lead in naval aviation, a larger strength in lighter warships, especially cruisers, and, according to the naval staff, a 'slight superiority' over the USN in the real strength of battleships and battlecruisers.[22] Although the treaty maintained British maritime security and did not prevent it from continuing to meet these needs, it was dangerous for an empire founded on seapower to define that strength by a treaty rather than strategic necessity, and certain aspects of the treaty did hamper Britain. The hiatus in the construction of battleships and battlecruisers harmed Britain's armament capacity, just as it did for Japan and America. As Japan and Italy violated some treaty clauses, Britain's maritime position became slightly worse than had been envisaged in Washington.[23] Moreover, Britain equalled two naval powers excluding the USN simply because the European fleets were obsolete. It might have a two power standard only on paper when France and Italy built modern warships, as they were entitled to do in the late 1920s, while Russia and Germany could also expand their fleets. As Britain's battleships and battlecruisers were older than those of Japan and the US, it would suffer more should the reconstruction programmes of the 1930s be deferred. In any case, since Britain could no longer hope to win quick victories against the USN, the IJN or any two powers, it would have to recast its naval policy.

The conference eased diplomatic tensions in east Asia, as Japan agreed to withdraw to its prewar position there. Yet new ones could easily develop, since China in chaos offered a standing invitation for Japanese intervention. The conference also weakened Britain's strategic position in the Pacific. British statesmen had sought some permanent means of cooperation with Japan or America. Beatty favoured 'a strong entente with U.S.A. at Washington' while Curzon hoped to retain the Japanese alliance in some form. Balfour, Britain's chief delegate at Washington, favoured an agreement between Britain, Japan and the US by which any two signatories (for example, Britain and Japan) could form a 'military alliance' against any fourth 'Power or combination of Powers' (such as Russia and Germany).[24] Unfortunately, the US would not enter an *entente* nor tolerate a continued Anglo-Japanese alliance while Balfour's suggestion did not interest Japan.[25] The conference's security treaties, the four and the nine power pacts, offered no support to Britain.

By 1922 Britain had weathered the US maritime challenge and furthered its aims in China. It could expect years of relative stability in Asia and of friendly relations with Washington, yet at a price. Britain had drifted into Imperial isolation, the very strategic position in the Pacific it least wanted, while Japan could overturn the order there whensoever it chose. The Foreign Office and the Admiralty realised that it could easily attack China or British possessions.[26] Although no minister regarded Japan as an active menace, they feared an eventual Japanese threat. Thus, they declined to entrust Britain's position in the Pacific entirely to Japanese goodwill.

During 1919 Britain hoped to establish hegemony over the Middle East. It expected to possess Palestine, Egypt and Iraq and to exert a sphere of influence over Persia, the Caucasian states, a rump Turkey, a Jewish national home, a greater Greece and the various Arab groups. This policy would be feasible only if Britain could continue to dominate the region militarily and if the strength of Russia could be crippled and that of Turkey shattered. By 1920 Britain's military capacity in the region had declined while the power of the Turkish Nationalists and Russia had risen. Churchill, Montagu and Wilson argued that Britain should respond by cutting its commitments, especially by making a generous offer to Turkey. Curzon and Lloyd George, supported by most decision makers, wanted Britain to pursue all its previous ambitions. Britain's failure to coordinate its aims and means to meet these new conditions compromised its policy in the Middle East.

When the Soviet regime grasped control over Russia Britain ceased to be the only great military power close to the Middle East. Whitehall expected Russia to challenge Britain's domination of the region or even to attack British possessions. It hoped to avert these dangers by turning the Caucasian states and Persia into a strategic barrier against the spread of 'Bolshevism', despite the army's warnings that Britain could not support this aim.[27] By 1921, however, pressure from Russia and the local states forced Britain to abandon its hegemony over Persia and the Caucasus. By then the Turkish nationalists had rejected the peace treaty for the Middle East, that of Sèvres, and thwarted British ambitions in Turkey. Throughout 1921–22 Britain waited on events and rejected the options which might have better suited its policy: to help Greece smash the Turkish nationalists or to abandon British aims in Turkey to gain Turkish friendship elsewhere. Even Lloyd George did not openly favour the former, nor did Churchill and Montagu advocate the latter.[28] British policy rested on Greek power against the Turkish nationalists. Only after 1922 and many embarrassments did Britain abandon its attempts to dominate Turkey. It retained control over much of the Middle East but failed to establish the hegemony of its dreams.

Historians of British policy towards Europe in 1919–22, like Orde and N.H. Gibbs, have not addressed the strategic aspects of that issue.[29] In particular, they have not explained why by 1922 Britain offered a security guarantee to France and simultaneously came to fear a French menace. British policy in Europe was shaped by the relationship between strategic and diplomatic issues, between its perceptions of threats to its security and of the best means to exercise influence.

The prewar balance of power in Europe had collapsed; Britain wished to build a new one. It hoped that the peace conferences would create a framework for this purpose, by slightly increasing French territory, weakening, without utterly alienating, Germany and Russia, forming a federation in central Europe and establishing a concert of the victor powers, including the United States.[30] The peace conferences did not establish these aims. Indeed, as Archibald Wavell wrote, after fighting "'the war to end war" they seem to have been pretty successful in Paris at making a "Peace to end peace"'.[31] America withdrew from European involvements, eastern Europe remained a power vacuum, Germany and Russia were alienated but only temporarily weakened, while France for the moment—but for the moment alone—dominated Europe. Britain perceived two great threats to its hopes to establish balance and stability in Europe. France might establish hegemony there in the near future or Germany and Russia might eventually combine to overthrow the European order.

By 1920 France was relatively far stronger than in 1914 while Germany and Russia, prostrate, were for the moment no longer 'Great Powers which had to be taken into account'. This situation, however, would not long endure. British statesmen held that French power would inexorably decline relative to Germany, which would become the greatest power in Europe. The general staff believed that Germany 'in a dominating position in Europe will be a natural enemy' to Britain. Balfour agreed that if Germany again pursued 'world domination, it will no doubt tax the statesmanship of the rest of the world to prevent a repetition of the calamities from which we have been suffering'. No French security system could make it 'anything but a second-rate Power, trembling at the nod of its great neighbours on the East, and depending from day to day on the changes and chances of a shifting diplomacy and uncertain alliances'.[32]   These developments posed obvious dangers, for which Britain saw central Europe as the tinder-box. As Balfour noted, if 'civilisation has to fear' the renewal of prewar German ambitions, 'it is in the East rather than in the West that the storm will first break'.[33] The small and squabbling states of central Europe could scarcely match Germany, particularly given the uncertainty surrounding Russia. Whatever their differences over intervention in the Russian civil war, during 1919 all British decision makers hoped that Russian power would be weakened permanently and that whatever regime emerged there would accept thc European order. By 1920 these aims too had failed. Britain believed that Soviet Russia would become a great power again, which would not actively support and might even seek to shatter the Euopean order. It held that Soviet and British interests clashed so directly that they could never work together in the foreseeable future. At best, they might accommodate their interests. At worst, Russia might join with Germany to upset the European order.

Britain's main concern was not with eastern Europe in itself, but that events east of the Elbe would affect the world west of the Rhine. Thus, to create a counter-weight on Germany's eastern frontier, France sought to create an alliance system with many of the successor states in central Europe. Such a situation might force Germany and Russia to combine in order to overthrow the entire order in eastern Europe so as to achieve the smallest of changes there, such as those which Germany would inevitably demand from Poland. This struggle could in turn spread to western Europe, forcing Britain to enter another great war, costly at best and deadly at worst, or to let a Russo-German alliance bestride the continent. British statesmen held that the foundations of the balance of power in Europe would shift dramatically over the next generation. For the moment, France could have greater influence than ever since 1812; ultimately, Germany and Russia would be stronger than before 1914. Britain wished to find some point of equilibrium to dampen the worst of the oscillations which would follow from this swing in Europe. That is, it favoured a stable order which could accommodate the growing strength and the legitimate demands of Germany and Russia without entirely upsetting the balance of power.

Consequently, Britain wanted to reform the European order. It hoped to let Russia re-enter the community of nations and to gradually satisfy the more moderate German demands for revisions in the Treaty of Versailles. It feared that France's desire to defend that entire treaty and to maintain military superiority over Germany might, in Hankey's words, 'leave France master of the Continent'. Alternately, this could throw Germany into Russia's arms and, so

Churchill wrote, concentrate 'all German thought and energy upon a war of revenge'.[34] Britain realised that under certain circumstances it would have to fight again in Europe to protect its security. Statesmen intended to use all their influence to prevent this need from arising, which, under the circumstances, meant above all else influence on France. Britain had to determine whether it could best convince France to adopt a different policy by maintaining its distance from Paris or by offering a commitment to French security. It was this issue which linked the strategic and diplomatic aspects of British policy towards Europe.

By late 1919 Britain hoped that America would remain involved in Europe, thus ensuring the stability of the general settlement. Consequently, Britain was willing to undertake major commitments there so to maximise its influence in detail. It pledged to guarantee French security, favoured the construction of a channel tunnel to prove Britain's determination to do so and also authorised negotiations for an Anglo-French commitment to Belgian security.[35] However, the US withdrawal into isolationism weakened the forces supporting the European order. British commitments now seemed strategically riskier if, in the worst case, even more necessary. These developments caused Britain to reconsider its policy in Europe.

At various times during 1920 some decision makers feared that the instability in Europe might lead to immediate dangers. At the height of these fears, during the Russo-Polish war, Hankey and Churchill thought that like the US, Britain might have to withdraw strategically from European entanglements, while Hankey, Wilson and Hardinge argued that either France, Germany or Russia could eventually threaten Britain.[36] However, the government did not perceive imminent dangers in Europe, believing that the strategic problems were long-term ones, which Britain could prevent from arising. Whitehall's psychological confidence in the strength of Britain's position in Europe was not shaken until 1922. In 1920–21 the debate was over how best to maintain and exercise that influence. One faction held that the road to Berlin led directly through Paris, that only by immediately guaranteeing French security could Britain hope to influence French policy and create the conditions for lasting peace in Europe. The other argued that for some time Britain could not hope to alter French policy and yet had time to wait, that it was precisely by avoiding such commitments that Britain could best achieve its ends. Lloyd George, acting on an idiosyncratic reading of history, wished to revive Britain's policy of 'isolation' after 1816, where 'we obtained a predominant influence on the Continent without committing ourselves too closely'.[37]

In 1920 the general staff advocated an alliance with France and Belgium, to guarantee British security against Germany and Russia, and to encourage France to agree to make concessions to Germany. The Foreign Office and Austen Chamberlain wanted Britain to guarantee Belgian neutrality in order to extend its influence in western Europe. The government, however, rejected these suggestions. Britain's guarantee to France was formally contingent on US ratification of its own commitment to that nation. When the United States reneged on its promise to France, Britain followed suit, and also rejected the channel tunnel and a guarantee to Belgium.[38]

Some decision makers mistrusted France and questioned the very principle of commitments in Europe. Thus, Hankey doubted that France 'could be bought, and even if she were bought, it is doubtful if she would stay bought'. He disliked any obligations which might 'prove inconvenient to fulfill, and from which it might be impossible to extricate ourselves'.[39] Yet the government opposed commitments not for these reasons but because it denied that its immediate diplomacy required them. Decision makers agreed that a commitment to France was a trump card which could force France to follow British foreign policy, but held that for the moment this card would be more valuable if retained in Britain's hand than if played. Churchill argued that while Britain must ultimately guarantee French security, it should not do so until such time as this would provide the greatest diplomatic return. Curzon stated that since America had abandoned its guarantee, France was 'exclusively dependent' on British support for its security against Germany. He did not even want Britain to discuss the future of its guarantee, since the less certain France was of British support, the more it must follow British policy so as to purchase British goodwill.[40]

Curzon's argument was not only cynical; it was mistaken, for, together with all of Whitehall, he underestimated the strength of France's position. Indeed, Britain's rejection of commitments probably served to hamper its policies in Europe. Its repudiation of a pledge for which France had sacrificed so much in 1919 certainly heightened France's need to establish a security system in eastern Europe, contrary to British desires. Britain also forced Belgium, reluctantly, to look to France alone for its security. These developments may have been inevitable, but Britain rejected the only means available to influence their development. This placed it in a position where it had to consider supporting French policy so as to purchase French goodwill.

By spring 1921 France had thwarted British aims in Europe and Turkey. Consequently, when it suggested that it would support British policy in the Middle East if Britain would return the favour in Europe, Whitehall had good reason to reconsider the strategic and diplomatic value of a commitment to France. Churchill, Austen Chamberlain and many Foreign Office officials argued that Britain could only further its European policies by guaranteeing French security. Crowe, the new permanent under-secretary, argued that Britain needed an ally, for which France was the only option. Therefore, Britain must 'fortify' the *entente*, sacrificing some immediate interests to secure its greater aims throughout the world. Although Curzon and Lloyd George again denied the value of obligations in Europe or of closer cooperation with Paris, changes in diplomatic circumstances soon led Britain entirely to recast its attitude towards France.[41]

In autumn 1921 France challenged crucial British diplomatic interests not only in Europe but at the Washington Conference and in Turkey. Precisely at this point, as Whitehall finally began to realise that France could use its diplomatic strength to hamper British aims all over the world, it started to perceive a French strategic menace. In October, as part of their preparations for the Washington Conference, the services gave the CID a tabular comparison between the world's air strengths. This paper noted nothing about the FAF which had not existed since 1919, when the latter already possessed the features which were later taken to demonstrate the reality of a 'French air menace': that an 'Air Division' commanded all French bomber squadrons and that the FAF was far larger than the RAF. As soon as he read this paper, however, Balfour told the CID with 'profound alarm' that, since the RAF was too weak to resist a French 'aerial invasion', Britain was 'more defenceless than it has ever been before'. Trenchard, sensing his moment, immediately and for the first time claimed that a French bombing attack could cripple Britain. Consequently, the CID established a 'Continental Air Menace' committee to examine the 'diplomatic possibilities' which might arise from Britain's vulnerability to air attack.[42]

Although Trenchard manipulated this issue to defend the RAF when its survival was at risk, his claims were not the cause of Britain's hysteria about France. His first reference to an air menace followed rather than preceded Balfour's formulation of this idea; he simply exploited an existing if latent fear. Whitehall needed little prompting to realise that with modern weapons France could threaten Britain, and was, indeed, initially more concerned with French submarines than its aircraft. Thus, on 23 November the CID stated that

> in the future a very dangerous situation might arise if France were strong on sea, land and air, while Great Britain were weak in all directions, and that in such circumstances, the Empire would be merely existing on the goodwill of its neighbour—a situation which had not been tolerated in the past and could not be tolerated in the future.[43]

Although the older services sought to exploit these concerns, the RAF had the most to gain from any fears of a French menace.[44]

Historians like Hines Hall have not examined this idea of an air menace nor its relationship to British foreign policy, particularly to Britain's simultaneous decision to offer a security guarantee to France.[45] The air menace theory was a diplomatic matter, but one which affected British strategy. France did not plan to attack Britain but then the latter did not expect France to do so. Its concern lay with the 'diplomatic possibilities' of France's strategic position, with whether France could further its diplomacy at Britain's expense by blackmailing Britain through the threat, explicit or not, of using superior French armed force. France already challenged British diplomacy far more than did any other power. Britain feared that the strength of the FAF would increase its ability to do so. The origins of Whitehall's fears of an air menace and its reconsideration of a commitment to France both sprang from Britain's need to overcome these diplomatic conflicts with France. Britain saw but two means to do so: air rearmament, which would avoid the danger of blackmail, or the offer of a guarantee to France, which might reduce the conflicts of interest.

Britain preferred to pursue the latter option. In November 1921 the Cabinet agreed that if, at the Washington Conference, France should refer to the Anglo-American guarantees, Britain would be 'honour bound' to support their ratification—if France reduced its naval and air strength. In December the French Premier, Aristide Briand, suggested closer ties between French and British policies. Although Lloyd George and Curzon rejected this idea, they favoured a ten-year security guarantee to France. The Cabinet refused to commit Britain automatically to take military steps in response to specific German actions, but agreed to consult with France about any German violations of Belgian neutrality or the military terms of the Treaty of Versailles. The Cabinet regarded this guarantee as an inexpensive way to further British diplomacy. It was expected to lead France to give Britain a 'free hand' with Germany, which was 'to us the most important country in Europe', and 'the key to the situation in Russia'.[46]

However, Briand's government fell and his successor, Raymond Poincaré, rejected Britain's offer as insufficient. Despite renewed pressure from Churchill, Crowe and Tyrrell, Whitehall abandoned the idea of guaranteeing French security because it doubted that this could increase British influence in Paris.[47] Britain had played its trump card only to find that it had mistaken the suit. Throughout spring 1922 Poincaré frustrated British diplomacy while Germany moved towwards Russia. Although Britain feared that the Rapallo Pact had forged a Russo-German military alliance, these concerns receded because it could find no proof of military cooperation between them.[48] Nevertheless, Britain's nightmares about Europe suddenly seemed to be nearing reality. France had established its hegemony there while Germany and Russia were beginning to conspire against the European order. Decision makers increasingly believed, in Curzon's words, that all the European powers were 'relapsing. . . into the deepest slime of pre-war treachery and intrigue'.[49] In particular, they regarded France as a potential menace.

By 1922 Britain had achieved much of its foreign policy and surmounted imperial disturbances at the loss only of southern Ireland. Yet Britain had not achieved its full ambitions of 1919: it had not secured hegemony in the Middle East, created its desired order in Europe or east Asia or retained its supremacy at sea. Nor had it established the concert of the powers which it had hoped would regulate the postwar world. Virtually every decision maker had wanted an alignment with one or another power to guarantee British security. Circumstances, not intent, had driven them into Imperial isolation. Since no ally or collective security arrangements offered it strategic support, Britain would have to deal with any dangers through its own strength alone. Although Britain did not perceive imminent threats, it did fear that France and to a lesser extent, Japan, might endanger British interests. These views lent strength to the RAF and the navy but not to the army against the government's pressure for economy.

The perception of a French air menace bolstered the RAF's position. Although the government might want to alter its naval decisions, which had already served their diplomatic purpose, the navy could defend its policies by reference to the one power standard, the naval treaty, and the latent fears of Japan. However, the Cabinet rejected the army's wish to prepare for an imminent war in the Middle East or an eventual one in Europe, leaving it with no role except Imperial policing, which, ministers maintained, would not require a large or modern army.[50] The government's views of Britain's strategic position shaped its formulation of a new strategic policy in 1922. Britain hoped that during the foreseeable future it would remain secure and further its foreign policy, but was not absolutely confident about these matters. Thus, it decided that it could cut service estimates and alter their policies but could not accept the full strategic risks recommended by the Geddes Committee.

7 The New Strategic Policy of 1922

By spring 1922 Lloyd George was in decline, for even if Austen Chamberlain remained loyal to him, many ministers and sections of the Conservative Party were no longer. These determinants shaped Lloyd George's strategic decisions. So as to overcome the controversy surrounding the Geddes Committee's recommendations, he had to establish Cabinet committees to examine its civil and armed service proposals. He made Churchill the chairman of the committee (including Montagu, Lord Birkenhead and Baldwin) to examine the service ones. Although the Geddes Committee's proposals were politically vital to Lloyd George, he had to give colleagues of questionable loyalty the power to challenge its recommendations. When Britain reached its decision on these matters, Lloyd George confronted another political danger, for his advisors warned him that should Churchill resign over Anglo-Soviet negotiations at the Genoa Conference, he would gain much die-hard Conservative support. Given Churchill's ties with some Asquithian Liberals and Cecilite Conservatives, he might even focus every Parliamentary faction which opposed Lloyd George and thus threaten the Coalition. Although Churchill probably had no such intention, he was ready to work with the opposition to defend the RAF had the Cabinet rejected his views on that question.[1] In any case Lloyd George could not trust Churchill but equally dared not antagonise him needlessly.

Due to this fact and his influence over his committee Churchill dominated the reformulation of service policies in spring 1922. He supported a strong RAF and navy and favoured the TA and mechanised forces, but wanted the army otherwise to prepare only for Imperial policing and to cut the elements which were necessary solely for major wars. Churchill demanded reductions in service spending and their support elements. He believed that Britain would be secure during the next decade, while 'before a great war can come there must be a period where the antagonisms of the principal nations will be revealed, and then as a precautionary measure' Britain could strengthen the services. Hence the latter should maintain the minimum strength necessary for deterrence and Imperial policing, with a nucleus for expansion.[2]

Churchill gave the services a chance to challenge the Geddes Committee, a task eased by the fact that the latter had made elementary arithmetical errors like counting twice over the same £1 000 000 cut in RAF estimates and 20 000 reduction in the army, and had not even specified the source of £19 500 000 of its proposed service economies.[3] However, the navy and the RAF also found support on the grounds of strategic principles and grand strategy. Consequently, they rolled the Geddes Committee's onslaught further back than did the army.

The Air Ministry emphasised the need for home defence and substitution. It offered to cut its estimates by £1 700 000 but argued that any real economies required a change in defence organisation: that instead of being 'purely auxiliary' to the older services, the RAF should replace them. Four army and navy squadrons in Britain should be reassigned to form a Home Defence Air Force (HDAF) while two army squadrons in Egypt should become a reserve under RAF control. The Air Ministry turned the financial pressure to support its aims: to form an HDAF, defend its independent role in Imperial policing and increase its control over the RAF.[4]

The Admiralty denied that finance should determine strategy. Instead, Britain should define policies to govern the services' 'power' and, after the latter had defined how much money these policies required, 'decide whether the policy is too costly to carry out' and, if so, select an 'alternative'. This approach would let the Admiralty dominate the formulation of naval policy. It claimed that its policy of 1921, subject only to the naval treaty, was needed to maintain the one power standard and maritime security. However, it offered to reduce 20 000 men and £19 750 000 from its estimates in 1922–23 to reach 98 750 men and £61 250 000.[5]

Although it offered no specific economies, the War Office realised that it must make cuts. Thus it defined a crucial priority: to maintain the forces necessary for Imperial policing by sacrificing all other elements. It expected to reduce its support services and the TA and to maintain only two infantry divisions and one cavalry division of the expeditionary force at full strength. Although the War Office opposed any cuts in cavalry, infantry or armoured units, it realised that these would be reduced. It opposed substitution, no doubt to minimise the threat to conventional units, but agreed that armoured forces had a crucial role in Imperial policing. The War Office conceded that this was the army's only role and that it was the least necessary service for any 'war with a Continental Power'.[6]

The Churchill Committee approved the RAF's proposals but cut the army's estimates by £11 800 000. Its greatest struggle came with the Admiralty. Beatty rejected further reductions unless the government would publicly reduce the one power standard to 'some smaller proportion'. This standard must override the ten-year period should any clash occur. However, Beatty offered to 'compromise by risking inadequacy in certain services', and extended the completion date for the fuel reserve from 1929 to 1931. Pressed by the Treasury Churchill defined economy as Britain's fundamental strategic need. Thus, expenditure on the Singapore base, the fuel programme and the treaty battleships should be deferred for several years. However, he wavered between the imperatives of economy and security. When Birkenhead argued that Britain must develop all these programmes to maintain its security, especially against Japan, Churchill adopted the Admiralty's proposals.[7]

The Churchill Committee established the basis for service policies until 1925. It argued that its cuts, the largest possible, were justifiable only on the assumption of a 'prolonged period of peace'. The Committee supported the proposals of the navy and the RAF, but believed that the army could 'very considerably' reduce its 'higher formations for immediate purposes on a great scale'. It recommended RAF estimates of £12 500 000, including the Colonial Office grant, naval ones of £61 750 000 and army ones of £58 500 000.[8] However large, these economies fell far short of the Geddes Committee's recommendations and of the hopes of the Treasury and Lloyd George.

Barstow conceded it was 'arguable that the Government has no right to put the national defences into any jeopardy, even remote', but claimed that Churchill had not seen the 'national problem as a whole, i.e. contrasting its financial with its defence requirements'. Barstow accepted Churchill's army and RAF proposals, but denounced Beatty's argument that the one power standard should override' the ten-year period. Barstow claimed that the 'national effort in regard of naval strength . . . so far as it can be expressed in percentage terms at all', should be 26–66 per cent less than in 1914. From this peculiar basis, he recommended naval estimates of £47 000 000. Although Lloyd George, Balfour, Chamberlain and

Horne demanded further service and pre-eminently naval cuts, the Cabinet supported Churchill's recommendations. After a further reduction of £500 000 each on the RAF and the army and £1 250 000 on the navy, these recommendations were adopted as the services' estimates for 1922–23.[9]

Although these estimates formally equalled £138 100 000, approximating the normal figure of August 1919, the real indicator of service finances, their current effective estimates, was below this level. Excluding expenditures on ephemeral purposes, like bounties to personnel who were prematurely retired, (which absorbed, for example, 11 per cent of army estimates), they received £123 930 000 for normal purposes. Their estimates of 1922–23 became the basis for future ones. £13 870 000 of these estimates went to cover extraordinary charges and were essentially surrendered to the Treasury once these had been met. Hence, in 1922–23 normal service estimates in effect fell by 10 per cent below those of August 1919. Although in global terms this merely accounted for declining prices, the army absorbed almost all of this loss and the RAF none of it.

Excluding non-effective charges, in 1922–23 the services received only £110 010 000 for current effective purposes (army £46 683 000; RAF £10 738 000; navy, £53 569 000). However, a Colonial Office grant of £1 750 000 actually paid for 25 per cent of the RAF's squadrons. Most of these cuts on the services would have occurred in any case, as they followed directly from political decisions of 1921, like the naval treaty. Nonetheless, these decisions established the Treasury's central aim against the services, to cut their estimates to £135 000 000. The Treasury also finally acquired some power over their estimates. It forecast that revenues would fall from £910 800 000 in 1922–23 to £827–£868 000 000 in 1923–24, necessitating more cuts in spending.[10] The services had to reshape their policies in the expectation of further pressure for economy.

The government had not determined the nature of British maritime requirements. The Churchill Committee claimed that its proposals provided the minimum level to maintain 'genuinely' the one power standard, which it defined in a political sense. The British and US fleets need not be 'exactly matched in every instance', but Britain's navy must not be perceived as being 'definitely inferior' to the USN. Such a situation would 'affect our whole position and indicate to our Dominions that a new centre had been created for the Anglo-

Saxon world'. By this definition, Britain's navy might be weaker than the USN so long as it was not seen to be. However, the committee hoped that American naval power would 'wane', allowing Britain to retain maritime supremacy.[11] Conversely, the Admiralty reverted to Long's definition of the one power standard, that 'our Navy should not be inferior to that of any other Power'. It used the naval treaty to define that standard in practice which, of course, entailed a reduction in Britain's absolute strength at sea.[12] Although Britain could maintain its maritime security on this basis, the question was whether it would. The Cabinet had barely approved the Admiralty's programmes and the latter had agreed to accept further economies '*during the next two years*, even at the cost of additional and temporary risks to national security'.[13] Yet despite intense pressure, Beatty had prevented any further cuts than were inevitable given the naval treaty. The navy was in a far better position to define and defend a new policy than was the army.

In 1922 postwar army policy was destroyed. It declined from 254 890 men in September 1921 to 218 718 a year later, losing 22 infantry battalions, eight cavalry regiments and 47 artillery batteries. Including units stationed in India, the army retained 136 battalions, 20 regiments, 170 batteries, two full and two cadre tank battalions and 13 armoured car companies. Its strength for emergencies and expansion was crippled. The War Office could despatch an expeditionary force of but one cavalry and two infantry divisions immediately and another infantry division six weeks after mobilisation. That force's support elements could not meet its mobilisation requirements while the TA was a weak cadre for expansion.[14]

Developments in India widened the gap between the army's strength and commitments. In 1919–20 the War Office had wanted the Indian army to be modernised and to be able to maintain internal security in India, defend the northwest frontier and provide four divisions for Imperial 'considerations'. The Indian authorities initially favoured similar ideas but, by 1920, facing financial problems of their own, they decided to postpone modernisation, to maintain no forces solely for Imperial purposes and to cut the British and Indian armies and the RAF in India.[15] In 1922 the Cabinet authorised a reduction of $1\frac{1}{2}$ divisions of Indian units but rejected any cuts in the British army or the RAF in India. The Indian army thus consisted of 28 Indian and eight British regiments; 45 British and 100 Indian battalions; 57 British and 12 Indian artillery batteries; 12 armoured car companies and six RAF squadrons. The Cabinet acted on

Churchill's contention that the 'main object of the Army in India today was to maintain British supremacy in India — neither to withstand external attack nor to provide Imperial reserves.[16] Instead of supporting the British army, India became another drain on it.

The army was left in a deplorable condition, barely able to meet normal Imperial policing duties or serve as a nucleus for expansion and unable to handle any great emergency. The Cabinet accepted these risks, on the assumption that

> we need not now contemplate fighting a European enemy equipped with all the latest mechanical appliances for war. We should now visualise a situation in which we might have to fight Indians and Arabs. This involved military operations of a very different class . . . no serious risks would be incurred by cutting off the ancillary services to form part of the higher tactical formations.[17]

It wanted the army to provide the smallest strength necessary for Imperial policing and prevented it from preparing modern forces. This policy might have been reasonable had it been absolutely necessary to cripple one of the services. However, as Britain's position was not so stark, these decisions were short-sighted.

When Wilson retired in 1922, the army had become the 'Cinderella service', a trap from which it never escaped before 1939. He bequeathed to his successors a compromised position, for he had proposed an excellent but overly ambitious policy and defended it poorly. He left the army without large or modern forces and shackled to one strategic role which could not justify their maintenance. Its estimates were vulnerable and it could subsidise new developments only by sacrificing other priorities. The army declined because Wilson had been a poor bureaucratic politician. The RAF thrived because Trenchard was a great one.

In 1919 the RAF had faced daunting problems; by 1922 it had surmounted them. The Cabinet accepted its independent role in Imperial policing and the RAF could hope to gain more through substitution. The Cabinet also assigned three squadrons to home air defence and soon favoured an HDAF. Alone of the services, the RAF avoided any cuts on its 1921–22 strength, preserving $31\frac{1}{2}$ squadrons and 31 176 men, with its economies coming entirely from ancillary areas.[18] In 1919 other organisations had some control over 23 of the 25 RAF squadrons. By 1922 the Air Ministry completely ran 17 of them, while the Indian army, the British army and the navy controlled 6, 3 and 5½ squadrons. Moreover, the RAF's position against the older services was strong. The Admiralty, believing that its bid to take over naval aviation was being compromised by its association with the War Office's arguments to abolish the RAF, rejected any further cooperation with the army. The Cabinet agreed to examine how the RAF should support the older services, but it rejected the abolition of the RAF or the establishment of a separate naval aviation force, because 'French air development constituted a formidable danger to this country'.[19]

The Air Ministry had overcome its gravest political problems of the 1920s, partly because of the older services' errors, the Treasury's relative friendliness and Churchill's support, but primarily because of Trenchard's cynical exploitation of every opportunity which opened to him. Thus, Trenchard had always offered a postdated cheque for substitution; even in spring 1922 he realised that the RAF could not yet control any part of Iraq.[20] He was manipulating Whitehall's fears of the need for defence against the FAF so as to establish an offensive bombing force. He had conciliated the older services by pledging them their own air arms, but may never have intended to honour that pledge. Certainly by 1922 he had different ideas about that issue, although he would not act on them until 1926.[21] Trenchard preserved the RAF at the cost of harming the older services.

In 1922 the imperatives of foreign and financial policies again briefly converged against the services. The Cabinet, assuming that Britain's strategic position had improved, hoping that it would remain secure during the foreseeable future and in hot pursuit of economies, enforced the August 1919 principles on the services. Britain also in effect adopted several principles defined by the Churchill Committee to guide service policies.

(1). . . the essential elements of fighting strength shall be maintained on such a scale as to ensure that we shall maintain the national security until we are able to achieve victory by bringing the mobilised war power of the Empire to bear;
(2). . . the peace establishments of the ancillary services shall be reduced to a nucleus; and . . . the war establishments of these services shall be created after a rupture [of relations with another power];
(3). . . adequate provision shall be made for scientific research

and for the maintenance of the technical staffs for the design and manufacture of warships and war material.[22]

The Cabinet, wishing to maintain the services at the minimum level needed for Imperial policing, reduced their insurance forces on the assumption that Britain would have a warning period in which to rebuild them as necessary. It wanted further cuts on service estimates, for once these had reached £135 000 000 that figure was no longer regarded as 'normal'.

However, ambiguities remained in this new strategic policy, for the Cabinet had not clearly chosen between the views of the Treasury or the services regarding how to maintain Britain's strategic insurance. Although the RAF and the navy were authorised to prepare a deterrent and defence against France and Japan, the Cabinet had not approved definite programmes for these purposes. It had not yet considered an HDAF programme in detail nor defined the nature of Britain's maritime requirements, while Whitehall differed over the meaning of the ten-year period. Lloyd George, Churchill, the Treasury and the War Office argued that Britain could expect ten years of security from 1922. They implied that Britain need not even begin programmes against major threats for many years. Conversely, the Admiralty and the Air Ministry argued that these programmes should be completed by 1929, and thus must begin almost immediately.[23] The answers to these questions of principle would shape the evolution of strategic policy.

As Britain's strategic position was not challenged until 1932, the Cabinet's belief that for some years Britain did not need to maintain large service programmes and could further reduce their estimates, were not unreasonable. Yet, like so many of the coalition government's decisions, those of 1922 stemmed from a failure to balance its aims and means. These decisions cut the margin for security against major threats and reduced the strength available for Imperial policing. These aspects of the new strategic policy were soon tested and found wanting, which exposed the ambiguities in that policy and led it to be altered in the services' favour.

In autumn 1922, after the Turkish nationalists had driven the Greek army from Anatolia, Britain faced its gravest military test of the 1920s. Scholars have treated the 'Chanak crisis' as a political or diplomatic issue, but not as a strategic one. Like many contemporaries, they have assumed that Britain's military strength was sufficient to support its diplomacy.[24] An examination of this question illuminates that crisis and the services' general ability to support British strategic policy.

Throughout the crisis Britain's aims were to preserve as much as possible of the Treaty of Sèvres, to retain its freedom to use the Dardanelles and to maintain British prestige. The Cabinet believed that Britain could achieve these aims only through the presence of force and was willing to run the risk of war to do so. The suggestions that Lloyd George, Churchill and Birkenhead courted war, however, are misleading.[25] They were more willing than other ministers to fight to achieve Britain's aims, yet even they did not want war. The Cabinet was not divided between war and peace parties but over diplomatic aims: between those who were and were not willing to let Turkey regain both Constantinople and Thrace. The entire Cabinet prepared for the possibility of war precisely because it was possible. On 29 September it ordered the British commander, General Harington, to inform the Turks that he would fire on their forces unless they ceased to threaten his position at Chanak. It did so because Harington had just requested authority to deliver such an ultimatum and because the Cabinet and the service chiefs interpreted his ambiguous telegrams to mean that Chanak would fall unless this were done.[26] If necessary, Britain was prepared to fight but its real aim was to show resolution so as to deter war and to force the Turkish nationalists to the negotiating table. This was the best possible policy and one which Bonar Law's government adopted.

In order to sustain this policy, Britain needed the military means to deter attack and to retain diplomatic bargaining chips, particularly control over Constantinople and the Dardanelles. Although it achieved these objectives, for some time it expected Turkey to attack. If this had occurred before 30 October, Britain's forces probably could not have secured its aims. The Cabinet realised that British forces could not prevent Turkish ones from rapidly seizing Constantinople, Britain's greatest diplomatic asset. In case of war Britain planned to evacuate that city but, in order to remain capable of threatening Constantinople and of using the Dardanelles, it intended to hold Gallipoli and Chanak, on the Asiatic shore of the Dardanelles.[27] Had Chanak fallen Britain would have lost men, prestige and the ability to use the Dardanelles.

By 2 October, Harington commanded 7300 fighting men which, five days later, reached a final strength of 9900. This overstretched and outnumbered force would have had difficulties everywhere but particularly at Chanak, where 4700 men held a four-mile perimeter overlooked by Turkish positions.[28] Britain estimated that Turkey could mass up to 36 000 infantrymen and 112 guns there, and had they ever once breached the Chanak perimeter, this narrow position would probably have collapsed. Recognising these problems, Lloyd George hoped to substitute 'mechanical superiority' for manpower, to hold Chanak through naval gunfire, howitzers and aircraft.[29] Such 'mechanical superiority' alone could have defended Chanak. It is doubtful whether this was more than a mirage.

Harington had far less artillery than needed to maintain his positions, especially at Chanak. Although this firepower was augmented by that from British warships, the latter probably could not have broken an infantry attack, while only the 23 howitzers on Gallipoli had a significant counter-battery capacity.[30] British land and naval guns alone probably could not. have defended Chanak and would have had little effect without aircraft direction. Ultimately the RAF was the key to defence through 'mechanical superiority'. Trenchard pledged that the RAF would gain air superiority, disorganise Turkish ground attacks and render 'useless' any Turkish artillery. He spent much energy in preparing to bomb the Turkish nationalist capital, Ankara.[31] Unfortunately the RAF could not have honoured Trenchard's promise.

It had 15 aircraft available for operations by 1 October and 38 by 22 October. All its squadrons had many untrained personnel, while over half its aircraft could not initially use their weapons because of technical problems. Against this Turkey had 30 to 60 French aircraft which, Trenchard admitted, outclassed those of the RAF, although Turkish personnel were presumably less competent than British ones.[32] Thus, on 1 October the RAF could have provided some ground support around Chanak but none had Turkish aircraft intervened. The latter might even have established air superiority throughout the theatre and attacked British land and sea forces. By mid-October the RAF could have prevented such operations and provided some ground support, but only by 30 October could it have begun to fulfill the functions on which rested the defence of Chanak.

The general staff regarded Britain's position during the crisis as a 'gigantic bluff'.[33] Had this bluff been called after 30 October, when its local forces reached their maximum size, Britain might have carried out its plans, but probably not before then. Heavy losses or a débacle were possible during the evacuation of

Constantinople. Chanak might well have fallen, as the general staff thought likely, although the garrison commander did not.[34] In any case, by 29 September Whitehall realised that nothing could stop the Turks from establishing batteries on the Asiatic shore of the Dardanelles, which could block the straits and trump Britain's last diplomatic card.[35] Had war occurred, Britain's forces could not have maintained Britain's political aims and might even have failed to defend themselves. Yet this strength — a large fleet, $6\frac{1}{2}$ RAF squadrons and one division — was the entire force Britain had available short of mobilisation. The maximum reinforcements it could have provided 25–48 days after mobilisation would have been another 10–12 RAF squadrons, one cavalry brigade and $2\frac{1}{2}$ infantry divisions.[36]

The Chanak crisis led to the collapse of the coalition government and demonstrated that Britain's forces could barely deal with major Imperial policing requirements. Among the services, the navy alone had a creditable force for emergencies. Moreover, the crisis challenged the tenets of British strategic policy, by showing that a great emergency could arise suddenly rather than waiting until 1929, and that in the interim other powers might threaten British interests. Britain believed that France had betrayed it during the crisis while the Cabinet had certain knowledge that Russia was pressing Turkey to attack Britain.[37] These events, followed by the Ruhr crisis, led Britain to doubt that it could safety cut its armed forces or assume that it would be secure during the foreseeable future. The questions for strategic policy became whether Britain must treat certain powers as threats and rearm against them.

8 Service Policies and Financial Policy, 1922–24

Although in 1922 Britain seemed ready to enforce the ten-year rule and Treasury control, this was soon forgotten. Between 1922 and 1924 Britain had four different governments, whose perceptions of its strategic position changed drastically, which cut service estimates but approved expensive rearmament programmes. Strategic policy entered its most dynamic phase of the 1920s. Since the imperatives of financial and service policies conflicted, by 1925 Britain had no choice but to support one against the other.

After March 1922, with an election imminent, Lloyd George's government pursued cuts on the services' 1923–24 estimates, particularly through a new committee under Churchill.[1] The Cabinet and the Treasury cooperated to increase the politicians's power over service policies and Treasury control over their spending, but they differed in one area. The Cabinet favoured service programmes which the Treasury opposed. After Lloyd George's government fell, Bonar Law organised his Conservative Cabinet. He appointed influential service ministers: Amery as First Lord, Lord Derby as War Minister and Samuel Hoare, Air Minister, although this did not become a Cabinet post until June 1923. Curzon remained Foreign Secretary, Baldwin became Chancellor while Salisbury, the Lord President, became responsible for the CID. In May 1923 Baldwin became Prime Minister and also remained Chancellor until August, when Neville Chamberlain succeeded him. Baldwin retained Bonar Law's Cabinet, although he added Cecil as Lord Privy Seal. Bonar Law and Baldwin cut service spending but as Barstow remarked in December 1922, a Cabinet 'elected on a platform of tranquility and peace' had already approved the completion of two battleships against the US, an HDAF against France and was considering the construction of the Singapore base against Japan.[2]

Prompted by inter-service conflicts, these governments re-examined British strategy. Lloyd George's Cabinet asked Churchill to settle the struggle over naval aviation. He proposed that this should remain under the RAF, with the navy defining the requirements for, paying for and controlling operationally all its flights. The RAF should administer these units while both services should supply personnel. Although Roskill has asserted that Trenchard's obstinacy destroyed these negotiations, Beatty was equally rigid, rejecting everything but complete Admiralty control. He ignored Trenchard's offer to install the RAF's naval aviation command within the Admiralty, which would have given the latter practical control over naval aviation and perhaps overcome the problem of dual authority.[3]

Bonar Law's attempt to settle this issue had wide repercussions. He set up a committee under Salisbury to examine 'National and Imperial Defence', particularly regarding the RAF's relations with the older services and the RAF 'standard to be aimed at' in home and Imperial defence. This committee proposed to examine three 'alternative, but not simultaneous, hypotheses': war against a European enemy, a naval power, or Turkey or Russia in the Middle East. As the older services did not exploit these opportunities to further their policies, it focused on the question of a French air menace. This committee produced a new proposal for an HDAF programme, rejected the army's demand that the RAF be abolished and gave the Admiralty no more control over naval aviation than Churchill or Trenchard had offered earlier.[4]

The Bonar Law and Baldwin governments left strategic policy in a state of confusion, particularly because Baldwin supported all sides at once and refused to assign priorities between security, economy and social reform. He claimed that finance should dominate all policies and favoured service economies so to prevent the public from believing that a Conservative government 'always wastes the taxpayer's substance in armaments and neglects his social development'.[5] Yet Baldwin allowed two services to expand and approved a final strength for the third.

After Baldwin's government fell, MacDonald's minority Labour Cabinet of 1924 was in a delicate position. Its Parliamentary survival depended on Liberal support, but MacDonald wanted Labour to replace them as Britain's leading party of movement. He favoured changes in strategic policy but also wanted to prove that Labour was responsible. If these changes were too radical, Labour would seem irresponsible; if insufficiently so, his attempts to dominate the left might be thwarted. For MacDonald, every strategic decision necessarily had complex political overtones. Trusting his own abilities and mistrusting his colleagues, he sought to run strategic policy himself, as Prime Minister and Foreign Secretary, leaving the CID under Lord Haldane, the Lord Chancellor, to handle technical issues. MacDonald appointed weak service ministers, Stephen Walsh as War Minister, Lord Chelmsford as First Lord and Lord Thomson as Air Minister. He sought to keep his Cabinet from even discussing strategic issues. Colleagues like Philip Snowden, the powerful Chancellor, initially challenged this situation, wishing to examine 'Defence policy as a whole', but finally they accepted MacDonald's decision to continue most of the service policies he had inherited.[6]

Each of these governments began, but did not complete, a new strategic policy yet altered its predecessor's work. This confused British strategy and altered the departmental balance over such issues. The Foreign Office achieved dominance in the formulation of foreign policy, affected only by the intermittent influence of the prime ministers and by the Treasury's role in international finance. However, the Foreign Office kept aloof from service issues. Moreover, the Treasury's power over the services declined from spring 1922, for the imperatives of diplomacy supported them against those of finance.

The Chanak and the Ruhr crises reminded Britain that international developments were unpredictable and that other powers could unexpectedly threaten its interests. The government ceased to believe that Britain would necessarily be secure during the foreseeable future. It did not fear immediate dangers from Germany or Russia while Anglo–US relations remained good, but the government decided to maintain Britain's requirements of insurance against France and Japan, on whose sufferance it was unwilling to live. Lloyd George's Cabinet approved an HDAF against France and gradual naval preparations against Japan. The Bonar Law and Baldwin governments increased these programmes while MacDonald's maintained them all except the Singapore base. Between 1922 and 1924 the Treasury did not control naval and RAF estimates. The ten-year rule was not enforced on them and insofar as it had any effect at all, supported them against the Treasury. Although the Air Ministry and the Admiralty believed that they should always be ready to meet any threat even if no state was seen to be one, they realised that they could not complete their programmes before the end of the ten-year period. They argued that these must begin immediately if they were to maintain security: that is, be fully ready for a great war by 1929. Conversely, Treasury control and the ten-year rule were enforced on the army. Cavan agreed that army estimates could fall by £10 000 000 during the 1920s, because no 'World War' was likely before 1929. Instead of using 1929 as the target by which to be prepared for a major war, Cavan merely implied that army policy should then be reconsidered.[7] The decline of the army demonstrated what could happen if Treasury control and the ten-year rule were strictly enforced on any service.

The War Office held that the army could not avoid the status of 'Cinderella service', a view which may have acted as a self-fulfilling prophecy. Since the army believed that it would lose any major policy battles, it chose not to fight and thus acquired that status. Although no Cabinet would have let the army prepare fully for modern and major war, the army's position could not have worsened had it fought for its interests. The War Office did not do so because it was willing to let the Cabinet's decisions of 1922 govern its policy. The army surrendered to financial pressure in the vain hope that it might gain favour by cooperating with the Treasury. It elected not even to try to reallocate to other purposes in 1923–24 £8 700 000 (or 13 per cent) of its net spending of 1922–23, including £3 000 000 from current effective estimates. This retreat completely stripped the army of the disposable income needed to finance any new programmes.[8] Moreover, the War Office feared that economies might be forced on it to 'set-off' RAF expansion should its strategic case be compared to that of the RAF. Thus, it chose to ignore its only opportunity to justify improvements in the army, by showing the Salisbury Committee that it could not meet important requirements like a major war in the Middle East. This retreat cost the army any chance to break its policy predicament. Instead, Cavan and Derby asked the Cabinet to approve 'a degree of finality' for army policy, to make permanent a position which, they knew, 'is far from being a scientific solution to the problem of our Imperial defence needs'. The Cabinet agreed that the army's strength could be cut no further without compromising 'national safety'.[9] Although better than nothing, this decision pinned the army to its current position, wherein it could meet no major tasks and pursue no new aims except by directly sacrificing others.

Cavan summarised the army's history between 1922 and 1925 in 17 words: 'I am cutting in all directions so as to keep the little Army at its present size'.[10] The War Office did consider expansion programmes (for example, by forming 14 cadre tank battalions and 20 close support artillery brigades for the TA, at £1 115 000, half the construction cost of one 8-inch gun cruiser) but abandoned them for lack of funds.[11] Under Cavan the army returned to real soldiering with a vengeance. Although it formed two more tank battalions and started to 'mechanicalise' two artillery brigades, it abandoned its plans to develop armoured forces for Imperial policing. The 1922 experimental brigade manoeuvres examined 'the tactics and conduct of all arms, based on existing resources'; that is, small colonial operations involving flying columns of traditional units. However, the army's exercises in 1923–25 provided useful studies of how traditional formations could work with mechanised units.[12]

The War Office's predicament prevented it from pursuing even good ideas. It warned that Britain needed a stronger army but settled for marginal improvements in all practical matters. A small change in army estimates, say of another £2 000 000 per year, could have greatly increased its value. Had the War Office fought more firmly, its position might have improved; it could hardly have become worse. Certainly the other services overcame similar problems and established large programmes, although these contained many flaws and rested on alarmist assumptions.

Between 1922–24 substitution fell into the back seat of RAF policy while its main concern became the HDAF programme. It justified this programme by asserting that strategic bombing could destroy any nation's 'morale' and war capacity and could be resisted only by counter-bombing. Given contemporary technical factors, it was reasonable to argue that 'passive defence' could not work. However, the Air Ministry distorted the moral and material effect of bombing, just as it did the facts about the FAF's threat. In 1922, for example, in implied that the FAF's striking force had a five-to-one superiority over the 15 squadrons which Britain could raise for home defence. That real strength would probably have been 19 squadrons, excluding another 5 squadrons committed to the older services in Britain. By the Air Ministry's calculations, however, army support and civil aircraft comprised over half the FAF's bombing strength.[13] Consequently, the paper odds shrank to three-to-one, and even this seemed so formidable only because the Air Ministry distorted the FAF's role.

In 1922 Britain's Air Attaché in Paris reported that the FAF had in France an Air Division of 30 fighter and 30 bomber squadrons. By 1925 France proposed to increase the FAF from 126 to 220 squadrons and to have two Air Divisions, each of 20 fighter and 20 bomber squadrons. The Air Division was deployed to support the army against Germany and the attaché stated that it was intended to 'attack enemy territory, hinder mobilisation and prevent inroads of enemy machines'. Nothing indicated that this was a strategic bombing force or one directed against Britain. Yet the Air Ministry told the Cabinet that the attaché's report showed the Air Division to be an 'essentially offensive' unit, which indicated that French policy towards Britain was 'offensive'. Moreover, by 1924 the FAF's expansion had slowed while the Air Division was concentrating even more on support for the army. Trenchard argued that France was probably taking these actions 'to make it appear that the whole of their Air Force is allocated to their Army for combined work. This may be so, or it may not be, but . . . we must make our own surmises'. He did not inform MacDonald's Cabinet of these developments, perhaps fearing that it would make surmises of its own.[14]

Although the HDAF was a relatively sound idea, the case for it was flawed. Yet Whitehall detected none of these weaknesses, leading two Prime Ministers to entirely misinterpret the situation. In 1922 Lloyd George stated that 'if we quarrelled with France', its 220 squadrons 'would be across the Channel in a few hours'. Yet these squadrons would not exist until 1925 and were actually built at a slower rate; just 194 (including but 48 bomber squadrons, the sole strategic bombing threat) would be in France, and few of these could have reached Britain within 'a few hours'. In 1924 MacDonald told the French Ambassador that the British people naturally regarded France's '1000 aeroplanes against our 80 . . . as a menace'. Yet 98 HDAF aircraft were formed with 132 forming, while only 308 bombers were in France.[15] Fears of France, stemming from suspicions of its foreign policy and the worsening diplomatic situation in Europe, led the government to adopt Trenchard's alarmist technical arguments about a French air menace.

Especially after France occupied the Ruhr, Britain believed that it was fomenting a situation which would lead to French hegemony or another war in Europe. Bonar Law and Curzon held that France was trying to shatter Germany and to occupy the Ruhr semi-permanently. Crowe described French policy as 'sickening and revolting'; Tyrrell stated that the 'mistakes the French are making about us remind me of those made by the Germans before the war: only the former are more clumsy and stupid than the latter!'.[16]

Warren Fisher, in his first direct attempt to influence foreign policy, reminded Baldwin that

> I have never pretended to the possession of a 'first-class brain'; and, lest there should be any misunderstanding as to my point of view, let me state . . . that I am an Englishman and quite devoid of sentimental predilections for foreigners collectively, German or otherwise.
>
> By the Treaty of Versailles, which we English helped to create and which we signed, we . . . deprived the Germans of all effective means of *armed* self-defence. We thereby assumed a responsibility for securing the Germans against armed brutality — unless of course we have ceased to be Englishmen and are prepared first to tie a man's hands behind his back and then encourage or allow someone to hit him below the belt. We are thus in the position of trustees, directly by reason of the Treaty and generally because of our English sense of fair play.
>
> I have read principally as a pastime and partly for examination at Winchester and Oxford a good deal of history; and, while I admit that the French from 1870 to 1914 had their tails well down and therefore assumed a veneer of moderation, during the rest of their centuries-old existence, they have played the part of bullies whenever they had or could make the chance, and they are doing so now. This view is neither anti-French nor pro-German — it arises solely from regard for English self-respect. We force a country to disarm; is it consistent with English traditions or Treaty obligations to connive then at armed coercion of it thus rendered defenceless . . .?
>
> We have a moral responsibility . . . to see that the ring is at least fairly kept.[17]

Whitehall feared that France might use the FAF to blackmail Britain and refused to live on French sufferance, because 'our diplomacy might be weakened if we were at the mercy of some other Power. An Air Force adequate to our national security was therefore essential'. Balfour told the Salisbury Committee that although France was unlikely to attack, he doubted 'if we possessed sufficient confidence in the French nation, who were at present in a somewhat hysterical condition . . . to say "We throw down our weapons; you can stab us in the back if you wish, but we are certain that you will not"'. Curzon noted the power of dictation which was conferred on nations by the possession of superior forces . . . to some extent the present enormous military strength of France allowed her to act as dictator to the rest of Europe. This explained why Belgium, the Little Entente, and Poland were constantly compelled to shape their policy at the present time at the behest of France. This country was not at present affected to the same degree because we entertained no military ambitions on the Continent; but give France a preponderance of air power and increased strength in submarines, and . . . it would be possible for her to dictate her policy to the whole world . . . it was impossible for this country to accept a situation which would make it impossible for us to contemplate even a remote possibility of war because we knew that we should be beaten.[18]

A bitter sense of impotence haunted Whitehall in 1923–24, a recognition that Britain lacked the influence to halt Europe's slide towards the dangers which it had most feared since 1919. However much they tried, decision makers could find no diplomatic means to overcome these problems, whether through commitments to western European security under the League, mutual arms limitation with France or a commitment to French security,[19] Statesmen perceived great problems in Europe but no means to overcome them. Since they were unwilling to trust on time and tide as their salvation, they turned to what they saw as Britain's only possible independent action, to begin an HDAF programme, a step which they believed public opinion demanded. Even Barstow, who opposed an 'insane' air competition, advised Snowden not to challenge the programme, for fear that this would inflame public opinion. Whenever this matter was raised in Parliament during 1922–24, the Cabinet immediately issued statements on the need for air strength.[20] Trenchard skillfully exploited these advantages to gain his objectives.

In 1922 the 'Continental Air Menace' committee concluded that Britain could not prepare 'against all the contingencies of war' but against 'reasonable possibilities' alone. The Cabinet must decide whether an air threat fell within that category. Balfour noted that

If France was regarded as a possible enemy, our position was one of extreme peril. The danger was greater than any threat the country has had to face for many years . . . If the Air Staff were correct in their forecast, it would be possible for an enemy to strike a blow which would render this country almost impotent.

The CID made Trenchard offer more squadrons than he had proposed and for less cost, but accepted his central contention that the HDAF would be a 'very powerful deterrent' to France. In August the Cabinet approved the formation of 20 HDAF squadrons to create a total of 23, at a cost of £2 000 000 (£900 000 of which would come from RAF economies). Trenchard claimed that this HDAF would have a real strength of 501 aircraft (266 regular and 235 second line machines) against the 596 in the Air Division. This government regarded a French air menace as a 'reasonable' possibility. As Lloyd George said,

> a war with France would be a calamity which seemed almost unthinkable, but it was necessary to make preparations against such a contingency, because even if it did not occur the fear of it would be a weapon in the hands of French statesmen which they could not refrain from using.[21]

There was no guarantee that the new government would adopt this attitude; indeed, Hoare and Boyle have stated that Bonar Law intended to abolish the RAF. However, their evidence for this claim is unreliable. At most Bonar Law may have toyed for a month with the idea and then abandoned it. All surviving evidence indicates that from December 1922 he increasingly opposed the elimination of the RAF and, moreover, linked Anglo-French relations to their air strengths. He feared a breach in relations with France and was 'fully seized of the dangerous disproportion between French and British aerial forces'. All this supported the need for an HDAF programme. The Treasury stated that in December 1922 this government reaffirmed that programme, although the Cabinet's records are silent on this point.[22]

Nevertheless, the RAF faced problems under Bonar Law. He wanted to evacuate Iraq, which would leave 8 squadrons unemployed, while he and the Treasury wished to defer any spending on the HDAF in 1923–24. Yet in March 1923 Bonar Law abandoned these proposals and asked Hoare to tell the Cabinet what a 'One-Power standard in Air' would cost. Hoare rejected such a standard due to its expense and probably because the Air Ministry did not want the strength of the HDAF to hinge exclusively on Britain's perpetually uncertain relations with France. Still, prompted by Trenchard, Hoare argued that only an increased HDAF could honour the ten-year period while an even longer one would be needed if France was actually regarded as a threat.[23]   The Cabinet let the RAF begin seven squadrons of the 1922 programme in 1923 and elected to take this public line against Parliamentary pressure about air defence:

> that the Government deprecate any talk of aggression by France toward this country; that they understand that in the present state of tension on the Continent of Europe, France is bound to take every precaution for her safety; that we have no knowledge as to what the ultimate French armaments will amount to; but that we can conceive nothing worse than a competition in armaments between France and this country.

Yet the Cabinet announced that it 'would not be behindhand' in air defence. By June it approved the Salisbury Committee's proposal for a new HDAF programme (incorporating that of 1922) of 600 regular aircraft. This would provide 334 more first-line machines while retaining all the second-line ones of 1922. The Cabinet implied that this programme might be increased should the FAF expand further. It also defined an air standard which linked the HDAF to Britain's fears of France. The HDAF must be able 'adequately to protect us against Air attack by the strongest Air Force within striking distance of this country'. Its standard was to be equality in first-line machines with 'the Independent Striking Force of the strongest Air Force within striking distance of this country'; that is, with the Air Division. Smith has erroneously asserted that this meant 'parity with the largest force within striking distance of British shores', which would have entailed equality with the entire FAF in France.[24]

Between 1923 and 1925 the government never defined a rate of completion for this programme but simply urged that it be finished as rapidly as possible. The RAF planned to form 52 squadrons by 1929, the estimated cost of which swelled from £14 850 000 to £17 845 000 in its first year. It received almost all the money it requested but failed to spend much of it. By 1925 the RAF was forming 25 squadrons but 18 months after the programme had begun, the HDAF had already fallen a year behind schedule, with the procurement of new models of aircraft even more so, as Barstow predicted, because of bottlenecks in the construction of bases, in the training of men and in the provision of equipment. Had the programme continued after 1925, it would probably have fallen further behind schedule.[25]

Whatever the flaws in the RAF's case, the HDAF was a far-sighted idea. Although there was no French air menace, the fear of one led Britain to take a crucial strategic step. Yet given its relative freedom, the RAF executed that programme poorly. In any case, given Trenchard's cynical use of the French air menace, in which he later claimed never to have believed, the programme naturally became vulnerable when this menace was no longer perceived. The only service between 1923 and 1925 which could pursue an expansion programme unhindered failed fully to exploit that opportunity.

During 1922–24 Britain temporarily sank to the status of the world's second naval power. As an economy measure in 1922 the Admiralty destroyed the battleships and battlecruisers due to be scrapped under the naval treaty, which no signatory had to do until the treaty was ratified. In the interim, the USN and the IJN scrapped none of their warships, leaving Britain with far fewer battleships than the USN and scarcely more than the IJN.[26] Fortunately, as these powers honoured the treaty once it was ratified, Britain remained secure at sea with an opportunity to maintain that position. The Admiralty did not fear the European navies, and the USN was not allowed to pursue the programmes which worried Britain. The USN wanted to increase the range of fire for its older battleships, but the Foreign Office skillfully convinced the US government not to do so over Britain's objections.[27] Although Congress approved a programme of eight Washington standard cruisers, it allocated funds for only two. The Admiralty did not disregard the European and US threats but its policy was directed primarily against Japan.

This stemmed from the fact that the naval treaty established a maximum size for cruisers of 10 000 tons with 8-inch guns (the 'Washington standard') which was larger than any existing cruiser. Historians such as Antony Preston have misinterpreted the origins of this decision. Although it was influenced by the USN's desire to build such cruisers, in 1921 Britain also favoured vessels of roughly this size.[28] In mid-1922 the Admiralty thought that all its new cruisers should be of the Washington standard but saw no immediate need to build them, since Britain had the most and best cruisers at sea. Although it wished to continue the Singapore base and the fuel programmes, it did not perceive an imminent Japanese threat. However, in July 1922 the IJN announced that by 1928 it would build 117 lighter warships, including four 10 000 and four 7100 ton cruisers with 8-inch guns. This galvanised British naval policy. The Admiralty decided that these 8-inch gun cruisers were proof that Japan was a threat which Britain must overcome by building

Washington standard cruisers of its own. Beatty soon gave the CID its first taste of a series of warnings which continued until 1925: that Japan was likely to attack India or Australia, that the navy alone could restrain these 'aggressive tendencies' and that until the fleet could operate in the Pacific, the empire would exist on Japan's 'sufferance'.[29] The fate of naval policy depended on whether the government accepted Beatty's arguments. Britain had a complicated perception of Japan. It knew that Japan dominated the western Pacific and yet faced economic crises, was restraining itself in China and had cut its armed strength. The question, as Wellesley noted, was whether Japan 'will take advantage' of its position, to which Tyrrell cheerfully added, 'even the Japanese may not know!' During 1922–23 the Admiralty and the Foreign Office dominated Britain's attempts to answer this question and the differences which emerged in their answers were to shape strategic policy in 1925. The Foreign Office believed that Britain had to maintain its security against Japan but perceived a threat only to British interests in China, where Japan might ultimately use its 'strong defensive position to defy the rest of the world in an expansionist policy'.[30] The Admiralty feared an attack on British possessions. In fact Japan was not preparing such an action but rather sought to defend itself against the USN. Although Britain had to maintain its security against Japan, the Admiralty misunderstood the nature of this situation. Consequently, it developed a politically unacceptable policy which could not have supported its strategy.

During 1922–23 the Admiralty established a new policy founded on its interpretations of the one power standard and of the ten-year period, which it took to mean that its preparations for major wars 'are to be spread over a period of years ending in 1929'. It approved 1923–24 sketch estimates of £61 850 000 and defined its priorities: to maintain its current size and to complete the treaty battleships, the Singapore base and the fuel programme.[31] Lloyd George's government challenged these aims. The CID again sanctioned the Singapore base but decided to complete the fuel programme in 1933 instead of 1931 because Balfour and Churchill denied that Japan was an imminent threat. The government wished to defer the start of the two battleships until 1923–24. When it was advised that according to the treaty the construction of these vessels must begin in 1922–23 or not at all, Lloyd George but not the Treasury favoured their construction. The Treasury and Churchill's economy committee claimed that naval programmes could be deferred because of the ten-year period and because Japan posed no threat.[32]

The Admiralty secured its programmes and broke the Treasury's challenge because Bonar Law's government was unwilling to compromise maritime security, to live on Japan's sufferance or to ignore a Japanese threat. The CID restored the completion date of 1931 for the fuel programme. After battles with Bonar Law and the Treasury, Amery warned the Cabinet that it must publicly abandon the one power standard unless the battleships were laid down immediately. The Cabinet capitulated on this point and approved naval estimates of £58 000 000 as well as a Singapore base scheme of £14 500 000 to begin in 1925–26.[33]

During 1923 the Admiralty refined its policy against Japan. It decided to redeploy the main fleet to the Mediterranean, whence it could most easily reach Singapore, and wanted to develop the infrastructure for fleet operations in the Pacific.[34] Captain Pound, the Director of Plans Division, also analysed the navy's construction needs between 1924 and 1936, both to replace aging warships and to provide the means for war with Japan. He wanted to complete Britain's needs in lighter warships before 1931, when the treaty's replacement schedule would begin. The current conversion of three new carriers should meet Britain's requirements, but it might also build another one. It should construct 72 destroyers, 32 submarines, eight Washington standard and 10 other, perhaps smaller, cruisers. This programme would cost £66 771 000, or approximately £8 000 000 annually, about 15 per cent (£17 424 000) for work on battleships and battlecruisers, 20 per cent (£14 000 000) for destroyers, 3–8 per cent for carriers (£2 457 000–£5 457 000), 33 per cent for cruisers (£22 000 000) and the remainder for auxiliary vessels.[35]

Some replacement programme was necessary as many British warships were becoming inefficient. All three of its existing carriers were obsolescent while only seven of its cruisers were suitable for oceanic war.[36] Pound's proposals were generally sound and Britain would also have been wise to replace its existing carriers. Even his cruiser proposals were a defensible proposition. He wanted the fleet to have 31 cruisers, or 25 per cent more than the total of 25 cruisers Japan would have by 1929. Britain's eight Washington standard and four large 7.5-inch gun cruisers would provide a 25 per cent margin over Japan's 8-inch gun ones. Britain also needed 38 normal cruisers for trade protection, a figure derived from the maximum cruiser strength used against surface raiders during the great war.[37] Thus,

Britain needed 69 cruisers, a figure rounded up to 70. By 1929 the empire would have 51 cruisers of less than 15 years of age. The 18 new cruisers would meet this deficit, while those replaced would go into reserve. This programme would give Britain far more cruisers than the USN or the IJN, but then it had greater needs for commerce protection than they did.

Although not unreasonable, Pound's cruiser calculations were arbitrary and could be altered in either direction. In 1919 the naval staff had wanted 92 cruisers and Admiral Jellicoe 89, while in 1921 Beatty had considered having only 50 and the naval staff had not rejected the idea of 60.[38] These construction needs could also have been safely reduced by extending the figure for the useful life of cruisers from 15 to 20 years, as was done by 1928.[39] Moreover, the Admiralty assumed that cruisers would most threaten Britain by acting as commerce raiders. Consequently, it exaggerated the degree to which British cruisers would serve to protect commerce and underestimated their role as fighting elements of the fleet. If, however, the Admiralty's construction programme overemphasised the importance of cruisers compared with carriers, it was right to note their value. Cruisers were the largest warships whose absolute numbers were not restricted by the naval treaty, and hence those vessels which could best strengthen the relative position of any naval power. During the Second World War cruisers fulfilled many traditional functions of battleships and battlecruisers. Pound's programme would have met Britain's maritime needs. Much less would have been dangerous and much more unnecessary, or even counterproductive. Any additions would make the programme more expensive than any government was likely to finance over the long term, especially since this would create the danger of a naval race in cruisers. Unfortunately, the Admiralty doubled the size of the programme because political developments led it to believe that the government would finance this expansion. In October 1923 Baldwin had the '"brainwave"' that a naval programme would reduce unemployment and improve his chances for the coming election. After the Cabinet approved this idea, Pound argued that Britain should build 30 cruisers between 1924 and 1929, at least 17 being of Washington standard. This would raise cruiser costs to £37 000 000 and the annual expense of the programme to £12 000 000. For the first time Pound also claimed that Britain needed nine Washington standard cruisers to protect its trade against Japan's 8-inch gun ones.[40] Although the latter could have attacked commerce, judging from their design they were probably intended for fleet use against the USN. The Admiralty wanted almost three times more cruisers than Japan; and twelve Washington standard or equivalent cruisers with the fleet and nine for trade protection against the same eight Japanese 8-inch gun cruisers. Although Britain needed to prepare both for fleet actions and trade protection, these proposals did appear excessive.

The Board justified this programme by citing the ten-year period and the one power standard. It wished to lay down a new carrier, eight Washington standard cruisers and 11 other vessels in 1924–25, and to replace 117 destroyers and 52 cruisers (at least 17 of Washington standard) between 1924 and 1935. Eight cruisers should begin annually over the next three years and four in each of the following years. The Admiralty even wished to pay for this programme through deficit financing. Baldwin's Cabinet allocated £5 000 000 for new construction, which would have financed the entire 1924–25 programme. MacDonald approved £1 800 000 to lay down five cruisers (which was all the Admiralty had wanted for 1924–25 before Baldwin's 'brainwave'). Although MacDonald did not rule on the full programme, Baldwin's second government would find it difficult to deny that it was committed in principle to one.[41]

The Admiralty had carried its policies of 1923 a long way, but several obstacles lay ahead. The first was cost. By 1924 the replacement programme had doubled in expense while that of the Singapore base had tripled since 1921. The Admiralty approved a £9 500 000 scheme for the base while its defences were expected to need another £3–4 000 000. These requirements soon rose to £21 000 000, which Beatty cut to £11 000 000, while Trenchard later suggested that it would cost £21–£30 000 000. These estimates varied with what was defined as part of the base and the period under review. The Admiralty secretly favoured a larger scheme and always implied that the base might cost more than had been stated.[42] Yet the Cabinet had not approved all these detailed proposals for security against Japan. It could be expected to balk when these costs finally began to bite, in 1925.

The second problem was that the 'Singapore strategy' itself was flawed. The navy's war plans were like those of 1921 although Britain lacked the paper superiority over Japan of that period. It wanted a fleet against Japan of 15 battleships and battlecruisers, four carriers, 37 cruisers and 81 destroyers, which only marginally exceeded the IJN's intended strength of 10 battleships and battlecruisers, three carriers, 40 cruisers and 144 destroyers. Under the Admiralty's plans, the fleet would reach Singapore and preferably Hong Kong, preventing any Japanese attacks on British possessions. However, the fleet 'would have to be reinforced' before it could operate in Japanese 'home waters'.[43] Britain would then advance a base north of Hong Kong and win by annihilating the IJN or through blockade. This strategy would have taken years to complete unless both parties risked a decisive engagement, in which Britain would have lacked real superiority.

Moreover, a naval threat at home would force Britain to cut the size of this fleet and its likelihood of victory. Although Britain's battleships, battlecruisers and carriers to be left in home waters during a war with Japan would have matched those of any European navy, France or Italy would exceed it in lighter warships. As the journalist Hector C. Bywater warned, so long as Britain had only a one power standard 'we shall do well to eschew strategic plans which connote a two-power standard of strength.'[44] The 'Singapore strategy' rested on the assumptions that Britain would be secure at sea elsewhere, could commit most of its navy to a protracted total war in the Pacific and could then crush a foe of roughly equal strength. These assumptions were scarcely realistic. The Admiralty was accounting neither for the most dangerous circumstances, a simultaneous naval war with Japan and at least one European power, nor for the most likely ones, in which Britain would neither care nor dare to allocate the bulk of its navy for such operations against Japan.

The third problem was the Admiralty's failure to analyse Britain's maritime needs against Japan. In 1924 Richmond argued that the questions were 'Why do we suppose that we might have to fight Japan?' and 'How are we going to make war?' Britain's strategy would be misconceived unless it examined how Japan could threaten Britain and how Britain could withstand these threats. Richmond argued that Japan could only do so by destroying Britain's fleet or capturing the Singapore base, and then occupying India or Australia. Britain must be able to prevent these occurrences but had nothing to gain from fighting to pursue greater objectives, such as its Chinese interests.[45] Like Bywater, Richmond implied that Japan and Britain could not easily damage each other. Britain could not crush Japan quickly, need not prepare currently for decisive offensive operations against it, and during the foreseeable future could preserve British maritime interests through lesser means. Had the Admiralty considered Richmond's critique, it might have better understood its strategic needs against Japan.

Finally, weaknesses were emerging in the Admiralty's political position. After his many victories in Whitehall Beatty believed that his only remaining tasks were to take over naval aviation and establish a 'reasonable' construction programme.[46] However, 1923 marked the turning point of his career as CNS. Contrary to his previous practice, he began to make ill-considered statements which weakened his general case. He told the Salisbury Committee that land-based aircraft could never affect any naval operations and informed MacDonald's government that should the navy be forbidden to prepare against either the USN or the IJN, 'it would be better to carry out that policy *in toto* and scrap at least half the British navy and save the taxpayers the cost of upkeep', advice which MacDonald followed in 1930. Furthermore, the Admiralty's uncompromising attitude as, for example, over naval aviation in July 1923, led statesmen to see sailors as petulant and unreasonable.[47] These perceptions ultimately cost the navy dear.

Many of the Admiralty's programmes were necessary but it misunderstood Britain's real maritime needs. It wanted to prepare for decisive offensive operations against Japan when its real task was to protect British interests in Imperial waters. During the 1920s Britain could have withstood Japan or any two naval powers except the United States but could not have defeated any two powers or Japan alone until after years of rearmament specifically directed to this end. Alarmist perceptions of an imminent Japanese threat led the Admiralty to exaggerate the rate and scale for the programmes needed to maintain British security, yet even these swollen proposals could not have sustained its strategy against Japan. There were many ways to challenge this policy. Richmond offered one while in 1925 Wellesley and Churchill proffered another: that since Japan was not a threat, Britain should not frighten it into becoming one through too rapid naval preparations. Moreover, the Admiralty's programmes would have been costly and could have sparked an arms race. They could only have been undertaken had the government entirely adopted Beatty's views about a Japanese threat which, beginning in 1924, Whitehall was unwilling to do. Yet the Admiralty's opponents were naive in their assumptions, arguing, like Snowden, 'that Japan in her Home Waters is in a different position from the British Empire in the West Pacific'.[48] Of course, Japan had security interests there but so too did Britain.

Unfortunately, the government was not debating Britain's real needs but the Admiralty's inflated estimate of them. In response to these demands, the government would be tempted not to meet Britain's real needs. By 1923, having finally mastered the budget, the Treasury defined a new financial policy. It wanted the 1923–24 budget of £853 000 000 to be £50–£56 000 000 smaller by 1925–26. Debt servicing should absorb 50 per cent of revenues while service estimates should decline to £110 000 000.[49] To achieve these aims the Treasury would have to cut the services' estimates of 1922–23 by 20 per cent, which it found difficult to do. Net service estimates fell from £138 000 000 in 1922–23 to £120 000 000 in 1925–26, or just 11 per cent, which was an even lesser victory than it appeared. This global cut masked real increases in RAF and naval spending, while their estimates were poised to climb dramatically after 1925–26.

About £14 000 000 of this global fall came from the elimination of the abnormal parts of the services' 1922–23 estimates, which did not affect their normal purchasing power. Their current effective estimates fell by just £7 000 000 (or 6 per cent) between 1922 and 1925, almost all of which came from the army and mostly in 1923–24. RAF and naval current effective estimates in 1925–26 together exceeded those of 1923–24 by £5 732 000. The services also received greater funds than they could spend: they lost more money from this cause than through all the Treasury's direct pressure. Moreover, between 1922 and 1925 they acquired a substantial but hidden financial bonus. By overcoming administrative inefficiencies, using up stocks of articles like clothing and accounting for declining prices (as their 1922–23 estimates had not fully done) the services could reduce their spending in various areas without affecting their policies. Any of these savings which remained in their hands would boost their purchasing power elsewhere, serving in effect as a real increase in their spending.

Consequently, as the Treasury well knew, its success against the services was not what it seemed. The army's current effective estimates fell by 10 per cent between 1923 and 1925, forcing it to forgo new programmes but not to cut any old ones or any unit. This indicates that the Treasury was right to see room for greater efficiency in the services. Although the navy's current effective estimates fell in face value by £5 750 000 between 1922–23 and 1924–25, it simultaneously received a hidden bonus of £10 283 000, while £2 000 000 of the reduction in 1924–25 was a shadow cut: money which previously would have been included in its estimates but not spent. In effect, by 1924–25 the navy's current effective estimates were £6 500 000, or 12 per cent, above those of 1922–23. This let the Admiralty finance the construction of four sub-Washington and five Washington standard cruisers, two battleships and three carriers without cutting its policies elsewhere. 1922–25 were boom years for the RAF. Other departments paid to maintain almost half its squadrons while its current effective estimates swelled by 43 per cent, excluding anything gained from hidden bonuses.[50] During 1922–24 the Treasury was not preventing real increases in naval and RAF expenditure, while the looming rise in their estimates threatened its entire budgetary policy. This stemmed from the failure of Treasury control.

Between 1919 and 1921, Treasury control over service spending had not existed. In 1922 it began to establish this, to uphold its right to examine service estimates and, subject to the Cabinet, to block specific expenditures. The Treasury did gain control over army estimates, because the army refused to fight. It conceded that the army was as small as possible but continually cut army expenditure to compensate for its failure to reduce that of the other services. Angered by its lack of political support, haunted by its inability to control naval spending in particular, the Treasury sought new financial means to control service spending. It asked the Salisbury Committee to empower the COSC, the Treasury and the CID to consider 'how the best value can be obtained for the total money that could be allocated for defence'.[51] The government gave the CID and the COSC, but not the Treasury, some influence over defence spending, a situation the Treasury tried to turn to its advantage. In what Barstow termed a 'shilling shocker', it told the Cabinet that the services wanted £127 157 000 for 1924–25, £8 274 000 more than in 1923–24. The Treasury wished to 'ration' the services to £112 500 000: navy, £52 000 000; army, £46 000 000; and RAF, £14 500 000. The CID might reallocate these rations within this global limit. The government, however, did not act on these proposals.[52]

The Treasury wanted to prevent the rise in RAF and naval estimates and to trim the fat from their organisations. It wished to cancel or defer indefinitely all the navy's programmes, which stemmed from an 'apprehensive view of the Yellow Peril', and to slow the HDAF programme.[53] Barstow appreciated that none of this could be achieved through financial control but only by attacking the foundations of service policies — grand strategy and strategic principles. He wished to redefine the ten-year period so that it would no longer justify the scale and rate of the services' programmes. He realised that the government had approved these programmes because it perceived a strategically uncertain world. Diplomatic changes alone could alter its view of the need for these programmes. So to initiate such changes Barstow favoured an air limitation agreement with France, even at the price of a British guarantee to its neighbour, and a new naval limitation agreement with Japan and the US.[54] Barstow had reconnoitered the battlefield. Whether the Treasury could triumph there hinged on matters beyond its control.

9 The Road to Locarno, 1924–25

In 1924–25 foreign policy held the balance between the clashing imperatives of financial and service policies, while the future of strategic policy came to hinge on the relationship between diplomatic and grand strategic matters. The government, concluding that Britain would be secure during the foreseeable future, created a new strategic policy and altered the services' expansion programmes. MacDonald began this process of revision. While he continued his predecessor's defence policies he feared their political consequences, believing that Liberal attacks on his service decisions would detrimentally affect Labour Party and public opinion and 'contribute largely to bringing us down prematurely'. His government had carried the cruiser programme through Parliament simply with Conservative support.

> I cannot repeat that. If I attempt it my hold on the Party will go. On a division a few of us will go with a united Tory Party into one lobby and Liberals and Labour under Liberal leadership will go into the other and that will be the beginning of the end not only of Government unity but of Party unity in the country.[1]

Between February and July 1924, for political and doctrinal reasons, MacDonald sought to alter strategic policy regarding Japan and Britain's relationship to France and European security.

He appointed a Cabinet committee to examine the Singapore base and the replacement programme. Speaking 'purely as a non-party' Foreign Secretary, MacDonald argued that the construction of the base would 'inevitably' foster 'a military situation in the East . . . similar to that in the North Sea in 1914'. Britain should instead pursue a different means of regional security, although when 'the balance of power became more settled, it might then be folly to hold our hand . . . He did not say that a base at Singapore should never be built, but not at the present moment'. The committee believed that while the base would be necessary against a Japanese threat, its construction would invoke that very danger. The government cancelled the base so as to gain 'international confidence' for its policy, although it recognised this to be just a first step towards achieving its greater aims in east Asia.[2]

MacDonald took two further steps in this direction. First, responding to a suggestion from Britain's ambassador to Tokyo that Britain could reach a systematic settlement with Japan, MacDonald considered a 'realist' arrangement whereby Britain would 'make our disinterested friendship axiomatic in the minds of Japanese Governments' by somehow letting Japan augment its position in China. He wanted to know 'what can be done not to prevent the expansion of Japan, but to give it limits which will curb its power of mischief in the Pacific'. MacDonald dismissed this idea when Wellesley demonstrated that it entailed special economic rights to Japan in China. Second, the Cabinet committee favoured a new naval limitation conference with Japan and the US. Due to MacDonald's mishandling of this issue, it became bogged down in disputes between the Admiralty and the Foreign Office, and he abandoned it in June.[3]

By then his European initiative had also failed. In February MacDonald asked the Foreign Office to help him form a 'comprehensive' policy towards French aims in Europe. Two junior officials, Harold Nicolson and John Sterndale Bennett, responded that France wished permanently to control the Rhineland, from which it could dominate Europe and threaten Britain. MacDonald incorporated their arguments into a policy intended to be 'European in the fullest sense of the word'. He wished to oppose this French 'historical craving', this policy motivated by 'much more' than fear of Germany. He requested the services' opinions on the 'military import' of French domination of the Rhineland, and also about 'what we might do as regards security of France'. He favoured demilitarisation and reconciliation between France and Germany, but without British commitments.[4] MacDonald flirted with the idea of raising a new approach towards European security with France before a reparations agreement was reached.

The other services agreed that French control of the Rhineland would threaten Britain but the general staff argued that France would not do so, while Germany would try to overturn the European order. It also demonstrated that no demilitarisation system was practicable. Influenced by these arguments, MacDonald abandoned his proposals, leaving France the initiative on the security issue.

After the reparations question was settled in August, France stated that its European policy would depend on a guarantee of its security. Consequently, until 1925 Britain was on the diplomatic defensive against a French proposal, the 'Geneva Protocol', which would have created regional security pacts under the League. MacDonald rejected this proposal, but many ministers and officials favoured a commitment to France or to mutual security. MacDonald refused to let any decision be reached on these topics during his last weeks in office.[5]

MacDonald's endeavour to control and to alter strategic policy himself had failed, but he caused one notable change. He used the Foreign Office as his executive agent on strategic matters in Whitehall and left it inextricably involved in issues which determined the future of service policies. MacDonald brought the Foreign Office into the heart of strategic decision making for the first time since the war while his diplomatic actions set the stage for those of his successors. After the Conservative victory in the election of autumn 1924 Baldwin made Amery the Colonial Secretary, Bridgeman the First Lord, Hoare, the Air Minister and Salisbury, Lord Privy Seal. Cecil, the Chancellor of the Duchy of Lancaster, became responsible for League affairs under the Foreign Secretary, while Curzon became Lord President and CID chairman. Worthington-Evans became the War Minister, Churchill, the Chancellor and Birkenhead, the India Secretary. Balfour became a CID member and Lord President after Curzon's death in March 1925.

All these ministers influenced the revision of foreign policy, but two of them in particular did so. Austen Chamberlain was an able Foreign Secretary, although in 1925 he usually followed his advisors' proposals. For example, he admitted that he was 'ignorant' regarding east Asia and mistrusted 'my own judgement' when it conflicted with that of his officials.[6] At all critical moments Baldwin dominated the reformulation of strategic policy. His government shared many of MacDonald's diplomatic views and, while favourably inclined towards the services, saw financial advantages to arms limitation. Baldwin's Cabinet adopted MacDonald's approach to naval limitation, his decision that Japan was not a threat, and continued his search for a European settlement without a British commitment.

The 'liberal' tendency in MacDonald's policy was not an aberration but rather the beginning of a change of emphasis in diplomacy. Hitherto 'liberal' attitudes had been a subordinate influence in strategic policy. For example, Britain had favoured naval limitation not because it regarded disarmament as a universal panacea but because this specific action was thought to suit certain British interests better than an arms race. However, 'liberal' views were slowly gaining influence in Whitehall. The government's strategic assessments of 1925 were largely 'realist' but it increasingly believed that international reconciliation and arms limitation could support Britain's needs as well as rearmament. This emerging partiality for 'liberal' solutions helped to shape a new strategic policy.

The debate on naval policy, which governed the formulation of strategic policy in 1925, turned on British diplomacy in east Asia. Britain perceived three threats to its interests there: that Japan might seek to dominate the area, especially China; that Russia and its local allies might take over China, which had become even more unstable; and that the strained relations between Washington and Tokyo might restore the situation which had existed before the Washington Conference. These diplomatic developments caused a split between the Admiralty and the Foreign Office over Japan. The former held that Britain must prepare against an imminent Japanese menace. Conversely, the Foreign Office thought that since Japan would shape the development of any danger in the Pacific, it was vitally important to retain good relations with Tokyo. It challenged the navy's policy in the Pacific because that threatened its own diplomacy in east Asia.

The Foreign Office wished to avoid alarming Japan which, Tyrrell noted, was in a 'very "sensitive' condition at present; we want her cooperation very badly in the Chinese crisis and we do not want to drive her into the Asiatic camp'. It believed that Japan would threaten Britain solely because of differences arising over China. That eventuality could be avoided only if China were to become stable, which would require cooperation between Japan, Britain and the US. Wellesley denied that Japan would attack the British Empire during the foreseeable future. Japan was 'really aiming' at

> military and naval preponderance in the Far East, not for aggressive purposes, but to be able to say 'hands off'. Japan has succeeded, in spite of her naval reductions, in increasing the strength of her military and naval position in the Far East. She has nothing to gain from a war with America, but a great deal by being in a position to say, if and when she wants to do

something in the F.E. contrary to the wishes of the other Powers, come and stop us if you can.

The Foreign Office recognised that Japan could ultimately threaten Imperial security, but feared that too rapid a strengthening of Britain's position in the Pacific would drive Japan to subvert immediate British diplomacy. For example, although it held that the Singapore base was needed to deter Japanese aggression, it wanted to complete that slowly so as not to provoke Japan.[7]

When the Cabinet asked for an analysis of the political situation in the Pacific, preparatory to its naval decisions, Chamberlain requested Wellesley's opinion 'on our relations with Japan in connexion with the Admiralty's shipbuilding programmes'. In a paper entitled *The Improbability of War in the Pacific*, Wellesley argued that Japan would not endanger Britain until *'another group of Powers asserted its influence in the Far East'*, which would be foreshadowed years in advance by movements towards a Russo-German-Japanese alliance. A 'policy of building against Japan' was 'provocative and dangerous', for that alone could cause Japan to become a threat.[8] The Foreign Office's decision to subordinate the imperatives of long-term naval policy to those of immediate diplomacy ultimately crippled British strategy. For in 1925–26 the Foreign Office and the Treasury shared similar perceptions of Japan, and cooperated against the navy. Moreover, the politicians did not regard Japan as a threat. Chamberlain could 'conceive of no subject' which could cause Anglo-Japanese hostilities. Influenced by Britain's decisions about European security, in March 1925 Baldwin favoured a 'liberal' solution to the entire Pacific problem.

At the moment, the world was full of talk of peace talks, pacts of guarantee and so forth. Why should not we, America and Japan conclude a peace treaty in respect of the Pacific? . . . some arrangement of that sort could only be to our advantage . . . there was a danger that America and Japan would heap up naval armaments against one another, ultimately there would be a clash; and . . . it was conceivable that we might be drawn in, however much against our will. But why should we not all three sign some instrument to the effect that there should be no resort to war? He really attached great importance to [this proposal]. If we could make one of these magnificent 'moral gestures' which everyone was talking about, showing that we were in fact strong supporters of arbitration, it seemed to him an easy way of doing it.[9]

Finally, decision makers, especially Beatty, came to regard Japan as a potential ally against Russia.[10] Yet Britain did not deal realistically with Japan. It ruled out Japan as a threat and reduced its preparations against that eventuality. It took no steps to turn Japan into a friend; its actions weakened Britain's ability to deal with Japan as an enemy.

During 1922–23 Britain had not perceived any way to overcome the diplomatic stalemate in Europe. By December 1924, however, this problem seemed close to solution. Consequently, Whitehall debated whether Britain should ensure this development by accepting a commitment to European security. It considered four kinds of commitment: an Anglo-French or Anglo-French-Belgian defensive alliance against Germany; a quadruple pact (under which Britain would defend Belgium, France and Germany against an attack by one upon another of them, while all these powers also signed a non-aggression agreement); a non-aggression treaty between these four states; and regional security pacts under the League. Decision makers frequently altered their position on these issues. The balance of opinion initially favoured an Anglo-French alliance or regional security pacts, then swung to oppose commitments beyond a non-aggression treaty or a loose quadruple pact. In the end Britain accepted a more definite quadruple pact.[11]

Many decision makers opposed commitments for fear that these might force Britain to enter a continental war, one which it might lose. They doubted that commitments could have any diplomatic value, believing that these would 'stereotype' the situation in Europe and not alter the conditions which might lead to war. Hankey and Miles Lampson, the chief of the Central Department, worried that a British commitment might actually encourage a more aggressive French policy and increase the likelihood of war.[12] The government rejected any commitments to eastern Europe and feared that one to France might force Britain to fight Germany for Poland's sake. It agreed that Britain must assist France and Belgium against German aggression, but no one wished to support France's security policy or send an army to a continental war. The doubts of the Dominions and British public opinion about commitments influenced Whitehall, as did the American attitude towards the Protocol.

Yet Britain saw arguments in favour of limited commitments in Europe, where the diplomatic situation might lead to another war. The general staff predicted that the danger period lay between 1935 and 1940, Churchill spoke of it as being 'decades' away while Austen Chamberlain believed that it would not arise before the 1960s.[13] The proponents of commitments argued that these alone could provide the leverage needed to alter French policy and to maintain the balance in Europe. Decision makers saw that German strength was rising and French strength falling, although many of them exaggerated this situation because they accepted naive extrapolations of the future demographic balance between these two nations.[14] Whitehall feared that Germany wanted to overthrow the European order and become a military power again, thus threatening Britain. Its debate was over what commitment, if any, could overcome these problems and establish British security within a stable and balanced Europe.

Britain wanted to reconcile France and Germany, to bring the latter into a concert of Europe and to detach the former from its eastern entanglements. It knew that these aims would require changes in the European order. Many statesmen were willing, in the worst case, to prevent German challenges in western Europe by leaving it free to expand eastward at Poland's expense. The Foreign Office and Churchill, for example, argued that Europe could become stable only after Germany had regained its *irredenta* from Poland. Britain hoped that this would occur peacefully but recognised that Germany might pursue these aims through force and that Britain had never fought to 'resist the dismemberment of Poland'. Lampson stated a common view, that

> the whole future of Poland is more than doubtful. She is between the hammer and the anvil: and when these two instruments are again in working order (as they will be some day) Poland will be in an unpleasant position between them. I should *not* care to stake my family fortune on the permanency of Poland as an independent state.[15]

Britain's discussions after it approved a commitment illuminate its earlier strategic attitudes. By May a Cabinet Committe favoured a powerful France to restrain German and Russian power. Churchill argued that only a large French army could underwrite the reparations agreement, which was the 'surest way of keeping down the strength of the German army'. Balfour stated that Britain would lose by French disarmament . . . and that the whole world would lose by the disarmament of the Little Entente so long as Soviet Russia was a possible source of trouble . . . The French army was not likely to be used as an aggressive force. Was it not possible that it would prevent other countries from going to war.

In July Cavan told the CID that 'it would be disastrous if Germany were driven to find a new orientation to the East' while Chamberlain offered three principles which had governed his European policy. The first

was to make it an absolute impossibility for Germany again to overrun Europe. The second . . . was to induce France to adopt a more friendly and reasonable frame of mind towards Germany. The third was to prevent a Russo-German understanding against the rest of Europe.[16]

A desire to prevent Russia or a Russo-German axis from challenging the European order affected Britain's decisions of 1925. It wished to ensure that during the coming gradual transition between French and German dominance in Europe the balance of power would remain stable. Britain wanted France to abandon its security system in Europe and yet to balance Germany; to loosen the bonds on Germany and yet to keep it from exploiting that situation to 'overrun Europe'. Britain's aims were complicated and so too was the debate over them. Of the departments, only the War and the Foreign Offices influenced this debate. However, the Admiralty favoured an Anglo-French alliance, mostly to let Britain strengthen its fleet against Japan. The Air Ministry also initially supported such an agreement but Trenchard, at one of the few moments during the 1920s when any decision maker referred to the possibility of an Anglo-German alliance, noted that in principle 'a pact with Germany' would give Britain as many advantages 'by keeping France in subjection' as would any ties with France. In any case, the Air Ministry's fundamental concern was to keep any political agreement with France from hampering the HDAF programme.[17]

The general staff argued that Germany would challenge the European order. German military strength already approximated that of France and would entirely exceed it by 1935. Yet British security turned on that of France.

The true strategic frontier of Great Britain is the Rhine; her security depends entirely upon the present frontiers of France, Belgium and Holland being maintained and remaining in friendly hands. The great guiding principle of the German General Staff in making plans for a future war will be, as in the last war, to try to defeat her enemies in detail. Any line of policy which permitted Germany (with or without allies) first to swallow up France and then to deal with Great Britain would be fatal strategically.[18]

The War Office favoured an Anglo-French alliance for strategic reasons, although it hoped that this might further general reconciliation in Europe by deterring German aggression and establishing French security. Like all decision makers, the generals assumed that France would provide the army for their joint security while Britain would offer only the navy and the RAF. The Foreign Office complained that the general staff exaggerated the inevitability of aggression from the German 'beast'. Still, the general staff presented a strikingly prescient analysis. Although its conclusions approached those of Crowe, he termed one general staff paper 'dangerous stuff'.[19] He feared that its forthright strategic arguments might lead the government to reject his own foreign policy.

By late 1924 the Foreign Office accepted Lampson's arguments that only a British commitment to France could create stability in Europe. Chamberlain agreed that France would never cooperate with Britain without such a commitment, nor would Germany so long as it could hope to split Britain and France. If Britain did not guarantee French security

what will be our position? We shall lose all influence over French policy. Do what we may, we shall win no gratitude from Germany. We shall be dragged along, unwilling, impotent, protesting, in the wake of France towards the new Armageddon. For we cannot afford to see France crushed, to leave Germany or an eventual Russo-German combination supreme on the Continent, or to allow any great military power to dominate the Low Countries.

Chamberlain also held that 'When we talk about the guarantee of the French eastern frontier, we are talking about the guarantee of our own frontier — the only place where we can defend our frontier'.[20]

Although Chamberlain shared his official's views, until March

1925 it was they, and especially Crowe, who formulated Foreign Office policy.[21] A memorandum by Nicolson represented their concensus on this issue. It argued that Germany would not directly challenge Britain or Russia so as not to force into being another Anglo-French-Russian alliance. Germany would, however, eventually attack Poland, which France would have to defend. Current conditions were leading straight towards the destruction of any acceptable balance in Europe: to a new great war and the defeat of France or to a Russo-German alliance. Only a new Anglo-French *entente*, involving a commitment to France, could restrain these dangers, maintain British security and foster European reconciliation.[22]

After some uncertainty about the nature of this commitment, by January 1925 the Foreign office advocated an Anglo-French alliance, but, unlike the general staff, simply as the means to an end. It really pursued a new concert of the powers in Europe, to be formalised in a quadruple pact. Since Paris would block this until London specifically guaranteed French security, Britain must first square France so as to reconcile Germany. The Foreign Office expected this commitment to encourage France to abandon its security policy and Germany its challenge to the European order. It did not consider the strategic implications of this commitment, believing that this would automatically create peace in Europe and would never have to be honoured. As Crowe wrote,

> the offer of a British pact of security has a twofold advantage;
> (1) it allays or mitigates French fears; (2) it provides against a danger which is really rather remote, so that the commitment involved for this country is smaller than might appear at first sight.[23]

Twelve ministers dominated the debate over European security. Amery, Birkenhead, Curzon and Balfour opposed any commitments; Austen Chamberlain, Worthington-Evans and Bridgeman favoured an alliance with France; while Cecil wanted Britain to pursue mutual security. Baldwin's attitude is uncertain but he probably was most affected by political considerations. Although their opinions changed, Churchill, Salisbury and Hoare initially accepted a commitment to western Europe under the League. Salisbury favoured a pledge of assistance to France against German aggression, which could become a non-aggression pact including Germany. Hoare and Churchill advocated a loose 'general military guarantee' in Europe, including several 'regional Pacts formed to meet special emergencies'.[24] Although they did not define Britain's commitment to this system, they implied that one would exist.

In December 1924 the CID established a committee of officials, including Crowe and Hankey, to consider British policy towards security in Europe. The committee rejected the Protocol but favoured an Anglo-French-Belgian alliance, which could later become a quadruple pact. Whereas Crowe supported this for diplomatic reasons, Hankey did so to eliminate a French threat to Britain.[25] By January 1925 few decision makers opposed commitments as a means to further British interests in Europe, while most who made their positions known favoured them. By February, however, diplomatic developments had caused a shift in these views. Germany offered a non-aggression pact to Britain and France, in which binding arbitration, but without any means of enforcement, would settle any differences between them. France did not reject this proposal but demanded a more definite guarantee of its security. The Foreign Office believed that France would accept this German idea only after Britain offered it a guarantee.[26] Conversely, most politicians thought that this signalled the end of the Franco-German deadlock. The CID, believing that Britain could gain its aims without a specific commitment to France, thus reconsidered the dangers of any commitments at all.

Cavan, Chamberlain and Cecil alone favoured strong commitments. Hankey, Trenchard, Hoare, Balfour, Birkenhead, Amery and Curzon opposed a guarantee to France. Churchill argued that without Russia or America as allies, France and Britain 'might get defeated' in a war with Germany. Yet Britain could 'stand alone. I decline to accept as an axiom that our future is involved with that of France.' Churchill argued that for several years Britain could not alter French policy in Europe and should simply state that whenever France and Germany made a 'real peace', Britain would form a 'genuine triple accord' with them.[27] The opponents of commitments were the larger party, but their views were inconsistent. They argued that a war in Europe was not imminent but that an alliance with France might lead to 'Armageddon No. 2'. They knew that Britain must defend France against German aggression but doubted that they could defeat Germany. They believed that German aggression was possible but favoured an agreement in which unenforceable arbitration alone could check that possibility.

The Foreign Office had wanted an Anglo-French alliance so as to create a quadruple pact. The government rejected the former but not the latter. Hence, Austen Chamberlain changed his policy to one of pursuing a quadruple pact from the outset.[28] On 2 March the Cabinet authorised this proposal but two days later, on the ostensible grounds that public opinion would reject any commitment to defend Germany against France, it issued new instructions 'severely limiting' Chamberlain's freedom of action. He was only allowed to tell Edouard Herriot, the French Premier, that if France would accept the German non-aggression proposals, Britain would do its 'best' to establish some 'quadrilateral agreement of mutual security'. The Cabinet neither stated whether it favoured a quadruple pact or a non-aggression one, nor defined Britain's role in this agreement. So confused was its discussion that Hankey reported that Curzon's 'opposition was to the proposed four-power pact rather than to Mr Chamberlain's proposal', ideas which the Foreign Secretary regarded as identical. Many ministers may have taken this stand sincerely but Curzon and Amery at least hoped that this approach would wreck Chamberlain's policy and avoid any commitment. Conversely, Chamberlain interpreted these ambiguous instructions as authorisation to pursue a real quadruple pact.[29]

When in response Herriot threatened to extend France's occupation of the Rhineland and in Chamberlain's absence, several ministers reconsidered the situation. Churchill, Salisbury, Birkenhead, Amery and Hoare argued that on 4 March the Cabinet had decided merely that Britain would agree to consult with France about countermeasures if it met legitimate German demands and if Germany later became aggressive. Although these ministers probably wished to wreck Chamberlain's policy, their interpretation of the Cabinet's decision was no less valid than his own. They were reacting to what they regarded as blackmail and can scarcely be blamed for trying to alter British policy. Crowe was attempting to do exactly the same by asking Baldwin to authorise the Foreign Office's old policy of first reaching a bilateral security arrangement with France and only subsequently with Germany.[30] Crowe's proposal contradicted the Cabinet's decision more than did that of the conference of ministers. However, when Chamberlain threatened to resign over this issue, Baldwin chose to support his policy. As the Foreign Office hoped, France negotiated on this basis since 'half a loaf is better than no bread'.[31]

After Baldwin's decision the Foreign Office controlled Britain's European policy. Hankey warned Chamberlain that his approach entailed commitments, that 'some day the cheque would be presented and we should have to honour it'. Chamberlain, however, rejected a CID examination of the strategic aspects of this issue. He believed that his proposals alone could avoid war in Europe and 'did not wish to wreck his policy on the technicalities of military consideration'. No doubt Chamberlain also feared that another enquiry might be turned against his policy. Yet his own and the similar arguments of Tyrrell, the new permanent under-secretary, were flawed.[32] They were intended to let the Foreign Office alone control a matter with obvious strategic connotations, issues on which, as usual, it was scarcely an authority.

By late 1925 the Foreign Office's diplomacy led to the Locarno Pact, under which France, Belgium and Germany signed non-aggression treaties while Britain agreed to defend any signatory which was attacked by another of them. Britain retained wide latitude for deciding when and how to act and accepted this commitment in the expectation that it would never have to be honoured. Furthermore, it could do so only through strong military forces and plans for their use with its potential allies. Yet the treaty led Britain to believe that Europe would remain peaceful during the foreseeable future and encouraged it to reduce its forces, while Britain's position as impartial guarantor between the signatories hampered the making of such plans. As Amery noted, Britain could scarcely send 'its officers simultaneously to Paris and Berlin to work up arrangements for fighting with the French and against the French!'[33] Britain soon rejected a Belgian request for staff talks about Belgium's defences because this would contravene Britain's 'special position'.[34] Although the treaty had a promising diplomatic effect, its value, should 'the cheque' ever be presented, was questionable.

In 1925 the government thought that Britain would not be threatened until the balance of power altered, through some arrangement between Japan, Germany and Russia. It held that immediate dangers had been surmounted while Germany and Japan were moving away from Russia. This led Whitehall to believe that the possibility of a menace from several powers had receded while France, Japan and Germany would not threaten Britain. Simultaneously, it came to see Russia as the most likely danger to British interests.

By early 1925 the War Office warned that Russia was poised to absorb the border areas of Persia, Afghanistan and China. The

Indian authorities began to regard Soviet influence in Afghanistan as a potential threat while the Foreign Office sought to strengthen British diplomacy against Russia in Afghanistan and Persia. The Cabinet approved this cautious policy although it noted that Britain might not fight Soviet attempts to absorb Persian frontier provinces because 'in present world conditions, careful stock has to be taken of our responsibilities and available resources'. By June these fears had increased because Britain believed that Russia was seeking to take over China. Trenchard, Hankey, Beatty and Hoare even favoured Japanese domination of north China to keep Russia out. Soon most decision makers regarded Russia as a threat to Britain; Churchill suggested that it might attack Britain within 'the next ten years'.[35]

Conversely, the Foreign Office denied that Russia was a menace. Chamberlain regarded it certainly as 'one of the danger points' of the future but saw little to be done except improve relations with Russia. He accepted his officials' view that Britain's best response to 'Bolshevism in the East is the perfectly above board method of strengthening the solid and stable elements in a particular country'; that at most Britain should break diplomatic relations should Russia press too far. Any stronger steps would simply heighten the Soviet *'drang nach osten'*. He argued that Russia, 'obsessed' with fears of an anti-Soviet bloc, would threaten Britain only should the latter overreact to Soviet provocation and cause it to fear encirclement. Chamberlain held off most of Whitehall, which regarded Russia as a threat, and favoured preparations to assist Afghanistan against a Soviet attack.[36] Even after the rupture of diplomatic relations with Moscow, he minimised any planning for war with Russia.

In 1924 the CID had decided that for planning purposes, France, Japan and Germany should be viewed as Britain's potential enemies.[37] During 1925 Britain decided that Russia alone was a menace but would take no measure to deal with it. These changed perceptions shaped the government's reformulation of strategic policy and placed the services' programmes at risk. If the diplomatic rationale which had supported them was to vanish, because the services were demanding so much more than seemed necessary, in an equal but opposite reaction the government might reject all their programmes. Foreign and financial policies were again converging against the services. Financial policy opposed their programmes while foreign policy no longer required and in some cases rejected them. Consequently, the more the government correlated the elements of strategic policy, the more justification it could find to cut service policies. During 1924–26 it did coordinate these elements more thoroughly than ever before, but through a struggle over parochial interests rather than an objective analysis.

Underlying this struggle was a debate about how to maintain Britain's strategic insurance. The RAF and the navy believed that Britain must meet its strategic needs regardless of the financial and diplomatic situation. As Trenchard wrote, 'Whatever happens for diplomatic and other reasons it is absolutely essential that this great Empire should stand by its own strength and not live by the goodwill of other countries'.[38] Pound opposed the formulation of a coherent strategic policy precisely because he believed that this might compromise the maintenance of security:

> It will of course be most useful for the departments to know what the Govt. policy is. If the departments work this Govt. policy it may not do much harm as far as the Army is concerned as whatever war comes the Army will have to be expanded, but in the case of the Air Force and Navy, but particularly in the case of the latter, this could only lead to disastrous results. Singapore is a case in point. A Govt. may believe that their policy will prevent war with any particular country but they cannot be certain of it.
>
> Surely naval preparations should be based on the principle that wherever our commitments demand that under certain eventualities we must exercise control in that area we must be prepared to do so and this in turn means that we must be prepared to fight the enemy in that area . . . If this argument is correct then all *possible* wars should be taken into account and each Service, as far as finance permits, should prepare for the one which demands the greatest effort.[39]

Pound's statement skated over the central issues of finance and the perception of threat. Unless Britain perceived dangers, it would not fund the services' programmes. Conversely, Warren Fisher asserted that 'the extent of [national] insurance should depend on (a) the measure of risk and (b) the purse of insured. What shd. we think of a man who insisted on insuring his life against drowning to an extent that crippled the resources necessary for his existence'.[40] This view that Britain should subordinate service to financial needs so long as the world seemed peaceful would lead to reductions in its military strength. During 1925–26 Britain chose between these ways of maintaining its strategic insurance and in doing so it finally began to enforce Treasury control and the ten-year rule on the services. The Treasury set the pace for these developments.

10 The Triumph of Treasury Control and the Ten-Year Rule, 1925–26

Although historians have criticised Churchill for harming the services as Chancellor, they have examined neither his actions nor the reasons why he gained his objectives.[1] His challenge to the services was legitimate and often progressive, as in pressing the army to replace cavalry with mechanised units.[2] He reduced service estimates between 1925 and 1929 far less than his predecessors had done either in 1921–22 or 1922–24 or his successors would do between 1929 and 1932, while he cut only some of the services' proposed programmes rather than their existing strength. Churchill also offered to reduce the Treasury's means of financial control over the services.

In implying that he bears total responsibility for Britain's service decisions of 1925, that defence paid 'the price of Churchill', scholars have misunderstood how Baldwin's government reached these decisions.Churchill achieved his aims only because the Cabinet accepted his warnings about the costs of the services' policies. Few ministers opposed his attacks on the services; those who did represented departments whose policies would not be hampered by the competing costs of the services' programmes. Churchill affected these decisions but no more than did Baldwin or Austen Chamberlain. Their support alone allowed him to win his victories over the services and they gave that support because it suited their interests. Baldwin's entire government placed social reform and political considerations above service needs.

It did so because the service decisions of Baldwin's first government bequeathed a financial crisis to his second. Between 1925 and 1930 the HDAF programme was expected to cost £15 000 000, the fuel one £10 300 000, the Singapore base £11 000 000 and the replacement programme £111 000 000.[3] Even on the unlikely assumption that these costs would not escalate, by 1929–30 RAF estimates would have been £5 000 000 and naval ones £25 000 000 above those of 1924–25. That 20 per cent increase in service estimates would necessitate cuts in civil ones. This conflict between guns and butter forced Britain to reconsider its priorities, and the Treasury's first success was to set the terms for this debate. Churchill and his officials disagreed over many issues. He demanded greater control over the Treasury than Warren Fisher would accept, while the latter's ties with Baldwin allowed him to work behind Churchill's back.[4] However, Churchill and Barstow made a formidable team in pursuit of the Treasury's central challenge to the services, to have the ten-year period both renewed and used to control their policies.

By November 1924 Churchill developed a policy for spending which soon became even more stringent when he cut taxation and returned Britain to the gold standard. He told the Cabinet that major economies would be necessary if it were to finance new goals. Since RAF and army estimates could not be reduced, naval spending must be cut. When Bridgeman asked the Cabinet to reauthorise the Singapore base, Churchill retorted that that body should examine the navy's programmes 'consistently from the political point of view' of avoiding increased service spending in 1924–25, and should reconsider the principles governing strategic policy, especially the ten-year period. The Cabinet compromised by approving the base, subject to examination of its details by a committee. It agreed that another committee might study Churchill's proposals about strategic principles.[5] Although Churchill was right to argue that Britain could not formulate sound service policies until it first defined a strategic policy, his proposals were intended to weaken the services by having the government adopt the Treasury's views about strategic insurance. On the basis of his ideas, Whitehall established a new strategic policy. This emerged from the struggle over naval policy.

The Admiralty sought approval for all its policies of 1923, but without informing the Cabinet of their costs. Thus, it stated the expense of its replacement programme only when Churchill forced it to do so.[6] Bridgeman never challenged the Chancellor's financial arguments because they were irrefutable. The First Lord demanded 1925–26 naval estimates of £65 000 000 (£9 700 000 more than in 1924–25) including £1 950 000 to begin eight cruisers and 25 lighter warships.[7] He warned of a Conservative backbench revolt should these programmes be rejected.

The Admiralty defended its programmes by reference to the one power standard, for which in effect it offered a new definition. The navy had to match the USN in battleships, battlecruisers and carriers, while to meet its 'special needs' Britain might require the world's largest strength in other warship classes. Although such superiority was unnecessary in submarines and destroyers, it needed the naval treaty's 5–3 ratio in cruisers over Japan. The Admiralty was irritated in 1927 when the USN used this logic to justify parity in cruisers. Moreover, Britain should be able to sustain a Pacific fleet superior to the IJN at its selected moment, as well as to maintain security in European waters.[8] Although the Admiralty denied that it was preparing for war with Japan or attempting to dominate Japanese home waters, men like Hankey and Austen Chamberlain did not accept this disclaimer.[9] Above all, Bridgeman asserted that Britain must always fill its maritime insurance premium. If it ever ran up a naval deficit by deferring its programmes, its strategic credit might never recover. He disliked

> the principle that it is for the Government to decide when there is going to be another war and then for the Services to have to prepare for it. Governments have not been particularly successful in forecasting wars in the past, and I do not suppose they are likely to be much more successful in the future . . . I think the only way we can approach it is from the point of view of ensuring ourselves against any reasonable risks wherever they may be in the world.[10]

The Admiralty's argument that it alone could define Britain's maritime needs conflicted with the Treasury's opinion that only it could define Britain's financial capabilities. By June 1925, when the question was whether four cruisers should be laid down in 1925–26, Beatty made this classic statement of the Admiralty's view of its own prerogatives. It could not alter its proposals

> if we are to be responsible, as we are to-day, for carrying out the policy of the Government. Therefore, the only alteration which must occur is that the Government must alter their policy, or they must tell the Admiralty that they are incapable of doing their job and get someone else to do it for them. . . if the Chancellor of the Exchequer says that the money is not forthcoming, and it is impossible to provide that number of ships and the Government come to us and say: "What are we going

to do?' we say: "We are very sorry; we say your policy is an expensive one — you must change your policy and have a cheaper one". It is up to the Government to say: "We do not believe you; we think that we can find someone else who can carry out your policy on the money that we think you ought to have". If that is the case, let us go and get these gentlemen and see what they can do.

Churchill retorted that Beatty really meant

"That is what we have to say", and when he has said this, you have this choice: either that you must raise from Parliament whatever money you require, or else you must recognise that your British Empire cannot be defended. . . the question whether the British Empire is to be adequately defended. . . does not depend upon whether there are 4 cruisers in this year or whether you drop one year behind, and certainly I do not think that we should be able to raise the money that we are told to do from Parliament. If the Admiralty were to go and make their case and work it out in the House of Commons, it would be different; but others have to do it and it is not a pleasant business, and others must have the right to be consulted as to the expenditure. . . with the 4 cruisers the Admiralty profoundly say "Britannia rules the waves", without 4 cruisers "We are at the mercy of Japan".[11]

The Treasury wanted the CID, advised by the Foreign Office, to forbid the navy to prepare for war with Japan before 1935, and to reimpose the ten-year period in 1925 on the navy. However, Churchill and his officials differed fundamentally over naval policy. The latter wanted to cancel or defer all the navy's programmes.[12] Churchill wished to reduce these proposals but still favoured large and rapid programmes.

His strongest suit was his warning of the political costs of the navy's programmes, which would

(a) prevent any appreciable relief of taxation during the present Parliament, (b) exclude any form of social legislation which involved finances, and (c) present naval estimates of about 80 millions in 1928–29 as the main issue for the consideration of the electorate. I believe that if this were the course of events, we should have taken the most effective steps to secure the return of the Socialist Administration, and the naval programme for which everything would have been sacrificed would thus have been broken up before it was complete.

Nor was Churchill wrong on these points, considering the naval consequences of the Labour Government in 1929–30. He also denied that there was 'the slightest chance' that Japan would attack Britain 'in our lifetimes', an argument which, however wrong, was shared by virtually every decision maker. Churchill also noted that if such a war did occur, it 'would last for years. It would cost Japan very little. It would reduce us to bankruptcy', and leave Britain vulnerable to pressure from other powers, especially the US.[13]

Churchill wanted to maintain British maritime security and, indeed, supremacy. Even in 1928 he claimed that if Britain did not provoke the US, the latter would eventually abandon parity because 'our needs for a navy are so much more real than theirs that we should probably make far greater sacrifices for sea-power'.[14] Churchill offered a different naval policy based on a redefined one power standard. Britain should not seek to 'dominate' American or Japanese waters. Instead, as he had argued in 1922, the navy must not be perceived as weaker than any other; and in reality it must 'over a long period of profound peace . . . taken as a whole, not be inferior' to any other. The best indicator of maritime power was naval spending. As real British naval expenditure equalled that of the US and greatly exceeded that of Japan, the one power standard already existed. Since Britain was already secure at sea, the navy's entire programmes were unnecessary; these might even reduce security by sparking an arms race.

However, contrary to the assertions of Roskill and Robert Rhodes James, Churchill still made generous proposals to the navy. He offered estimates for 1925–26 £1 850 000 larger than in 1924–25, and thereafter favoured a large construction programme. He proposed to finance half the navy's proposals, including three cruisers in 1925–26, guarantee future naval estimates of £60 000 000 and let the navy transfer directly to construction any savings from internal economies. He also supported the gradual completion of the fuel and Singapore base programmes, by 1933–34 and 1939–40 respectively.[15]

Churchill and Bridgeman opened a fundamental debate on strategic policy. The decisive issue was Whitehall's perception of their cases. The Cabinet wanted maritime security but, accepting Churchill's financial arguments and not regarding Japan as a threat, on a slower scale and at a smaller rate. At all crucial moments

Baldwin and Austen Chamberlain supported Churchill against Bridgeman. Chamberlain backed Churchill's challenge regarding the ten-year period and a Japanese threat while Baldwin played a canny role which aided the Chancellor. Baldwin promised Bridgeman, a political friend, that he would 'do my best even at the 11th hour to find a way to ease a very difficult situation for you'.[16] This encouragement fed Bridgeman's uncompromising political tactics, but Baldwin pursued every means to limit the need for Bridgeman's programmes such as naval limitation negotiations, 'moral gestures' and changes in strategic principles.

In February Baldwin approved naval estimates of £60 000 000 with an additional £2 000 000 shadow cut, midway between the proposals of Churchill and Bridgeman. The Cabinet also approved a proposal by Baldwin intended to defer its naval decisions; to accept in principle a replacement programme but to have a committee determine its details. Additional funds would if necessary be granted to cover any construction this committee might recommend to begin in 1925–26.[17] This committee was not biased in Churchill's favour. It was chaired by Birkenhead who, although Churchill's closest political friend, supported a powerful navy, as did its other members, Salisbury, Lord Peel and Edward Wood. Prompted by Baldwin, the Treasury and the Foreign Office, the Cabinet also elected to pursue a naval limitation conference, which would have reduced the need for construction.[18]

During March the Admiralty presented its replacement proposals: that between 1925 and 1931, Britain must build 31 cruisers, 2 carriers, 44 submarines, 92 destroyers and 42 auxiliary vessels, costing £111 000 000, while between 1931 and 1936 it should begin 7 battleships, 15 or more cruisers, 45 destroyers, one carrier and 40 submarines, costing at least another £137 300 880. It demanded the construction between 1925 and 1931 of three times more lighter warships than in Pound's original programme.[19] Although the Admiralty may have raised these demands simply for bargaining purposes, it did not use them in that fashion. It never offered to cut its proposals to gain a compromise, but did so only when ordered to. Although the Admiralty's real aims remain unclear, it probably wanted what it said it wanted — to replace virtually all its lighter warships over the next decade, at a real cost equal to that of Britain's largest peacetime naval programmes in history. This case was so excessive as to be counterproductive. In order to justify its rejection, the Cabinet would have had to accept Churchill's request to redefine strategic principles and adopt Beatty's logic and 'have a cheaper' policy.

The Admiralty offered three arguments about cruisers, the main issue in dispute; first, that Britain required 70 cruisers and must build 46 new ones by 1936; second, that these must all be of Washington standard since one such vessel outclassed any number of smaller cruisers. This argument was incorrect. Although one Washington standard vessel was stronger than any single existing cruiser, a few of the latter could match one of the former. Nor were Washington standard cruisers necessarily more cost effective than lighter 8-inch or 6-inch gun ones; third, that Japan's cruiser programme threatened Britain. The Admiralty distorted this situation, claiming that by 1929 Japan would have 39 cruisers (of which 18 would have 8-inch guns) rather than 25 (eight with 8-inch guns) which it had identified previously. This figure included 10 obsolete coastal defence cruisers with 8-inch guns.[20]

Churchill, ably briefed by Barstow, successfully challenged these arguments. Beatty conceded that the programme must be increased should, as he expected, Japan build more warships, and that naval estimates would soon reach £80–85 000 000. Churchill insisted that the Admiralty's intention to maintain the whole fleet on 'virtually a war basis' would require £90–100 000 000. These proposals were too costly to sustain and yet too weak to meet the Admiralty's case. For if war came, with Britain's best cruisers tied to the fleet, Japan might refuse an engagement while its surface raiders demolished British commerce. Churchill pressed this alternative:

> Everything turns upon this — the desirability or undesirability of basing a Battle Fleet on Singapore to wage war against Japan in the Pacific. If the Government were to decide . . . that during the next ten years no preparations were to be made . . . [to do so] . . . our task must be instantly simplified and lightened. The Japanese Fleet cannot come around the world to attack our fleet in home waters or the Atlantic Ocean, and they would place themselves at an enormous disadvantage if they attempted to fight a decisive fleet action in the Indian Ocean. Therefore a general battle between the British and Japanese Fleets cannot take place unless we ourselves send our fleet around the world into the Pacific . . . no fleet action can take place unless both sides wish it . . .

Churchill advocated a defensive and long-term strategy. The fleet should stay out of the Pacific for the initial years of a war, while its cruisers protected commerce and Britain created a 'fleet of almost measureless power'. Indeed, the mere knowledge that 'the last word would be with us' would deter any Japanese attack. Therefore, Britain need not develop the Singapore base and required only 50 commissioned cruisers with more in reserve. It should build 16 cruisers between 1926 and 1936 on an alternating basis of one and two annually.[21] Churchill exposed the flaws in the Admiralty's case and formulated the most sophisticated version advocated in the 1920s of the 'home waters' argument. These proposals were just an opening bid, since both before and after Churchill offered much more. Yet they were ludicrous: Britain could not safely grant the IJN total control over the western Pacific in a war, while Churchill's proposals to defer most naval preparations would have compromised British security. Nonetheless, by paralysing the Admiralty's case, Churchill achieved his aims.

By March the Cabinet's hopes for a naval limitation conference were dashed.[22] It immediately found another means to limit the naval programme. It asked the CID to rule on the fundamental points in dispute: the interpretation of the one power standard, Britain's strategic needs regarding Japan and the renewal of the ten-year rule. Crowe told the CID that all strategic forecasts were 'speculative to a certain extent' but that war with Japan would be unlikely for ten years. The Foreign Office could provide five years warning of the most probable signal of danger, the development of a Russo-German-Japanese alliance. The CID decided that before 1935 the navy should not prepare for a Pacific campaign. In May the Cabinet accepted this recommendation and redefined the one power standard on the basis of a formula originated by Baldwin.[23] This did not require Britain to dominate another power's home waters:

Even before the War it was recognised that the two-Power standard did not necessarily imply that our fleets were able simultaneously to deal with the concentrated fleets of two first-class Naval Powers in different parts of the globe. This is equally true of the one-Power standard today. The requirements of a one-power standard are satisfied if our fleet, wherever situated, is equal to the fleet of any other nation, wherever situated, provided that arrangements are made from time to time in different parts of the world, according as the international situation requires, to enable the local forces to maintain the situation against vital and irreparable damage, pending the arrival of the main fleet and to give the main fleet on arrival sufficient mobility.

The Cabinet decided that the navy would equal the USN and exceed the IJN by 60 per cent but that, before 1935, Britain should not prepare to maintain in the Pacific a fleet equal to Japan's commissioned navy. It defined the one power standard to mean that the navy could be weaker than the USN or the IJN in their waters so long as it was superior in imperial seas. The Foreign Office was made responsible for providing a warning period to let Britain strengthen its strategic position in the Pacific when necessary.[24] Although the government reversed the foundations of naval policy, this need not have crippled the latter. The Cabinet forbade the Admiralty from preparing for offensive operations against Japan but expected the navy to complete by 1935 its preparations for maritime security, including the fuel, Singapore base and replacement programmes. The redefinition of the ten-year period and the one power standard forced the Admiralty to recast its policies but left it room to claim large programmes.

Thus, the Admiralty reduced its construction programmes by only 33 per cent. Its 'revised' programme demanded that between 1925 and 1931 Britain should build 48 submarines, 45 destroyers, one carrier, 35 auxiliary vessels and 21 cruisers.[25] The committee rejected these demands but wished to grant the navy as much as possible. On 25 June Wood stated its dilemma:

> I find myself in a position of great difficulty. In all the discussions I have felt what one anticipated, that the Admiralty can make a very good case on all the various things which come up. On the other hand, I am sure that the Chancellor of the Exchequer from my own instinct and feeling, is right that even the amended programme of the Admiralty, if it were submitted to the House of Commons next year, would be frankly impossible from the political and financial points of view. I do not easily see how we are going to arrive at a conclusion, and I wondered whether the Chancellor might give them a sort of indication of the extreme limit to which he might be able to go. Having got that, the Admiralty could tell us . . . what would be the tolerable sacrifices it would impose upon them.

Churchill offered to guarantee naval estimates of £65 000 000 beginning in 1926–27, including £10 000 000 for construction; to let the Admiralty transfer any unspent funds for construction from one year to the next; and to use for construction all savings from other economies. On the basis of no construction in 1925–26, Churchill proposed several large programmes, including the entire 'revised' one if it began in 1926–27.[26] He offered to cut the Treasury's formal control over naval spending; to guarantee naval estimates £9 200 000 above those of 1924–25, roughly equal to those of 1914 and larger than those actually received between 1926 and 1929; and more money for construction than the navy had requested in autumn 1923. His proposals would have let the Admiralty begin as many cruisers by 1929 as it actually did and to complete more vessels than Pound had wanted in July 1923.

Churchill's offer must be judged in its chronological context. The decisions which crippled Britain's naval position came not in 1925 but in 1930. In 1925 Britain had a far greater qualitative and quantitative strength in cruisers than the US or Japan. Churchill's proposals would have let Britain build far more of them and more rapidly than any other navy was planning to do. His offer was generous while there was no strategic need for the programme to begin in 1925 instead of 1926. Nor does it seem that he was trying to trap the navy with an offer which he intended to repudiate, although the Admiralty could not be sure of this. Churchill's offer could not bind any future government and the Admiralty would require a firm pledge that Baldwin's administration would honour it. However, Birkenhead commended this offer in terms which indicate that the committee would have tried to persuade the government to do so.

> Instead of each year having wrangles, having another conflict with the Treasury, and perhaps another Cabinet Committee set up, which means three months' more delay in the building programme of the country, [the Admiralty] become masters of their own household; it is their money. They know for the first time over a sustained period of years where they are, and they know that by every economy they are successful in making, they are the gainers and they alone.[27]

Yet Bridgeman rejected the best naval offer ever made by the Treasury between 1919 and 1934. He offered to cut projected naval spending but denounced anything less than its 'revised' programme to begin in 1925 and demanded £68 500 000 for estimates, including £13 500 000 for construction. Bridgeman claimed that Churchill's proposals would defer most construction until the next election, thus offering no 'security'. Yet only 33 per cent of Churchill's programme would begin after that date, compared to 25 per cent of the 'revised' one. Bridgeman wanted to lay down cruisers during 1925 rather than receive promises that these would begin later. As Birkenhead remarked, any naval programme necessarily rested on the presumption that the government would honour its promises.[28]

The Admiralty rejected a compromise with important guarantees because it refused to cut its projected estimates by £3 500 000 and to delay its programme by one year. Ultimately it received a worse settlement than Churchill's offer. In July the committee recommended that between 1926 and 1932 Britain should build 20 cruisers, one carrier, 45 destroyers, 35 submarines and 23 auxiliary vessels, (66 per cent of which should begin before 1930–31) for £68 873 000. This compromise between Churchill and Bridgeman excluded the Chancellor's guarantees and included his 'blank year' for construction in 1925–26.[29]

The Admiralty pursued the entire 'revised' programme. Bridgeman thought that the Cabinet would be 'mad' to override the views of 'the Admiralty experts . . . but some of my colleagues are such knaves and others such fools that I doubt if the wisdom of the few will prevail'. He believed that Churchill's proposals were part of a political conspiracy: that Churchill, Birkenhead and possibly Austen Chamberlain had cynically selected an issue to divide Baldwin from his loyalists, who would be forced to resign, thus shattering the Prime Minister's position.[30] However, nothing supports this view and all circumstantial evidence goes against it. Birkenhead did not accept Churchill's original demands, Chamberlain backed the Chancellor on Foreign Office advice, Peel, Salisbury and Wood decided against the Admiralty while Baldwin, who was scarcely naive, supported Churchill. Moreover, Bridgeman threatened to resign over this issue which, according to the conspiracy theory, was precisely what Churchill wanted.

Bridgeman received little support from the Cabinet. Although Chamberlain refused to give an 'absolute guarantee . . . as to the permanence of good relations with any Power', he stated that war with Japan 'during the next ten years is not a contingency seriously to be apprehended'. The Cabinet, however, offered to let part of the Birkenhead Committee's construction for 1926–27 begin in 1925–26. Bridgeman rejected this compromise and, fearing a Conservative backbench revolt over this issue, Baldwin conceded slightly more to the Admiralty, probably to avoid difficulties over the coal subsidy. The Cabinet agreed to lay down four cruisers in 1925–26 but in every other respect adopted the Birkenhead Committee's recommendations.[31]

The Admiralty received far less than it had demanded and little more than Churchill had offered. Although it gained the 'accelerated' construction of four cruisers in 1925–26, ultimately it had to finance through other economies their entire cost — £5 000 000 — and had no guaranteed level of estimates or construction funds. Roskill's claim that this was a major Admiralty victory is tenable only on the supposition that the latter had vastly exaggerated its demands and never wanted more than its 'revised' programme or that it was right to reject Churchill's compromises.[32] Even if these suppositions are correct, which is doubtful, the Admiralty had won a Pyrrhic victory. Its intransigence had alienated the Cabinet and even its supporters in Parliament, weakening its position against the looming counter-attack of the Treasury. As a result of the Admiralty's actions the Cabinet formed the 'Colwyn Committee' to cut the 1926–27 service estimates.[33] This body began the process of establishing Treasury control over all the services.

During 1925 Trenchard helped Churchill to attack the navy, in order to further a new RAF policy. His actions hampered naval policy at the price of crippling his own. With the HDAF programme on course the time seemed politically ripe to open a second front for the RAF. For the first time since 1922 Trenchard challenged both older services at once with the claim that the RAF could fulfill all their main functions. He also evolved a systematic theory that the RAF was Britain's central service, that airpower had replaced seapower as the pillar of Imperial security.[34] The cutting edge for Trenchard's policy was his decision to work with Churchill against the older services to make aircraft rather than 15-inch guns the foundation of the Singapore base's defences. Trenchard was less interested in Singapore itself than in using that issue to 'open up the wider one of the application of airpower for overseas defence'. In his plan of action India was as important a target as Singapore. He pursued his aims regarding India by exploiting the Indian authorities' fears of an 'Afghan Air Menace'; fears which he did not take seriously.[35]

Trenchard wanted the Air Ministry to control all RAF units, including those attached to the older services, and to begin a new substitution campaign. Multi-purpose RAF squadrons should replace several kinds of forces, simultaneously doing the work of infantry in India, 15-inch guns at Singapore and cruisers in adjacent seas.[36] The RAF should dominate Imperial defence just as it did home defence. Trenchard's proposals became the basis for RAF policy until 1931. In order to further this aim, he helped Churchill challenge the Singapore base and secretly launched his greatest attack to date on the naval aviation programme. By provoking a new round of inter-service struggle, Trenchard overreached himself, letting the RAF become, as Hoare had warned, Churchill's 'storm troops in a financial battle with the Admiralty'.[37] Trenchard embittered the older services while, in using the Treasury to further his interests against the navy, he helped the exchequer create a change in strategic principles which it used against the HDAF.

In early 1925 Barstow and Churchill wished to slow that programme. By September they pursued a radical deferment when it finally became vulnerable to financial pressure.[38] Given Britain's improved relations with France, it no longer feared French diplomatic blackmail. Hoare reminded the Cabinet that even if the programme were completed by 1929, the HDAF would be 50 per cent weaker than the existing FAF in France. Of course, the HDAF had never been intended to match this strength but that of the Air Division, which had been so altered that it no longer was an 'Independent Striking Force' if it ever had been. However, Hoare emphasised that Anglo-French relations might worsen and that

> The relations between England and France are as friendly as they could be, Germany is altogether deprived of an Air Force, yet France continues to maintain an air strength more predominant than was ever her military strength under Napoleon or Louis XIV. Are we justified in remaining for many years in a position of such numerical inferiority. . .?[39]

Hoare's linkage of the programme with Anglo-French relations remained a strong card, for Hankey, Salisbury, Balfour and Austen Chamberlain were unwilling to ignore entirely the possibility of a French menace. This was, however, no longer a trump card. In November a Cabinet committee was ordered to examine the HDAF programme. Trenchard and Hoare recognised that it would be slowed and fought simply to ensure its completion as quickly as possible. Chamberlain declined to say that 'war was permanently impossible' but denied that France would threaten Britain during the foreseeable future. Although he and Churchill wanted to complete the HDAF only by 1940, the committee approved 1935 for that purpose and approved RAF estimates of £16 000 000 in 1926–27. Three HDAF squadrons would form in 1926, one between 1927 and 1929, and three and four in alternate years after 1929; 32 HDAF squadrons would exist by 1930 and 52 by 1935.[40] The committee reduced the HDAF's standard, for it would not equal the front-line machines of the Air Division. However, as Trenchard had wished, Britain placed the RAF 'on the same terms as it has its Navy'; unfortunately, these terms were not what he had expected.[41] The government applied to the HDAF the precedent of its changes to naval policy. It denied that France would be a threat during the foreseeable future and decided that the ten-year period on the programme should end in 1935 rather than 1929.

During 1922–24 Britain had not followed a systematic strategic policy. In 1925 it began to do so. Britain was justified in reassessing the ten-year period, since 1925 was the mid-point in its original duration, while international developments gave sound reasons to reconsider strategic policy. Yet these particular far-reaching decisions arose simply from the struggle over naval policy. Since the Admiralty chose to fight without compromise for extraordinarily expensive proposals, the government needed a defensible rationale to reject them. Thus, an alliance of convenience between Churchill, Baldwin, Chamberlain, the Treasury and the Foreign Office resurrected the half-forgotten ten-year period of 1919 and altered the principles which governed all the services' policies.

Underlying these decisions was the assumption that Britain would be secure during the foreseeable future. The government ignored Balfour's warning that risks were involved in reducing defences because of faith in 'prophecies' of the behaviour of other powers.[42] It overlooked the fact that the services could barely ensure Britain's aims against lesser powers, whether in the Mosul crisis of 1925 or the Chinese one of 1927. Although these specific weaknesses did not endanger vital interests, they did raise questions about Britain's ability to defend such interests against major threats. Yet this modification of strategic principles need not have hampered British security. Even under the redefined naval and HDAF standards and the extended ten-year period, the services were authorised to maintain large programmes to defend British interests. Nor were their new policies unreasonable ones. Unfortunately, these changes in strategic principles would be used to prevent these policies from being enacted. They provided the foundation for a new strategic policy which finally enforced Treasury control and the ten-year rule on all the services.

That period became an independent factor in strategic policy while the government rejected the services' definition of strategic principles. However, its rulings remained open to debate. Contrary to the Colwyn Committee, Britain had not yet decided that no great war would occur 'for a *minimum* of ten years' from 1925.[43] The government had simply redefined the ten-year period to cover two special cases: that Britain should not prepare before 1935 for wars with Japan or France. No general ruling prevented the services from preparing against other powers before 1935 or from making large current preparations to maintain security. The RAF and the navy were still authorised to complete their programmes by 1935 while the original ten-year period governed all the services' general preparations. Britain had not defined whether the services should be ready for major war by 1929 or 1935; or should just begin such preparations in 1929 or 1935; or at whatever date the Cabinet ordered.

These ambiguities left the services with the leeway to defend large programmes. Thus, the Admiralty agreed that the Cabinet had not 'in so many words' prolonged the 1919 ruling that Britain 'will not be engaged in *any* great war during the next ten years' for a new ten-years period'. The navy planned to complete all its general preparations by 1929, deferring until 1935 only those *'peculiar to a Far Eastern War'*. In 1926–27 the army and the RAF were encouraged to plan for a limited war against Russia.[44] Although the government rejected the services' definition of how to maintain strategic insurance, it had not yet accepted that of the Treasury. These decisions weakened the services but were not a complete Treasury victory. They were, however, a crucial step in that direction. Between July 1925 and July 1926 the imperatives of foreign and financial policies would converge still further against the services while Britain would form a strategic policy on the basis of Treasury control and the ten-year rule.

In 1925 the Treasury extended its claims regarding its role in the formulation of strategic policy, arguing that it should be the pre-eminent department in that process and that finance should dominate that policy. For the first time it stated officially that finance was a more important component of power than military strength.

Niemayer claimed privately that the Treasury's 'duty' was to be 'the central department to view expenditure *as a whole* and concentrate on the big issues for whose sake the steady drip of smaller things must be firmly stemmed'.[45] The Treasury pursued these ends through its attempts to control the 1926–27 budget, which led to the formation of the Colwyn Committee and a Cabinet Economy Committee.[46]

In these actions Baldwin was close to Warren Fisher, who frequently clashed with Churchill.[47] Yet they all cooperated against the services, whose draft estimates equalled £129 500 000: navy £64 500 000; army £44 500 000, and RAF £20 500 000. On Baldwin's authorisation Lord Colwyn stated that their estimates would be £115 250 000. Britain must cut 'our existing standards of defence' and 'our insurance against War Risk in view of the far greater risk to our financial stability of defence expenditure on the present scale'. Churchill and Baldwin encouraged an inter-service struggle by allowing the older services to challenge Britain's air organisation.[48] In pursuing these rivalries before the Colwyn Committee the services weakened themselves against the Treasury.

The army and the navy each demanded their own separate air services.[49] They did not coordinate their cases and wished only to take over a few squadrons. Trenchard, however, assuming that they were conspiring to destroy the RAF, sought heavy cuts in naval aviation while Hoare asked the committee to approve a new principle: 'An independent Air Ministry to administer a single unified air service which should carry out all air work'.[50] This, the first formal repudiation of Trenchard's pledge that the older services should control some RAF units, marked the start of the 'unified air' campaign, by which the Air Ministry sought absolute control over all RAF squadrons, in order to increase its ability to replace the older services.

The Colwyn Committee reported that service estimates had risen dramatically from real spending in 1923–24 of £111 000 000 to 1926 draft estimates of £127 000 000. This comparison between different matters was misleading; for example, one between draft estimates would have shown no increase. The committee proposed army estimates of £42 500 000, navy of £57 500 000 and RAF of £16 000 000. It recommended that the navy's programmes be cut by £10 480 000 between 1926 and 1928 and adopted the RAF's proposals about 'unified air' and naval aviation.[51] Although inter-service rivalries furthered Trenchard's interests, they also bolstered those of the Treasury. The 1926 service estimates equalled £116 600 000

(RAF £16 000 000; army £42 500 000; navy £58 100 000). Their current effective estimates of £100 097 000 were only £3 895 000 below those of 1925–26 and above those of 1924–25, but the policies of two services had hinged on the assumption that in 1926 their estimates would be far larger than this. Under these circumstances the services reformulated their policies, and in the process were each forced to make sacrifices so as to finance their first priorities.

The Admiralty hoped that its estimates would reach £70 000 000 in a few years and retained its aims of 1923.[52] Yet the obstacles which destroyed that policy were already clear. The government's desire to avoid naval competition could be expected to impede construction, the development of the Singapore base was falling behind schedule while the CID in effect extended the completion date for the fuel programme. Moreover, the need to finance the replacement programme, especially the 'accelerated' cruisers, led the Admiralty to initiate real cuts for the first time since 1922. It drastically reduced ancillary spending and decided that all warships outside the main fleet should have only 75 per cent crews. It also cut its projected spending on naval aviation, and Britain began to lose its lead in that area.

Underlying these decisions was a calculated gamble: that '1926–27 will be the most critical financial year since the Armistice' and that these economies would 'bear fruit' by 1928.[53] The Board hoped to reduce normal spending to subsidise construction in coming years and then reallocate these savings to finance other programmes. It adopted Churchill's proposed economies of 1925 without his guarantee that this money could be kept for other purposes. These policies could 'bear fruit' only if the navy's programmes continued unhindered, for if these were deferred it would lose these surplus funds. By Beatty's last year as CNS the navy's policy was vulnerable and its political strength waning. It began to lose decisive battles only under Beatty's successors, but he bequeathed them a compromised position. For the first time since 1922 the War Office developed an ambitious policy. In spring 1926 the new CIGS, Milne, told the COSC that

At the present moment, the Army was completely out of date. In the late war it might be argued that the main struggle against Germany was abnormal, but at the same time that there were a number of subsidiary struggles going on simultaneously in various parts of the world which more resembled the normal kind of war in which the British Empire had been engaged in the past and was likely to be engaged in the future . . . our wars usually commenced by a small force becoming committed to hostilities, to extricate which force, reinforcements, first of a division and ultimately of a corps, were probably necessitated. For such a kind of war the Army was not prepared at the present time. Attempts had been made to prepare for mobilisation for another Continental war, and considerable expenditure was being incurred in paying retaining fees to men who might be but were very unlikely to be required for any such eventuality. . .[54]

Milne was resurrecting the general staff's armoured policy of 1921. He sought to prepare a modern expeditionary force not for European wars but for Imperial ones, which became linked to the plans to defend Afghanistan against Russia. On the road to this ambition stood obstacles which only the will of a Trenchard could have surmounted, and iron was scarce in the souls of any CIGS of the interwar years. Since Milne inherited no surplus funds, he could finance this programme only by cutting something else. As Churchill insisted, the obvious candidate was cavalry. Despite his progressive attitudes towards mechanisation, however, Milne, and even more the other generals, opposed this unprecedented step. He held that cavalry retained value in Imperial policing and feared that Churchill would seize some of the fruits of such an economy, leaving the army with smaller estimates, no cavalry and just a few more mechanised units.[55] Consequently, Milne sought to finance this programme by reducing spending from areas like the TA which were useful only for another great war, which, as Churchill noted, was an undesirable sacrifice. Ultimately Milne could not achieve his aims because he could not find enough ancillary savings while no strategic role justified this programme once the fears of a Russian menace receded.

Still, the army hoped to develop modern forces through Imperial policing. So, too, did the RAF. During the disastrous year of 1925 the HDAF programme had been deferred and the substitution campaign stalemated. Trenchard realised that the RAF could expand only through his substitution and unified air proposals. Since for the moment this required better relations with the older services, he became more conciliatory towards them. This was, however, but a temporary settlement. The substitution campaign necessitated an attack on the older services while under unified air the same units would meet three functions: home defence and support for the expeditionary force and the fleet. As Trenchard's first priority was home defence, this triple pledge would lead him to undermine the older services.

In spring 1926 Whitehall was more interested than ever since the armistice in coordinating strategic policy.[56] The services, seeking to exploit this interest to further their individual aims, for the first time all favoured the formulation of an inter-departmental grand strategy. The COSC stated that service policies required 'some definite background of a determined and agreed defence policy': a COSC review of imperial defence policy, to be presented before each year's estimates were drafted.[57] Churchill used the desire to formulate a systematic strategic policy so as to resurrect the Treasury's aims of 1923. Service estimates should fall to £110 000 000 and the COSC should be given responsibility 'for the outlay of the limited resources available to the best possible advantage'. Churchill's contemporaries accepted a link between service economies and strategic rationalisation. Thus, Hankey told Tyrrell that service estimates 'will hinge to a considerable extent' on the COSC review, and told Churchill that his £110 000 000 limit would be 'particularly valuable' in shaping that review.[58]

The imperatives of foreign policy decided the clash between service and financial policies, since Britain's minimum level of military strength turned on the nature of likely threats. The Foreign Office gave the COSC a paper intended for the coming Imperial Conference, which defended its own position in all the current battles about foreign policy. It defined Britain as a *status quo* power and supported the Treasury's views on the role of finance in strategic policy. Although Britain needed armed forces to speak 'with authority', their cost might hamper the economy, the basic element in British strength. Without 'our trade and finance, we sink to the level of a third-class Power. Locarno and the unemployed have an immediate connexion'. In effect, the Foreign Office agreed that financial imperatives could dominate military ones. It predicted a stable world during the foreseeable future and denied that any nations were potential threats.[59] The Foreign Office did not support the services' plans because these might compromise its diplomacy.

Each service rejected this assessment precisely because it would hamper their policies. Beatty and Trenchard claimed that Japan or France might be threats while Milne stated that the commitments of India and Locarno necessitated an army 'central reserve'. Hankey noted that no views of 'political security' could override the COSC's duty to *advise the Government as to the cases in which national security is required, and the extent to which it should be provided, having regard to all relevant circumstances'*. After much bickering, the service chiefs formed a united front to further their individual interests.[60] The first review, of June 1926, defined the 'Problem' which, with unintentional irony, simply explained that Britain needed each service. It noted that manpower and industrial mobilisation alone could meet great requirements and that the maintenance of that ability was of paramount importance. Britain's defence priorities were to complete the Singapore base, defend its maritime communications and maintain home defence.

While reaffirming the navy's policies the review outlined new ones for the other services. It favoured a modern army for Imperial defence and stated that the HDAF could serve as a strategic reserve while the RAF's main role was the technical development of aerial forces. The COSC insisted that a Soviet or Japanese menace was possible and in the first of many such statements, drew the CID's

> earnest attention . . . to a consideration which has consistently impressed itself upon our minds . . . namely, the smallness of our defence forces when compared with the vast extent of our Imperial responsibilities and commitments. We wish to place on record our view that the forces available for Imperial defence are now reduced to a minimum and are barely capable of dealing with the problems that are liable to arise· either singly or simultaneously.[61]

The convergence of diplomatic and financial imperatives led Britain to ignore this warning. When it considered the review the CID regarded no power, save possibly Russia, as a threat. It shared Balfour's view that the review stressed imperial weaknesses 'too much' and that the empire might be best defended 'by spending less money on actual defence measures and thereby improving our economic position'. Austen Chamberlain wanted the Cabinet to consider how Britain's resources 'could best be husbanded for another great war'. The CID asked the Cabinet to consider how Britain 'can afford' to meet the responsibilities outlined by the review. The Cabinet responded by ordering the services to cut their 1927 estimates below £110 000 000, 'having regard to the requirements of Imperial defence as a whole', as defined by the review.[62] Ironically, the latter led the Cabinet finally to adopt the

Treasury's arguments regarding the role of finance in strategic insurance.

Between 1926 and 1930 the services tried to further their policies. Seeking to concentrate its resources on the development of a modern expeditionary force for Imperial defence and to defeat Churchill's pressure for changes in its policy, the War Office asked that the ten-year period be specially redefined for the army. The Cabinet agreed that it should not prepare for a continental war before 1937 but instead for an 'extra-European war.[63] Trenchard opened his last great substitution campaign while for the final time the navy pursued the concomitants of its policies of 1923. The prevailing trends in strategic policy prevented the services from achieving these aims. By 1926 Britain had established the basis for a strategic policy which did not alter until 1932. Only in 1925–26 did strategic policy acquire the features which historians have attributed to that of the entire decade, the emphasis on disarmament and reconciliation as the best means to settle international conflicts; and the assumption of security and financial strength as the central elements in strategic planning.

Before 1930 service estimates never fell below £110 000 000, but the Treasury gained control over their spending. Moreover, the government believed that Britain would be secure during the foreseeable future and should husband its resources by minimising service spending. In 1928, at the prompting of Churchill and Austen Chamberlain, it redefined the entire ten-year period: '. . . it should be assumed, for the purpose of framing the Estimates of the Fighting Services, that at any given date there will be no major war for ten years'.[64] This, the triumph of Treasury control and the ten-year rule, was possible only because of the decisions of 1925–26, the decisive years for strategic policy between 1919 and 1932.

11 Conclusion: Men, Money and Diplomacy, 1919–26

During the 1920s Treasury control and the ten-year rule did not always dominate strategic policy. They became decisive only in 1926–28 and then as a convenient means for the government to enforce the policy of its choice. A dynamic inter-relationship between foreign, financial and service policies instead determined the formulation of strategic policy. Britain believed that any service programme which was not absolutely essential for security would be economically and diplomatically counterproductive. It placed a higher marginal value on social reform and debt redemption than on service spending yet fully intended to preserve its security. The requirements of foreign policy determined Britain's answer to the question of strategic policy: how to draw the balance between the military forces Britain appeared to need and those which it seemed able to afford. These answers varied widely, as they had always done.

Historians have divided strategic policy during the interwar years into two periods, viewing the 1920s as a time of arms limitation and the 1930s as one of rearmament. This convention obscures the underlying consistency in Britain's approach to strategic matters throughout those years. In both decades Britain, refusing to live on the sufferance of other states, was willing to rearm, in order to prevent them from developing military strengths which could threaten vital British interests, and to maintain the diplomatic position needed to make them alter their policies. There are especially striking parallels between Britain's strategic response to France in 1921–24 and to Germany between 1934–37. In both cases Britain's concerns were primarily diplomatic. It mistrusted other powers and intended to match their air strengths which, like naval forces before 1914, were seen as the means by which they might hold British diplomacy to ransom. Britain did so not because it regarded these powers as

179

immediate threats but to deter them from becoming such, not so much to prepare for war as to preserve the peace on its own terms. Air rearmament seemed necessary to maintain a bargaining position which would let Britain achieve its fundamental aim, a systematic settlement with these powers, although secondarily to protect its security should that fail to emerge.

When seen across the range of years between 1816 and 1939, the period 1921–27 stands as a peak of British military preparations in peacetime, not as a trough. Its real military expenditure exceeded that of any other time except 1904–14 and 1935–39 and at least equalled that of any other state. It built as much new naval and air equipment as any other nation, for example, forming 39 RAF squadrons (more than doubling that service in strength) and laying down 18 Washington standard cruisers.

Britain was then far more than usually willing to take actions like rearmament and alliances to preserve its security. Until 1926 Britain met its naval and RAF needs well. Even its decisions to slow their programmes were acceptable because these were larger than necessary in 1925. These decisions would have provided an adequate basis from which to meet Britain's needs, had it adopted different policies between 1926 and 1935.

However, 1925 was the last time for a decade that a large expansion of the services was politically possible for the imperatives of foreign and financial policies then converged against them. In that year Britain finally presumed that the world had become stable, that it would remain secure during the foreseeable future and that it would have a warning period of several years in which to strengthen its position should the need arise. Nor was this assessment wrong. It took the catastrophic breakdown of the international economic system in 1929–30 to destroy the possibility that a stable world might follow from the Washington Conference and the Locarno Pact and to unleash the dangerous forces which British had always known existed in other states. Even then it still had a warning period of seven years to improve its position. However, this analysis led British governments to take a strategic gamble, which they lost. Between 1926 and 1933 they cut first their projected and then their actual service spending, so to free resources for other purposes and to increase British power by assisting economic growth. They subordinated service policies to social, financial and diplomatic considerations; they deferred programmes for Britain's security until threats actually became imminent. In order to maintain British strength and Whitehall's confidence in it, the government would have to react immediately and with little margin for error once this warning period began. These decisions placed Britain's strategic position at risk.

Between 1926 and 1929 Baldwin's government let the army carry out the world's most advanced study of mechanised warfare, let the RAF build 16 new squadrons and laid down as much new warship tonnage as any other single power, for example, nine Washington standard cruisers. Nor did it cut service estimates any further than was warranted by the fall in prices. Nonetheless, the government feared the diplomatic consequences of expansion programmes, holding that arms limitation in Europe could alone prevent Germany from denouncing the military clauses of the Treaty of Versailles; that too rapid British rearmament might stampede Russia, Japan or the United States into taking dangerous counter-measures. Consequently, it deferred a moderate amount of the approved service programmes of 1925 and prevented the navy from maintaining its lead in naval aviation. While unfortunate, these actions were anything but fatal; by 1929 the services were more effective than in 1925. Britain retained a powerful strategic position, with the strongest navy on earth and a reasonably large and modern army and RAF.

It was the actions of the governments between 1929 and 1936 which created the deadly predicament of the later 1930s. By 1932 the services' current effective estimates fell £9 990 000 (or 11 per cent) below those of 1929, and virtually every service programme was deferred.[1] Moreover, MacDonald's second government made Britain's single gravest strategic error of the interwar years. At the London naval conference of 1930, for no compelling reason, it destroyed the navy's ability to match the IJN and any European power. It forced the navy to scrap many warships, its actions precluded any major naval rearmament until 1937 and it again cancelled the Singapore base. Altogether, this hamstrung Britain's maritime position, which was still the foundation of Imperial security. Further, Britain's desire not to hamper its fragile economy, and its fears that rearmament would wreck any chance of preventing Japan and Germany from turning against the world order, paralysed any attempts to overcome these dangers until 1935. Men like Churchill and Lloyd George had used the warning period to govern strategic preparations because they expected subsequent governments to respond appropriately: they had not accounted for the nature of Baldwin and MacDonald.

This predicament was the cumulative product of many discrete decisions which stemmed from an underlying cause: the question being, which? The prevailing answer points to an alteration in British attitudes, the decline of the 'realist tradition', which was embodied by a generational change in Britain's leadership, as new men replaced those who had come to intellectual maturity in the 1880s and had been in office before and during the great war.[2] This argument has some power. The strategic attitudes of the British governing élite did change between 1816 and 1939. The Treasury and the Foreign Office, the first departments to have such a generational change in the postwar period, were those bodies between 1925 and 1929 which most pressed for arms limitation and international reconciliation, carrying the politicians and other departments in their wake. A similar change occurred in the political leadership between 1919 and 1929. Moreover, around 1930 Whitehall's psychological confidence in British strength finally began to erode, as the depression, the collapse of the world economic system and the rise of potentially deadly international circumstances demonstrated that Britain had not truly won the great war, that its losses had definitively outweighed its gains.

However, it was precisely these new men of the Treasury and the Foreign Office who, in the early 1930s, were the spearhead for a hard and immediate response to Britain's predicament, supported by many of these new politicians. By 1935 British strategic policy returned in nature to that of 1919–25, which was scarcely different from that followed between 1866 and 1914. Statesmen who contemplated the Hoare-Laval Pact and a possible deal with Japan over the corpse of China were closer in spirit to Henry than to Woodrow Wilson. The attitudes of the British governing élite changed most significantly in the 1860s and the 1940s, not between 1914 and 1939. Indeed, their attitudes remained strikingly similar between 1816 and 1939, throughout the 130 years in which the world rested on foundations created above all else by Britain. Changes in attitudes and in generations did affect strategic policy in the interwar years, but they are only part of the matter. At its heart was the need to choose between the strategies of the British Empire — the means by which statesmen could rationally hope to use Britain's power to influence its environment.

Rarely since 1816 had decision makers believed that Britain had anything to gain from major war, Palmerston being the main exception. Otherwise, and unanimously after 1866, they were always willing to bluff, to use overwhelming force to overbear another state, and to fight when necessary; not, however, to seize something new from another great power, but rather to hold what already they held. This attitude was entirely rational: Britain could rarely hope to gain more than it might expect to lose through a great war. As Britain's power declined, and the scale of that which it had to lose swelled, statesmen became more cautious, but no less resolute. They intended to protect vital British interests and against two distinct dangers: of a direct challenge to Britain or of a war between other powers which might indirectly threaten it. Between 1816 and 1939 British policy towards the great powers swung between two poles, which might be called the 'deterrence' and the 'reconciliation' strategies. So to overcome direct threats and to demonstrate that nothing could be gained from challenging British interests statesmen adopted means such as rearmament or alliances. To reduce the likelihood of a spillover war, they tried to persuade other states to accommodate their interests, and to keep such conflicts limited so that they would not destroy the world order. As one Foreign Secretary, Lord Malmesbury, wrote in 1858, Britain, seeking to maintain 'the General Peace', knew that 'Peace cannot be disturbed in any quarter without a risk of the disturbance becoming more general'. Hence Britain 'will always be ready, by [its] good offices, to contribute to moderate angry discussion, to avert hostile collision, or to remove estrangements which may threaten to alienate one nation from another'.[3]

Each of these strategies could further one aim at the price of potentially compromising another. While the deterrence strategy could deal with a direct threat or minimise the damage to Britain in a great war, it could not entirely prevent such damage and could increase the tensions leading to war. Although the reconciliation strategy might weaken Britain's ability to deal with war, it also helped to reduce international tensions and the likelihood of war. Each strategy dealt with a different set of problems. During the interwar years Britain followed whichever of them seemed best to suit the problem at hand. Between 1919 and 1925 Britain, fearing an immediate direct threat and involvement in the wars of others in the distant future, followed a deterrence strategy so as to keep what it held and maintain its ability to ameliorate the causes of a future great war. By 1926, believing that this approach had already served these purposes, it turned to reconciliation to surmount the long-term dangers, although retaining the means to sustain a deterrence strategy. Between 1929 and 1934 statesmen swung entirely to reconciliation, subordinating their ability to pursue a deterrence strategy whensoever the two conflicted. They held that this approach alone could help to counter the drift towards a new war which might wreck the British Empire. They reduced Britain's ability to deal with a great war in the hope that this very action would reduce its likelihood. This approach was not, however, the norm for strategic policy in the interwar years but the exception. By 1935, perceiving the dangers of a direct threat and of a spillover war in equal and immediate proportions, Britain reverted to a mixture of the deterrence and the reconciliation strategies. It was by then far less able to sustain them than it had been in 1929 while the dangers which it confronted had risen in scale.

When considering Britain's strategic predicament of the 1930s one must distinguish between the legacies of 1929 and 1934. They were bequests of different value. In the 1920s strategic policy met Britain's immediate and its vital needs but was less successful with its secondary ones. Excluding Ireland, the services secured Britain's interests in Imperial policing, but failed to preserve its zones of informal control beyond the empire, in Afghanistan, the Middle East and China. Their ability to deter a major threat or withstand a sudden blow were not tested, which may indicate that they served their deterrent function. By 1929 the services were well placed to mobilise Imperial resources against long-term threats, with a fair margin for error. By 1932 they were barely able to serve this role and only if the government reacted immediately, which it did not. Consequently, without strong allies Britain faced several threats which its military strength did not match while weaknesses in its armament industries and services hampered its ability to rearm. Certain of these problems arose from factors beyond the governments' control, from the decline in British power and from international developments, yet some of its strategic decisions between 1919 and 1929, and especially between 1929 and 1934 weakened Britain further than was necessary and magnified the effect of these problems. This dilemma was not the inevitable result of a slide in British strength. It occurred because no government saw the need to take those steps which could have countered the effect of that decline. The failures in strategic policy stemmed from the government's misunderstanding of Britain's strategic position.

During the 1920s Britain helped to create an international order which, under different circumstances, might have led to a stable world. Yet it did not properly consider the strategic consequences of changes in the balance of power, such as Japanese domination of the western Pacific or the drift from French to German dominance in Europe. Although the government knew that an alliance between several states could threaten Britain, it took no steps against this danger, nor did it adequately consider the possibility that the postwar order would not lead to a stable world. It preferred best to worst case planning, assuming that Britain's currently secure circumstances would continue indefinitely. Just as these predictions proved inaccurate, so its preparations proved inadequate.

Whitehall did not realise how easily the balance of power could shift against Britain, that this balance could not be preserved through an invisible hand but only by an active commitment to its maintenance. The government hoped to sustain security on the cheap, without large financial expenditure or commitments to other nations. It had an unjustified faith in Britain's power, and particularly disregarded the strategic limitations of the British economy which had manifested themselves in the great war. It minimised service spending in the belief that this would strengthen Britain's economic and hence its grand strategic power. As a result, by the 1930s neither Britain's services nor its economy met its needs. In strategic terms Britain would have done better to strengthen its armed services in order to counter the limits to its economic strength rather than to limit the services in order to bolster its economy.

None of the governments of the 1920s could have completely foreseen Britain's predicament of the 1930s, but had they perceived its position more accurately, they had the strategic resources at hand to surmount these problems. For example, Britain's service needs of 1934 would have been met by an RAF which matched the world's strongest air force, a navy which equalled the next three strongest fleets excluding the USN, and an army corresponding to the general staff's proposals of 1919. During the 1920s Britain had the absolute financial and the spare industrial resources necessary to sustain these policies, which might have required service estimates of £300 000 000: roughly that portion of its national wealth which Britain has devoted to defence since 1945. Yet this course of action would have caused the utter sacrifice of other important aims and would have seemed unnecessary. These forces would have exceeded the relative military strength which Britain had ever before maintained in peacetime. No government could have so reversed Britain's traditional strategic policy, but certain steps were politically feasible which could have significantly strengthened its position for the 1930s.

During the 1920s the government accepted that Britain must risk the initial loss of some possessions in war yet left the services officially responsible for the defence of untenable interests, pre-eminently Hong Kong. Britain would have gained some strategic leeway had it explicitly decided not to defend its Chinese interests against Japan. It could not, however, have eliminated any other commitments if it wanted to maintain the empire as a whole.

Conversely, Britain could have strengthened its position by gaining allies. The only powers it saw in this light were France, Japan and the United States. An Anglo-American *entente* was never possible, while Japanese and British interests may have been so divergent as to preclude the maintenance of their alliance. Britain could never have supported a Japanese attack against the United States nor offered more than benevolent neutrality to Japan in the unlikely case of American aggression. Nonetheless, it was Japanese emnity which rendered insoluble Britain's three-power problem of the 1930s; and yet these two states had much to offer each other in strategic terms. They might have sealed a pact which gave Japan some sort of hegemony over China; it was never compunction but rather calculation which restrained Britain from this step. Britain would have gained from retaining a Japanese ally and even more a French one. French and British security were indivisible: the fall of the British Empire was a necessary if delayed concomitant of the fall of France. Only by an understanding with France could Britain have achieved its central aim in Europe: to revise the Treaty of Versailles in such a way as to reconcile Germany while maintaining an acceptable balance of power in Europe. Moreover, until 1936 an Anglo-French alliance would have been the strongest military force on earth, dominant in Europe and easing indirectly Britain's problem of the Pacific. Even after 1936 such an alliance would have remained a formidable combination.

By 1934 each service suffered from major deficiencies, although their own miscalculations and inefficiencies had caused some of these problems. Large scale mechanisation could have been financed by abolishing cavalry; by placing more warships in reserve the Admiralty would have had greater funds available for other matters; between 1923 and 1925 a better organised RAF could have carried the HDAF further than it did. Nonetheless, the primary cause of the services' difficulties was the governments' decisions on their policies and estimates. Extra money would not have been a sufficient condition to solve all their problems but it was a necessary one. A marginal increase in their estimates during the 1920s would have improved their positions significantly for the 1930s.

The army's financial predicament precluded it from developing the general strength and the modern units needed by Britain, for which the best, if arbitrary, standard, was the prewar policy of a modern expeditionary force of six divisions and a large TA. Although this probably would have required estimates around £70 000 000, even an investment of £60 000 000 would have overcome many of its problems. After 1922 the RAF's relative financial position was always better than those of the other services. Even between 1929 and 1932 its current effective estimates were larger than in 1925, the peak of the HDAF programme. Nor were the government's decisions on the RAF's strength notably poor. All that it need have done differently was to hasten the completion of the HDAF once it was clear that powers like Italy were pulling significantly ahead in numerical terms. Britain could probably have done so with average net estimates between 1925 and 1934 of £19 000 000 instead of the £17 000 000 which was spent.

British maritime security required a two power standard against the IJN and a European navy. Given the weaknesses in the European fleets, Britain retained this standard during the 1920s, although this was likely to worsen when they strengthened their forces. The Admiralty's proposals were excessive and its priorities often misguided, but still many of its programmes were necessary for maritime security. The government's deferrment of these programmes after 1926 and above all its decisions of 1929–30 were the primary cause of the navy's weaknesses, which brought Britain closer to destruction than ever it came through the air. The simple expedient of not signing the London naval treaty of 1930 would have eliminated most of these problems. Beyond this, Britain would have been wise to complete the Singapore base and the fuel programmes on the 1931 or 1935 schedules, together with a replacement programme along the lines originally suggested by Pound. During the 1920s the navy could have achieved these objectives with estimates of around £60–£64 000 000.

Britain could have financed all these policies through estimates of £153 000 000. It could have improved their position to a lesser but important extent had at least their deficiencies been prevented. Britain could probably have done this with real estimates equal to those of 1914, or around £135 000 000; that is, £21 800 000 (or 15 per cent) more on average than the services received between 1923 and 1932. Britain could have done this without abandoning other aims and could have spent even £153 000 000 without too many other sacrifices. Nor did Britain need larger estimates in order to give the services more funds. They lost much money because it could not be spent in the financial year. A more flexible accounting system could have let them carry such funds over and so use fully their authorised estimates. Moreover, due to administrative inefficiencies and extravagance in certain areas, throughout much of the 1920s the services wasted money which could have been used to better purposes. They had no incentive to do otherwise if the Treasury was going to confiscate such savings. Had any government defined approximately how much money each service would receive during coming years and let them transfer savings from one area to another, a system which Churchill offered to the navy in 1925 and which governed the Indian army between 1928 and 1931, they might have used their resources more economically and efficiently.[4]

Certain other steps might also have strengthened Britain's strategic position. A defence ministry might have better coordinated the services' policies in the 1930s. More significantly, the scale of Britain's industrial base of the 1920s was better suited than that of the 1930s to the strategic circumstances of that decade. In the 1920s Britain's staple industries suffered from excess capacity, which was heavily run down by 1932, creating the shortage of capacity which, together with its psychological effect on management and unions, crippled rearmament more than did financial restraints. Britain could have helped its armament industries survive a lean period in better shape by subsidising them or by providing a moderately larger number of orders spaced evenly throughout the 1920s, and especially between 1929 and 1934.

Either individually or in tandem grand strategic steps during the 1920s, such as the formation of alliances with France, Japan or both and a moderate increase in service estimates, would have gone a long way towards mitigating the psychological and physical effects of the three-power problem which haunted Britain in the 1930s. Britain had the means to manage the strategic problems which it faced, and could have done so basically by retaining its policy of 1902–14. In any case, its actions between 1919 and 1929 were not a failure. Britain then followed its traditional strategic policy, which was to maintain the minimum possible military strength and to rely on subsequent expansion to match major requirements. This policy met Britain's immediate needs and did not eliminate its margin for security. Compared to other powers its position was not unusual in 1929; even by 1932 Britain had the means to respond to emerging threats. Its failure to do so was not the result of British strategic policy during the 1920s.

Notes

1. Parliamentary Debates (Third Series) (P.D.), Volume 76, column 309, 4 July 1844.

Introduction

1. Four excellent studies of such topics are: Stephen Roskill, *Naval Policy Between the Wars, Volume I: The Period of Anglo-American Antagonism, 1919–1929,* (1968), Brian Bond, *British Military Policy between the Two World Wars* (1980), James Neidpath, *The Singapore Naval Base and the Defence of Britain's Eastern Empire, 1919–1941* (1981) and Malcolm Smith, *British Air Strategy Between the Wars* (1984). Neither Correlli Barnett, *The Collapse of British Power* (1971) nor N.H. Gibbs, *Grand Strategy, Volume 1, Rearmament Policy* (1976) have systematically examined strategic policy during the 1920s as a whole.
2. Paul Kennedy, *The Rise and Fall of British Naval Mastery* (1976), p. 273; John Darwin, *Britain, Egypt and the Middle East, Imperial Policy in the Aftermath of War, 1918–1922* (1981) p. 28.

1 The Politics of Strategic Policy, 1919–26

1. Gordon Craig, 'The British Foreign Office from Grey to Austen Chamberlain' in Gordon Craig and Felix Gilbert (eds), *The Diplomats 1919–1939* (1953) pp. 15–33; A.J. Sharp, 'The Foreign Office in Eclipse, 1919–22', *History,* vol. 61 (1976); Anne Orde, *Great Britain and International Security, 1920–1926* (1978) pp. 4–5. For more accurate reappraisals of this issue, see Christopher Thorne, *The Limits of Foreign Policy, The West, The League and the Far Eastern Crisis of 1931–33* (1972) p. 97; R.M. Warman, 'The Erosion of Foreign Office Influence in the Making of Foreign Policy, 1916–1918', *Historical Journal,* vol. 15 (1973) and M.L. Dockrill and Zara Steiner, 'The Foreign Office at the Paris Peace Conference of 1919', *International History Review,* Vol. 2 (1980).
2. Lord Ronaldshay, *The Life of Lord Curzon, Volume III* (1928) pp. 259–61; Crowe to Hardinge, 8 November 1919, FO 800/243; Hardinge to Queen Mary, 20 March 1920, Hardinge of Penshurst papers, vol. 40; Vansittart to Curzon, 20 March 1921, Curzon of Kedleston papers, F.112, vol. 221 B.
3. This view is held even by G.C. Peden's revisionist *British Rearmament and the Treasury* (1979) pp. 7–8.
4. Memorandum by Niemayer, 6 April 1925, T 176/21; minute by Warren

Fisher, 29 December 1923. T 161/217 S. 21914.
5. Minute by Supply Services Branch, 15 July 1919, T 1/12469; memorandum by Fraser, 29 December 1927, T 161/285 S. 23101/3.
6. Warren Fisher to Lloyd George, 3 September 1919, T 171/155; Warren Fisher to Baldwin, 26 May 1925, Stanley Baldwin papers, vol. 3.
7. Barstow to Blackett, 25 November 1923, Basil Blackett papers, E.397, vol. 3.
8. Memorandum by Warren Fisher, 25 November 1931, T 199/50 B.
9. Roskill, *Naval Policy*, pp. 25–6 and 30–49; Bond, *Military Policy*, pp. 11–44.
10. Roskill, ibid., p. 386, note 1.
11. Salisbury to Austen Chamberlain, 15 April 1927, FO 800/260.
12. Warren Fisher to Baldwin, 30 February 1923, T 172/1309; same to same, 15 January 1925, Baldwin papers, vol. 2, Defence; Barstow to Blackett, 26 July 1923, Blackett papers, vol. 3.
13. Viscount Templewood, *Empire of the Air* (1957) pp. 41–2; H. Montgomery Hyde, *British Air Policy Between the Wars, 1918–1939* (1976) pp. 57, 113–14.
14. Andrew Boyle, *Trenchard, Man of Vision* (1962) pp. 336, 348–50, passim.
15. Roskill, *Naval Policy*, p. 243; Robert Rhodes James (ed.), *Memoirs of a Conservative, J.C.C. Davidson's Memoirs and Papers, 1910–1937* (1969) pp. 220–23.
16. Sixth meeting of the Imperial Conference, 24 June 1921, CAB 32/2; minute by Crowe, 20 May 1924, Colonial Office to Foreign Office, 17 May 1924, FO 371/9617.
17. Minute by Lampson, 29 January 1925, FO 371/10065.
18. AIR 8/7 contains the papers of this committee; Hugh Trenchard papers, C.11/12/1, unsigned memorandum for Trenchard, May 1919.
19. Minute by Radcliffe, 28 March 1919, WO 32/5355; memorandum by general staff, October 1919, WO 33/943.
20. Memorandum by Cox, ca. 29 May 1919, L/MIL 5/806; Board meeting, 14 August 1919, ADM 167/59; 3rd Interdepartmental conference, 17 May 1919, AIR 8/7.
21. Churchill to Lloyd George, 1 May 1919 and 14 July 1919, Lloyd George papers, F/9/1; Henry Wilson diary, entries 11–12 July 1919, Henry Wilson papers.
22. Beatty to de Robeck, 12 August 1919, John de Robeck papers, 6/24.
23. Wilson diary, entries 14 July 1919, 16 July 1919; Wilson to Lloyd George, 15 July 1919, 16 July 1919, Lloyd George papers, F/47/8.
24. Lord Riddell, *Intimate Diary of the Peace Conference and After* (1933) pp. 139–40.
25. W.S. Chalmers, *The Life and Letters of David Beatty, Admiral of the Fleet* (1951) p. 411; 133rd CID meeting, 29 June 1920, CAB 2/3; 214th CID meeting, 10 June 1926, CAB 2/4; Trenchard to Geddes, 11 November 1921, AIR 8/42; report of Geddes Committee, December 1921, AIR 8/41.
26. Stephen Roskill, *Hankey, Man of Secrets, Volume 11, 1919–1931* (1972) passim.

27. Hankey diary entry 14 January 1921; Hankey to MacDonald, 18 March 1924, Hankey to Churchill, 19 March 1926, CAB 21/469.
28. Haldane to Richmond, 31 August 1924, Herbert Richmond papers, RIC 7/4; memorandum by Hankey, 12 October 1954, Maurice Hankey papers, vol. 24/1.
29. CID paper 257–B, CAB 4/7; Beatty to Hankey, 22 May 1920, CAB 21/468; Boyle, *Trenchard,* pp. 347–48; 133rd CID meeting, 29 June 1920, CAB 2/3.
30. Conference of ministers, 27 September 1922, CAB 23/36 Pt. 1, S.65.
31. Beatty to de Robeck, 1 February 1920, de Robeck papers, Volume 6/25; Wilson diary, entry 18 August 1920; Barstow to Blackett, 26 July 1923, Blackett papers.
32. Haldane to Richmond, 31 August 1924, Richmond papers, RIC 7/4.
33. Minute by Nicholson, 9 July 1920, FO 371/4713.
34. Sixth COSC meeting, 8 January 1924, CAB 53/1.
35. 187th CID meeting, 28 July 1924, Appendix, CAB 2/4; 229th CID meeting, 14 July 1927, CAB 2/5.
36. Beatty to Hankey, 17 December 1923, ADM 1/8464; Hankey to Salisbury, 20 December 1923, CAB 21/291; Keyes to Richmond, 8 July 1924, Richmond papers, RIC 7/3e; minute by Steel, 29 October 1924, AIR 5/605.
37. Wilson to Esher, 14 November 1919, Wilson papers, 73/1/13/34B.
38. Wilson to Rawlinson, 6 July 1921, Wilson papers 73/1/19/13 D.
39. CP 3619, CAB 27/164.
40. Orde, *Britain,* p. 4.

2 'Treasury Control' and the 'Ten–Year Rule', 1919–24

1. John Ferris, 'Treasury control, the Ten Year Rule and British service policies, 1919–1924', *Historical Journal* (1987) vol. 30.
2. Smith, *Air Strategy,* p. 32, has misconstrued the meaning of the HDAF standard of 1923, as Roskill, *Naval Policy,* pp. 21, 219–2I, has done regarding the origins of the one power standard (below, pp. 60–3, 130–1). N.H. Gibbs, *Grand Strategy,* p. 23 and Paul Haggie, *Britannia at Bay, The Defence of the British Empire Against Japan, 1931–1941* (1981) pp. 6–8, have cited the Cabinet's definition of the one power standard of 1925 as if that governed naval policy throughout the 1920s.
3. Memorandum by Treasury, 10 February 1922 (unsigned but by Barstow, according to internal evidence) T 171/1228; minute by Barstow, 20 February 1923, T 161/184 S.16984.
4. Warren Fisher to Lloyd George, 3 September 1919, T 171/155.
5. Herbert Richmond, *Statesmen and Sea Power* (I946) p. 328; minute by Warren Fisher, 16 November 1922, T 161/119 S.9627/01; note 3 above.
6. Memorandum FC(3), CAB 27/72; 3rd (20 August 1919) and 18th (30 January 1920) Finance Committee meetings, CAB 27/71.
7. Memorandum No. 2064, ADM 167/72; Board meeting, 2 July 1925, ADM 167/71; CID paper No. 892–B, CAB 4/17; 236th CID meeting, 5 July 1928, CAB 2/5; minute by Wilson, 2 June 1929, T. 161/618

S.33420; Hankey to Vansittart, 14 May 1931, CAB 21/2093.

8. Memorandum by Hankey, 17 July 1919, Hankey papers, vol. 8/8.

9. Lloyd George to Austen Chamberlain, 9 January 1919, Lloyd George papers, F/7/2.

10. GT 7729, CAB 24/84.

11. Memoranda by Finance Branch, 10 February 1919, John Bradbury, undated, and Niemayer, 11 April 1919, T 171/157.

12. Minute by Barstow, 28 July 1919, T 1/12353; minute by Barstow, 26 June 1919, passim, T 1/12469.

13. Cabinet meeting, 15 July 1919, CAB 23/11; Cabinet meeting, 5 August 1919, CAB 23/15.

14. Minute by Churchill, 1 July 1919, AIR 2/89 B.7442; Churchill to Lloyd George, 4 August 1919, Lloyd George papers, F/9/1; Wilson diary, entry 15 August 1919; Trenchard to Churchill, 30 July 1919, Trenchard papers, C.11/1.

15. AIR 2/89 B.7442, ibid; Board meetings, 16 July 1919, passim, ADM 167/56; memorandum No. 874, passim, ADM 167/57; memorandum by Churchill, 6 August 1919, WO 32/3510.

16. Memorandum by Grey, 5 August 1919, Curzon papers, vol. 211; memorandum by Grey, 29 July 1919, Lloyd George papers, F/12/1; *F.R.U.S., The Paris Peace Conference, 1919, Volume XI* (1943) pp. 620–23, 630–31.

17. P.D., vol. 119, Columns 610–702, 7 August 1919.

18. Second Finance Committee meeting, 11 August 1919, CAB 27/71.

19. Cabinet meeting, 15 August 1919, CAB 23/15.

20. Hankey diary, entry 25 August 1919.

21. Bond, *Military Policy,* pp. 23–6; Peter Silverman, 'The Ten Year Rule', *Journal of the Royal United Services Institute,* no. 661 (1971); Stephen Roskill, 'The Ten Year Rule—The Historical Facts', *JRUSI,* no. 665 (1972; Ken Booth, 'The Ten Year Rule, An Unfinished Debate', *JRUSI,* no. 663 (1971); N.H. Gibbs, *Grand Strategy,* pp. 3–4; Roskill, *Naval Policy,* p. 215; Barnett, *Collapse,* p. 278; J.K. McDonald, 'Lloyd George and the Search for a Postwar Naval Policy' in A.J.P. Taylor (ed.), *Lloyd George, Twelve Essays* (1971).

23. Bond, *Military Policy,* pp. 23–6; Hankey to Speed, 14 Deember 1923, WO32/9314.

24. CID paper No. 892–B, CAB 4/17.

25. 236th CID meeting, 5 July 1928, CAB 2/5.

26. Chalmers, *Beatty,* pp. 376–77; memorandum no. 2064, ADM 167/72; minutes by Wakefield (21 March 1928) and Upcott (1 May 1928), T 162/136 E.18938.

27. Trenchard to Wilson, 7 January 1920, Trenchard papers, 11/27/163;. GT 7846, GT 7882, CAB 24/85.

28. Warren Fisher to Lloyd George, 3 September 1919, passim, T 171/155; memoranda FC (7) and FC (13), CAB 27/72.

29. 11th and 12th Finance Committee meetings, 22 October 1919 and 24 October 1919, CAB 27/71; memoranda FC (12) and FC (22), CAB 27/72; P.D. vol. 120, Columns 732–52; memorandum by Treasury, 28 October 1919, T 171/155; Cmd 779.

30. Trenchard to Wilson, 7 January 1920, Trenchard papers, 11/27/163.
31. 15th and 19th Finance Committee meetings, 6 November 1919, 9 February 1920, CAB 27/71; FC (18), CAB 27/72.
32. Wilson diary, entry 15 August 1919; GT 8039, CAB 24/87.
33. 33rd Finance Committee meeting, 25 February 1921, CAB 27/71; Chamberlain to Churchill, 14 October 1919, T 161/228 S.23365; compare Long to Law 20 February 1920 with draft for same, ADM 116/1677.
34. Minute by Barstow, 21 March 1920, T 171/1116.
35. Memorandum FC (69), CAB 27/72.
36. 165th and 168th CID meetings, 30 November 1922 and 14 December 1922, CAB 2/3.
37. 3rd Salisbury Committee meeting, 17 April 1923, AIR 8/63.
38. 3rd Churchill Committee meeting, 12 January 1922, CAB 27/164; minutes by Geoffrey Salmond, 13 April 1923, and Trenchard, 16 April 1923, AIR 5/282.
39. Minute by Barstow, 28 December 1923, T 161/227 S.23175.
40. Memorandum by Niemayer, 6 April 1925, T 176/21.
41. Minute by Warren Fisher, 28 November 1928, T 161/292 S.34216; memorandum by Waterfield, 1 January 1931, T 161/486 S.34610/31.

3   The Elements of Strategic Policy, 1919–26

1. John Darwin, 'Imperialism in Decline? Tendencies in British Imperial Policy Between the Wars', *Historical Journal,* vol. 23 (1980); John Gallacher, *The Decline, Revival and Fall of the British Empire* (1982) pp. 73–153.
2. Keith Jeffery, *The British Army and the Crisis of Empire, 1918–1920* (1984) pp. 11–12; Orde, *Britain,* p. 4.
3. Memorandum by Keynes, 4 February 1920, T 172/1384.
4. Memorandum by Montagu, 9 December 1921, Churchill to Horne, 30 February 1922, T 171/202;CP 3947, CAB 24/136; minute by Barstow, 5 May 1922, T 161/119 S.9627/1; memorandum by Hankey, 9 February 1925, CAB 63/37; 9th Birkenhead Committee meeting, 2 July 1925, CAB 27/273.
5. Barstow to Blackett, 25 November 1923, Blackett Papers, vol. 3..
6. CID paper No. 599–B, CAB 4/12.
7. Appendix.
8. Booth, 'Ten Year Rule'; Correlli Barnett, *Britain and Her Army, 1509–1970. A Military, Political and Social Survey* (1970) p. 412; Basil Liddell Hart, *Memoirs, Volume One* (1965) pp. 107–37, 325–29.
9. Minute by Waterfield, 19 September 1919, T 161/228 S.23365; minute by Harington, 1 September 1920, WO 32/5550; Air Ministry to Treasury, December 1921, T 161/151 S.13829; Game to Trenchard, 17 May 1923, AIR 5/248; minute by Bagnell-Wild, 5 April 1923, AIR 5/362.
10. Memorandum by Beatty, 28 April 1924, ADM 1/8666.
11. Minute by Warren Fisher, 20 February 1923, T 161/184 S. 16984; CP 67, CAB 24/171.

12. CP 437, CAB 24/175; 10th Salisbury Committee meeting, 16 May 1923, AIR 8/63.
13. Minute by Barstow, 18 July 1921, T 161/119 S. 9627/1; minute by Barstow, 31 January 1924, T 161/227 S. 23175; memorandum by Barstow, 21 February 1924, T 161/800 S. 18917/2.
14. Martin Gilbert (ed.), *Companion Volume No. 1* to *Winston S. Churchill, 1874–1965, Volume 4, 1916–1922* (1975) pp. 1190–94; CP 1724, CAB 24/110; 173rd CID meeting, 29 June 1923, CAB 2/3.
15. Memorandum by Balfour, 18 March 1919, Lloyd George papers, F/3/4.
16. Minute by Chamberlain, 3 January 1925, FO 371/10984.
17. Lloyd George to Law, 31 March 1919, Lloyd George papers, F/30/3.
18. Wilson diary, entries 17 February 1919, passim; two memoranda by Trenchard, 18 February 1919, P.R.C. Groves papers (IWM); H.M.V. Temperley (ed.), *A History of the Paris Peace Conference, Volume II* (1920) pp. 124–40.
19. Memorandum by Hankey, 17 July 1919, Hankey papers, vol. 8/18; minute by D.M.O., 28 January 1920, WO 32/5758.
20. Memorandum by Barstow, 29 June 1919, T 1/12469; minute by Keyes, 22 December 1923, ADM 1/8702; D. Cameron Watt, *Succeeding John Bull, America in Britain's Place, 1900–1975,* (1984) p. 59.
21. John Ferris, 'A British "Unofficial' Aviation Mission and Japanese Naval Developments, 1919–1928', *Journal of Strategic Studies,* vol. 5 (1982); 158th CID meeting, 5 July 1922, CAB 2/3.
22. Minute by Hirtzel, 26 May 1921, L/PS/10/431; memorandum by Wellesley, 1 September 1920, FO 371/5361; Rawlinson to Cavan, 21 January 1925, Henry Rawlinson papers, vol. 22; Chalmers, *Beatty,* p. 410; Beatty to Baldwin, 1 March 1926, David Beatty papers, vol. 8, no. 8.
23. Meeting of ministers, 11 January 1920, CAB 1/29; Churchill to Lloyd George, 12 February 1920, WO 32/5620; Montagu to Curzon, 17 February 1920, FO 800/157; Hankey diary, entry 3 January 1921; CP 412, CAB 24/96; CP 3619, CAB 24/132; memorandum by Gregory, 3 December 1923, Curzon papers, vol. 236.
24. Report of the Inter-Departmental Committee on Eastern Unrest, 1922, CO 537/835.
25. COS 36, CAB 55/12.
26. CID paper No. 251–B, CAB 4/7.
27. F.S. Northedge, *The Troubled Giant, Britain Among the Great Powers, 1916–1939.* (1966) pp. 618–22; Charles Loch Mowat, *Britain Between the Wars, 1918–1940* (1955) pp. 52, 112; E.H. Carr, *The Twenty Years Peace, 1919–1939* (1980 reprint) passim; Martin Gilbert, *The Roots of Appeasement* (1966) passim; and D.C. Watt, *Personalities and Politics, Studies in the Formulation of British Foreign Policy in the Twentieth Century* (1985) p. 27; Patrick Kyba, *Covenants Without the Sword, Public Opinion and British Defence Policy, 1931–35* (1983) pp. 9–15; Thorne, *Limits* pp. 101–09; Kennedy, *Mastery* pp. 272–73; Barnett, *Collapse* pp. 237–43; Paul Kennedy, *The Realities Behind Diplomacy, Background Influences on British External Policy, 1865–1980* (1980) pp.

240–42. Michael Howard, *The Causes of War* (1983) pp. 40–1 and A.J.P. Taylor, *Rumours of Wars* (1952) pp. 75–81, offer excellent accounts of this issue.
28. Second Singapore Committee meeting, 3 March 1924, CAB 27/236.
29. Minutes by MacDonald, 3 July 1924, and Crowe, 4 July 1924, FO 371/9818.
30. Memorandum by Wellesley, 1 September 1920, FO 371/5361; 134th and 173rd CID meetings, 14 December 1920 and 29 June 1923, CAB 2/3; 2nd Singapore Committee meeting, 3 March 1924, CAB 27/236.
31. Memorandum by Headlam-Morley, 8 October 1920, passim, FO 800/149.
32. Memorandum by Cecil, 10 April 1919, Lloyd George papers, F/6/6; Martin Gilbert, *Companion Volume* to *Winston S. Churchill, 1874–1965. Volume V. 1922–1939* (1976) pp. 390–91; MacDonald to Thomson, 10 March 1924, FO 800/219.
33. CID paper No. 431–B, CAB 4/10; minute by Crowe, 25 May 1924, FO 371/9671.
34. Gilbert, *Roots* passim; Kennedy, *Realities* pp. 259–63.
35. 193rd CID meeting, 5 January 1925, CAB 2/4.
36. Kennedy, *Realities* pp. 223–36; Barnett, *Collapse* pp. 237–43.
37. Hankey diary, entry 4 December 1920; H.A.L. Fisher diary, entry 30 December 1920; undated marginal notes by MacDonald on George Trevelyn, *British History in the 19th Century, 1789–1901*, PRO 30/69/1; minute by Austen Chamberlain, 19 March 1925, FO 371/10756.
38. Circular letter by Castlereagh, 1 January 1816, FO 83/81.
39. Taylor, *Rumours* pp. 75–81; Paul W. Schroeder, 'Munich and the British Tradition', *Historical Journal*, vol. 19 (1976).

4 Strategic Principles and Service Policies, 1919–20

1. Roskill, *Naval Policy* pp. 103–16; Arthur Marder, *From the Dreadnaught to Scapa Flow, The Navy in the Fisher Era, Volume V: Victory and Aftermath (January 1918–June 1919)* (1970) passim; McDonald, 'Search'.
2. Although battleships and battlecruisers are often termed 'capital ships', that phrase is misleading. The authority on naval construction between 1919 and 1939 has termed battlecruisers 'semicapital ship types' and large 8-inch gun cruisers as 'a kind of junior capital ship' (Norman Friedman, *U.S. Cruisers, An Illustrated Design History* (1985) pp. 1, 111). Aircraft carriers were also gradually usurping the traditional functions of battleships. Finally, as Richmond stated about the concept of 'capital ships', 'you have to consider the whole of the ships together. They all act in unison. It is not one particular type that is the dominant unit'. (Third Bonar Law Committee meeting, 5 January 1921, CAB 16/37).
3. William Braisted, *The United States Navy in the Pacific, 1901–1922* (1971) pp. 171–209; David F. Trask, *Captains and Cabinets, Anglo-American Naval Relations, 1917–1918* (1972) pp. 356–59.
4. Kennedy, *Realities* pp. 259–63; Barnett, *Collapse* pp. 258–63.

5. Lloyd George to Law, 31 March 1919, Long to Lloyd George, 16 February 1919, Lloyd George papers, F/30/3, F/33/2; Wemyss to Long, 5 April 1919, Wester Wemyss papers, vol. 11/1.
6. Churchill to Curzon, 29 September 1921, Curzon papers, vol. 220 B; Lloyd George to Long, 14 December 1920, Lloyd George papers, F/34/1.
7. Roberta Allbert Dayer, 'The British War Debts to the United States and the Anglo-Japanese Alliance', *Pacific Historical Review*, vol. 45 (1976).
8. Minute by Wemyss, 26 February 1918, passim, ADM 116/1748; ADM 116/1745, passim.
9. Memorandum P.D. 0129, Admiral Fremantle papers, FRE 311; Board meetings, 6 February 1919, 13 February 1919, ADM 167/56; Memorandum M. 06366, ADM 167/57; Long to Lloyd George, 7 March 1919, Lloyd George papers, F/33/2; GT 6979, CAB 24/76; Wemyss to Long, 5 April 1919, Wemyss papers, vol. 11/1.
10. Madden to Beatty, 28 March 1919, Beatty to Admiralty, 1 April 1919, passim, ADM 116/2017.
11. Board meeting, 6 March 1919, ADM 167/56.
12. Wemyss to Hope, 6 June 1919, Wemyss papers, vol. 11/1.
13. Minute by DOD (F) 2 March 1919, ADM 116/2017; minute by Fremantle, 9 April 1919, Fremantle papers, FRE 315; memorandum no. 755, ADM 167/57.
14. Memorandum by Long, 25 March 1919, ADM 167/58; Long to Lloyd George, 8 April 1919, Lloyd George papers, F/33/2.
15. Cecil diary, entries 8 and 10 April 1919, Robert Cecil papers, Add. Mss. 51131, Lloyd George to Law, 31 March 1919, Bonar Law papers, 97/1/17; Long to Lloyd George, 6 and 8 April 1919, Cecil to Lloyd George, 10 April 1919, Lloyd George papers, F/33/2 and F/6/6; memorandum, 29 March 1919 (unsigned, but by Wemyss, according to internal evidence), F/192/1.
16. Board meetings, 29 May 1919, 18 June 1919, ADM 167/56; GT 6517, CAB 24/82; Long to Lloyd George, 2 May 1919, Lloyd George papers, F/33/2.
17. Churchill to Lloyd George, 1 May 1919, Lloyd George papers, F/9/1; memorandum by Hankey, 17 July 1919, Hankey papers, vol. 8/18; memorandum by Barstow, 29 June 1919, T 1/12469.
18. 16th Finance Committee meeting, 24 November 1919, CAB 27/71; minute by Long, 23 October 1919, ADM 1/8571.
19. Board meetings, 18 August 1919, 22 September 1919, ADM 167/56; Admiralty memorandum, M.03710, ADM 1/8549; FC (18), CAB 27/72.
20. *F.R.U.S., Paris Peace Conference, 1919, Volume XI*, pp. 675–76; Curzon to Grey, 9 September 1919, Grey to Curzon, 13 September 1919, Curzon papers, vol. 211.
21. Beatty to de Robeck, 30 November 1919, de Robeck papers, 5/13; Beatty to Lloyd George, 15 March 1920, Lloyd George papers, F/4/4.
22. Beatty to de Robeck, 4 January 1920 (according to internal evidence), de Robeck papers, 6/30; memorandum by Beatty, 7 January 1920,

ADM 167/61; Board meeting, 14 January 1920, ADM 167/60.

23. CP 645, CAB 24/98; Long to Law, 8 February 1920, Bonar Law papers, 98/7/3; 20th Finance Committee meeting, 18 February 1920, CAB 27/71; Board meeting, 18 February 1920, ADM 167/60; Long to Law, 20 February 1920, passim, ADM 116/1677; conference of ministers, 25 February 1920, CAB 23/20; Long to Austen Chamberlain, 17 March 1920, passim, T 171/1116; P.D. vol. 126, Columns 2300–01, 17 March 1920.

24. Memoranda by Murray and Chatfield, 1 May 1920, 6 May 1920, ADM 167/61; Board meetings, 12 May 1920, 13 October 1920, ADM 167/60; Field to d'Eyncourt, 14 May 1920, passim, Tennyson d'Eyncourt papers, DEY 27; N.J.M. Campbell, 'Washington's Cherry Trees. The Evolution of the British 1921–22 Capital Ships', *Warship*, vol 1 (1977) minute by Beatty, 8 July 1920, passim, ADM 1/8602; CP 2176, CAB 24/115.

25. Montgomery Hyde, *Air Policy* p. 46; Charles Webster and Noble Frankland, *The Strategic Air Offensive Against Germany* (1961) pp. 5–20.

26. Barnett, *Army* pp. 410–12; Liddell Hart, *Memoirs* pp. 100–01; Bond, *Military Policy* pp. 127–32; George Patrick Armstrong, *The Controversy Over Tanks in the British Army 1919 to 1933*, University of London Ph.D. thesis (1976).

27. Basil Liddell Hart, *The Tanks, Volume 1, 1914–1939* (1959) pp. 207–10, is the only historian to have noted that the army's loss of the role of substitution in Iraq negatively affected its mechanised policy.

28. Austen Chamberlain to Churchill, 3 November 1919, T 161/228 S. 23365; T 1/12373, passim.

29. Minute by Cox, 6 August 1920, passim, L/MIL 7/17133; Rawlinson to Wilson, 5 January 1921, Wilson papers, 73/1/9/13 C; Montgomery-Massingberd to Elles, 30 March 1920, General Montgomery-Massingberd papers, vol. 123.

30. Haldane to War Office, Aylmer Haldane diary, 17 April 1920, Aylmer Haldane papers, CP 1467, CAB 24/107; CP 2006, CAB 24/114.

31. Memorandum by Trenchard, 19 August 1920, Trenchard to Churchill, 6 March 1922, Trenchard papers, C/11/1 and C/11/8; memorandum, undated and unsigned but by Trenchard and *ca.* January–February 1922 according to internal evidence, AIR 9/14; Trenchard to Churchill, 9 September 1921, CO 730/16.

32. Churchill to Austen Chamberlain, 11 and 30 October 1919, T 161/228 S.23365.

33. Haldane diary, entries 15 and 25 April 1920; G.O.C. Ireland to War Office, 2 May 1919 WO 32/9522; Liddell Hart, *Tanks* pp. 203–06; Wilson to Rawlinson, 5 January 1921 and 26 January 1921, Wilson papers, 73/1/9/13 C; CP 1320, CAB 24/106.

34. CID paper, No. 255–B, CAB 4/7; Keith Jeffery, 'Sir Henry Wilson and the Defence of the British Empire, 1918–22', *Journal of Imperial and Commonwealth History* vol. 5 (1977).

35. Churchill to Lloyd George, 29 December 1918, Lloyd George papers, F/8/2.

36. Memorandum by Barstow, 28 July 1919, T 1/12353; Air Council meeting, 4 March 1919, AIR 6/14.
37. Churchill to War Office, 31 August 1919, WO 32/11286.
38. Memorandum by Sykes, 21 October 1918, passim, AIR 2/71 A.6446; Air Council meetings, 23 October 1918, and 14 December 1918, AIR 6/13; GT 6477, 6478, CAB 24/71; GT 6591, CAB 24/72.
39. Churchill to Seely and Sykes, 12 January 1919, passim, Frederick Sykes papers, vol. 62; Montgomery Hyde, *Air Policy* pp. 54–61; Boyle, *Trenchard* pp. 327–42.
40. Minutes by Churchill and Trenchard, 27 July 1919, 29 July 1919, passim, AIR 2/109 A.20010; minute by Churchill, 1 July 1919, AIR 2/89 B.7442; Churchill to Trenchard, 7 September 1919, passim, Trenchard papers, C/11/1.
41. Barstow to Trenchard (two letters), 5 September 1919, AIR 8/19.
42. Minutes by Trenchard, 10 and 17 September 1919, and Churchill, 11 September 1919, AIR 2/109 A.20010.
43. GT 8404, CAB 24/90; Boyle, *Trenchard* p. 346; 15th Finance Committee meeting, 6 November 1919, CAB 27/71.
44. Air Council meeting, 13 November 1918, AIR 6/13.
45. Smith, *Air Strategy* pp. 28, 31.
46. Trenchard to Churchill, 30 July 1919, Trenchard papers, C/11/1.
47. CID paper No. 258–B, CAB 4/7.
48. Cabinet meeting, 26 July 1919, CAB 23/11; memorandum by Barstow, 28 July 1919, T 1/12353.
49. Cabinet meeting, 18 November 1918, CAB 23/8; GT 6292, CAB 24/69; memorandum by general staff, December 1918, WO 32/4643; War Office conference, 20 December 1918, WO 106/345; memorandum by general staff, 1 February 1919, WO 106/316; minute by Chetwode, 3 March 1922, WO 32/5297.
50. Churchill to Austen Chamberlain, 30 October 1919, T 161/228 S.23365; minute by Furze, 22 July 1919, WO 32/4955; minutes by Kirke and Harington, 17 April 1919 and 6 May 1919, WO 32/5685; Churchill to Chamberlain, 22 July 1919, T 1/12373.
51. Minute by Wilson, 26 July 1919, WO 32/4955; Army Council meeting, 28 November 1919, WO 163/24.
52. War Office to India Office, 16 June 1920, L/MIL 7/17133; Army Council meetings, 11 August 1920, passim, WO 163/25.
53. Chetwode to Montgomery-Massingberd, 30 December 1920, Montgomery-Massingberd papers, vol. 122.
54. War Office to Treasury, 25 March 1924, T 161/228 S.23365; Robinson to Cobbe, 11 October 1921, 12 January 1922, L/MIL 7/17132.
55. Wilson to Rawlinson, 2 April 1921, Wilson papers, 73/1/9/13 C.
56. CP 586, CAB 24/97; CP 3231, 3259, CAB 24/127; memorandum by general staff, January 1922, passim, CAB 27/164.
57. CP 385, 386, CAB 24/97; 19th Finance Committee meeting, 9 February 1920, CAB 27/72.
58. Minutes by Churchill, 9 and 17 May 1919, WO 32/5222; minute by Churchill, 6 August 1919, passim, WO 32/3510; Churchill to Austen

Chamberlain, 30 October 1919, T 161/228 S.23365; minute by Churchill, 30 August 1919, WO 32/4955.

59. Memorandum by general staff, 15 October 1919, passim, CAB 27/72; CP 585, 586, CAB 24/97; 20th Finance Committee meeting, 17 February 1920, CAB 27/71.
60. Minute by Churchill, 14 January 1920, WO 32/5942; Haldane diary, entry 6 February 1920.
61. CP 707, CAB 24/99; memorandum by D.M.O., 9 February 1920, WO 32/5227.
62. Civil Commissioner, Iraq, to India Office, 19 January 1920, L/PS/10/ 766; memorandum by British general staff, September 1919, L/MIL 7/ 16907.
63. Boyle, *Trenchard* pp. 365–69; Leo Amery, *My Political Life, Volume 2: War and Peace, 1914–1929* (1952) pp. 201–02; Lord Ismay, *Memoirs* (1960) pp. 29–35; John Barnes and David Nicholson, (eds) *The Leo Amery Diaries. Volume I, 1896 to 1929* (1980) p. 263. The best published sources are Geoffrey Archer, *Personal and Historical Memoirs of an East African Administrator* (1963) pp. 96–114 and Patrick Kitabura Kakwenzire, *Colonial Rule in the British Somaliland Protectorate, 1905–1939,* University of London Ph.D. thesis (1976).
64. Cabinet meeting, 21 January 1919, CAB 23/9; CO 535/52, CO 535/54, CO 535/55, CO 535/56, CO 535/41, passim; minute by Bottomley, 5 September 1919, CO 535/58; 111/18b–111/1/60b, Lord Ismay papers; Milner to Wingate, 7 August 1919, Archer to Milner, 9 December 1919, 3 May 1920, Lord Milner papers, Dep. 702 and 387; 'Z' squadron diary, January–February 1920, AIR 5/1309; undated, unsigned, 'History of the Somaliland Camel Corps', WO 106/272; memorandum by air staff, June 1921, Trenchard papers, C.11/10.
65. Scott to Trenchard, 19 January 1920, AIR 9/14; Churchill to Trenchard, 29 February 1920, AIR 2/145 202903/20; Trenchard to Wilson, 18 March 1920, Trenchard papers, C/11/8. Cabinet meeting, 23 February 1920, CAB 23/20.
66. 23rd Finance Committee meeting, 22 July 1920, CAB 27/71; CP 1647, CAB 24/107; CID paper No. 258–B, CAB 4/7; Air Ministry to War Office, 24 August 1920, AIR 5/210.
67. Warren Fisher to Austen Chamberlain and Lloyd George, 16 June 1920, T 171/180; minute by Barstow, 10 July 1920, T 161/81 S.6288; Hankey diary, entry 14 January 1921.
68. Hankey diary, entry 4 December 1920.

5 Service Policies and Financial Policy, 1921

1. FC(52), CAB 27/72; 28th and 29th Financial Committee meetings, 29 November 1920, 7 December 1920, CAB 27/71; Cabinet meeting, 8 December 1920, passim, CAB 23/23; CP 2274, CAB 24/116.
2. 30th and 31st Finance Committee meetings, 21 December 1920, 4 January 1921, CAB 27/71.
3. CP 2919, CAB 24/123; Cabinet meeting, 11 May 1921, CAB 23/25.

4. Austen Chamberlain to Lloyd George, 13 June 1921, Geddes to Chamberlain, 10 June 1921, Lloyd George papers, F/7/4.
5. Wilson to Rawlinson, 6 July 1921, Wilson papers, 73/1/9/13 D.
6. CID paper no 142-C, CAB 5/4; memorandum by general staff, January 1922, CAB 27/164.
7. CP 2274, CAB 24/116.
8. Memorandum by Barstow, 18 July 1921, T 161/119 S.9627/1; 134th and 135th CID meetings, 14 December 1920, 21 December 1920, CAB 2/3; 29th Finance Committee meeting, 7 December 1920, CAB 27/71.
9. Memorandum by naval staff, 9 November 1921, ADM 1/8615; report of Geddes Committee, December 1921, AIR 8/41.
10. Richmond, *Statesmen* p. 328; Third Bonar Law Committee meeting, 5 January 1921, CAB 16/37.
11. Beatty to de Robeck, 4 January 1920, de Robeck papers, 6/30.
12. Minute by Domville, 5 February 1920, ADM 1/8507; ADM 1/8577, passim; Cabinet meeting, 17 January 1919, CAB 23/9; GT 6594, CAB 24/72; memorandum by Domville, 12 May 1921, ADM 1/8607.
13. CID paper, No 143-C, CAB 5/4; 143rd CID meeting, 22 July 1921, CAB 2/3.
14. Naval staff, draft war plans, 4 January 1921, Beatty papers, vol 8, no. 1; memorandum by naval staff, 9 November 1921, ADM 1/8615; memorandum No. 1352, ADM 167/64.
15. ADM 167/64, ibid.
16. 134th CID meeting, 14 December 1920, CAB 2/3; memorandum by Barstow, 4 June 1921, T 161/119 S.9627/1.
17. CAB 2/3, ibid.
18. Memorandum by Barstow, 18 July 1921, T 161/119 S. 9627/1.
19. Beatty to Richmond, 26 February 1921, Richmond papers, RIC 7/4.
20. Hankey diary, entry 15 December 1920.
21. Report of Bonar Law Committee, February 1921, CAB 16/37.
22. Alan Clarke (ed.), *'A Good Innings'; The Private Papers of Viscount Lee of Fareham* (1974) pp. 205–08.
23. 32nd Finance Committee meeting, 17 February 1921, CAB 27/71; Kenneth Young, *Arthur James Balfour, The Happy Life of the Politician, Prime Minister, Statesman and Philosopher, 1848–1930* (1963) p. 419; Balfour to Bonar Law, 3 March 1921, Bonar Law papers, 100/3/3; 140th CID meeting, 10 June 1921, CAB 2/3.
24. Cmd 467; Trenchard to Wilson, 18 November 1919, AIR 2/108 A.18840; Air Ministry to Admiralty, 17 November 1919, ADM 116/1836; Trenchard to Beatty, 22 November 1919, AIR 8/17; same to same, 9 December 1919, Trenchard papers, 11/27/16.
25. Minute by Harington, 10 December 1919, WO 32/5222; Wilson diary, entry 30 December 1919; Churchill to Wilson and Trenchard, 22 December 1919, passim, WO 32/5942.
26. Hankey diary, entry 14 January 1921; minutes by Miller and Upcott, 20 December 1920, T 161/104 S.8076; 30th and 31st Finance Committee meetings, 21 December 1920, 4.1.21, CAB 27/71.
27. 32nd Finance Committee meeting, 17 February 1921, CAB 27/71.
28. Trenchard to Churchill, 11 January 1921, AIR 5/552.

29. Trenchard to Rawlinson, 15 April 1921, Trenchard papers, C.11/27/139.
30. Minutes by Trenchard and Churchill, 24 February 1921, 25 February 1921, AIR 5/231.
31. 134th CID meeting, 14 December 1920, CAB 2/3; memoranda by Brooke-Popham and Game, 14 December 1920, AIR 8/30; Ninth Bonar Law Committee meeting, 26 January 1921, CAB 16/37.
32. Report of the Bonar Law Committee, February 1921, CAB 16/37; draft memorandum by air staff, with amendments by Churchill, 5 February 1921, AIR 5/552; CID paper No. 135–C, CAB 5/4.
33. Minutes by Domville and Brock, 8 April 1921, ADM 1/8605; memorandum by Braine, 10 February 1921, WO 32/5942; Barry Domville diary, entries 21 April 1921, 2 June 1921.
34. 139th CID meeting, 27 May 1921, CAB 2/3.
35. CID paper No 149–C, CAB 5/4.
36. Minute by Cox, 10 August 1920, and Hirtzel, 16 August 1920, passim, L/PS/10/766; CO 534/41, nos. 6691, 12115; Haldane diary, entries 10 March 1920, 25 April 1920, Wilson diary, entry 30 December 1919; Elizabeth Burgoyne, *Gertrude Bell, From Her Personal Papers, 1914–1926* (1961) pp. 134–35, 145; Minutes by Crowe and Curzon, 2 April 1920, 7 April 1920, FO 371/5071; memorandum by Hankey, 28 May 1920, Lloyd George papers, F/24/2; memorandum (mutilated) by Montagu, 10 April 1920, Trenchard papers, C/11/8.
37. CP 2275, CAB 24/116.
38. Cabinet meeting, 22 March 1921, CAB 23/24; Cabinet meeting, 26 April 1921, CAB 23/25; CP 2472, 2473, CAB 24/121.
39. Jeffery, 'Wilson'; minute by Wilson, 23 February 1921, WO 32/5233; CP 2608, CAB 24/120; CPs 2964, 2965, CAB 24/123.
40. Chetwode to Montgomery-Massingberd, 22 March 1921, Montgomery-Massingberd papers, vol. 124.
41. Army Council meetings, 25 May 1921, passim, WO 163/26; minute by Worthington-Evans, 9 August 1921, WO 32/11306; minute by Wilson, 9 June 1921, WO 32/11305.
42. Wilson to Rawlinson, 2 April 1921, Wilson papers, 73/1/9/13 C.
43. CP 2925, CAB 24/123; CP 2992, CAB 24/124; CP 3197, CAB 24/126; CP 3240, CAB 24/127; War Office to G.O.C. Iraq, 3 May 1921, CO 730/12; minute by de Radcliffe, 28 July 1921, WO 32/11305.
44. Cabinet meeting, 18 August 1921, CAB 23/26; CO 730/14, CO 730/15, CO 730/27, passim; Inter-Departmental Conference, 30 December 1921, WO 32/5899; Churchill to Trenchard, 10 September 1921, Trenchard papers, C/11/8.
45. Memorandum by Steel, 20 July 1921, AIR 8/34; minute by Meinertz-hagen, 14 October 1921, CO 730/13; Air Ministry-Colonial Office Conference, 15 September 1921, CO 730/16; conference of ministers, 21 December 1921, CAB 23/28; conference of ministers, 10 February 1922, CAB 23/29.
46. Worthington-Evans to Horne, 21 December 1921, T 161/150 S.13677; Liddell Hart, *Tanks* pp. 217–19; minute by Wilson, 9 June 1921, WO 32/11305; Chetwode to Montgomery-Massingberd, 12 January 1921,

and 6 September 1921, Montgomery-Massingberd papers, vols. 122 and 133; undated lecture, 'Experimental Brigade', Walter Kirke papers, Section 3 (LHCMA, KCL); Wilson diary, entries 9–10 August 1921.

47. Montgomery-Massingberd papers and T 161/150 S.13677, ibid.
48. Minute by Warren Fisher, 6 June 1921, T 161/119 S.9627/1; report of Churchill Committee, 4 February 1922, CAB 27/164; report of Geddes Committee, December 1921, AIR 8/41.
49. Cabinet meetings, 2 and 15 August 1921, CAB 23/26; Austen Chamberlain to Lloyd George, 11 August 1921, Chamberlain to Horne, 8 August 1921, Lloyd George papers, F/7/4,F/27/6; Geddes to Horne, 3 August 1921, T 172/1228.
50. Minute by Domville, 8 April 1921, ADM 1/8605; minute by Beatty, 21 September 1921, ADM 1/8611; CID papers nos. 150–C, 151–C, CAB 5/4; minutes of meetings of Geddes Committee, autumn 1921, T 172/1228.
51. Minute by Barstow, 24 June 1921, T 161/119 S.9654.
52. Memorandum by Treasury, October 1921, T 163/11/3; memorandum by same, T 163/11/4; T 161/119 S.9627/1, T 161/125 S.10233, passim.
53. Report of Geddes Committee, December 1921, AIR 8/41.

6 Strategic Policy and Diplomacy, 1919–22

1. Ian Nish, *Alliance in Decline, A Study in Anglo-Japanese Relations, 1908–24* (1971) pp. 295–96.
2. *D.B.F.P., Volume XVII,* no. 38; memorandum by Crowe, 26 December 1921, FO 371/7000; CID paper no. 98–A, CAB 3/3; Wilson diary, entries 22–23 March 1919; CP 1782, CAB 24/110; H.A.L. Fisher diary, entry 12 August 1920; CPs 410, 455, CAB 24/96; memorandum by general staff, October 1919, WO 33/943; CP 337, CAB 24/95.
3. Memorandum by Hankey, 4 November 1927, CAB 21/334; note from Lloyd George to Curzon, 12 August 1920, Curzon papers, vol. 317.
4. Roskill, *Naval Policy* pp. 218–29; Neidpath, *Singapore* pp. 45–6; Nish, *Alliance* pp. 319–32; J. Kenneth MacDonald, *British Naval Policy in the Pacific and Far East: From Paris to Washington, 1919–1922,* University of Oxford Ph.D. thesis (1975).
5. Barnett, *Collapse* pp. 258–63; Watt, *Succeeding* pp. 49–50.
6. Nish, *Alliance* pp. 294–318; memorandum by Beatty, 7 January 1920, ADM 167/61; memorandum by general staff, October 1919, WO 33/943; 140th CID meeting, 10 June 1921, CAB 2/3; memorandum by Wellesley, 1 September 1920, FO 371/5361; memorandum by Foreign Office, 10 October 1921, FO 412/118; undated note by Churchill, probably 30 May 1921, Lloyd George papers, F/101; Gilbert, *Companion III to Churchill Volume IV* pp. 1539–42.
7. Cabinet meeting, 30 May 1921, CAB 23/25; minute by Curzon, 8 March 1920, FO 371/5538.
8. CID paper no. 124–C, (no author cited, but apparently by Hankey), CAB 3/5.
9. Barnett, *Collapse* pp. 258–63; Hosaya Chihiro, 'Britain and the United

States in Japan's view of the international system, 1919–37' in Ian Nish (ed.), *Anglo-Japanese Alienation, 1919–1952* (1982).

10. Memorandum M.03710, September 1919, ADM 1/8549; 134th CID meeting, 14 December 1920, CAB 2/3; Wilson diary, entry 23 December 1920.
11. Minute by Hardinge, undated but *ca.* May 1917, passim, FO 371/3119; Balfour to Wiseman, 5 July 1917, FO 800/209; War Cabinet meeting, 22 May 1917, CAB 23/2; War Cabinet meeting, 3 July 1917, CAB 13/3.
12. *D.B.F.P. Volume VI,* no. 789; minute by D.M.O., 28 January 1920, passim, WO 32/5758; Board meeting, 14 January 1920, ADM 167/60; minutes by Hardinge, undated, and Curzon, 8 March 1920, passim, FO 371/5558.
13. Nish, *Alliance* pp. 319–21; *D.B.F.P. Volume XIV*, no. 162; minutes by Tyrrell, 11 and 26 February 1921, passim, FO 371/5616.
14. Cabinet meeting, 30 May 1921, CAB 23/25.
15. Cabinet meeting, 16 June 1921, CAB 23/26.
16. Sixth Imperial Conference meeting, 24 June 1921, CAB 32/2; Cabinet meeting, 30 June 1921, CAB 23/26; M.G. Fry, 'The North Atlantic Triangle and the Abrogation of the Anglo-Japanese Alliance', *Journal of Modern History*, vol. 39 (1967).
17. 13th Imperial Conference meeting, 4 July 1921, CAB 32/2; Cabinet meeting, 20 July 1921, CAB 23/26; Cabinet meeting, 1 November 1921, CAB 23/27.
18. Memorandum by Foreign Office, 10 October 1921, passim, FO 412/118.
19. CID papers, nos. 277–B, 280–B, CAB 4/7.
20. *F.R.U.S., 1922, Volume 1* pp. 1–235; *D.B.F.P. Volume XIV* pp. 466–645.
21. Cmd 1627.
22. Minute by Sperling, 1 February 1924, FO 371/9616.
23. Antony Preston, *Cruisers, An Illustrated History, 1880–1980* (1980) pp. 74–5, 83.
24. *D.B.F.P. Volume XIV*, no. 405; Balfour to Lloyd George, 11 November 1921, FO 412/116; Domville diary, entry 30 September 1921.
25. Balfour to Lloyd George, 24 and 29 November 1921, FO 412/116.
26. Minute by Wellesley, 28 November 1921, FO 371/6681; minute by Domville, undated but late 1921 by internal evidence, ADM 116/3300.
27. Inter-Departmental Conference, 12 January 1920, L/PS/10/807; Wilson diary, entry 26 December 1919; Beatty to de Robeck, 1 February 1920, de Robeck papers, 6/25; Hardinge to Rumbold, 6 January 1920, Hardinge papers, vol. 42; Cabinet meeting, 6 January 1920, CAB 23/20.
28. Minute by Churchill, 9 December 1920, WO 32/5743; Ist Constantinople Committee meeting, 1 June 1921, CAB 27/133.
29. Orde, *Britain* pp. 6–15; N.H. Gibbs, *Grand Strategy* pp. 35–44.
30. M.L. Dockrill and Douglas Goold, *Peace Without Promise: Britain and the Peace Conferences, 1919–23* (1981) passim; Schroeder, 'Tradition'.
31. Wavell to Dawnay, 23 February 1920, Guy Dawnay papers, 69/21/5.

32. CAB 23/25, Cabinet meeting, 30 May 1921; WO 155/3, memorandum by general staff, 31 October 1921; Hankey diary, entry 3 January 1921; memorandum by Crowe, 26 December 1921, FO371/7000; memorandum by Balfour, 18 March 1919, Lloyd George papers, F/3/4; CID paper no. 98–A, CAB 3/3.
33. Lloyd George papers, ibid.
34. CP 1724, CAB 24/110; CP 2855, CAB 24/122.
35. CP 117, CAB 24/93; Cabinet meetings, 26 November and 2 December 1919, CAB 23/18; Sally Marks, *Innocent Abroad, Belgium at the Paris Peace Conference of 1919* (1981) pp. 286–97; Roskill, *Hankey* pp. 133–34.
36. Hankey to Lloyd George and Balfour, 10 November 1919, CAB 63/25; Hankey diary, entry 16 November 1919; CID papers, nos. 98–A, 101–A, CAB 3/3; CP 1724, CAB 24/110; Gilbert, *Companion I* to *Churchill IV* pp. 1190–94.
37. H.A.L. Fisher diary, entry 30 December 1920.
38. CP 919, CAB 24/102; CP 1782, CAB 24/110; CID papers no. 240–B, passim, CAB 4/7; Cabinet meeting, 30 June 1920, CAB 23/21; Keith Middlemass (ed.), *Thomas Jones, Whitehall Diary, Volume I* (1969) pp. 115–17; Marks, *Innocent* pp. 300–01.
39. Hankey to Lloyd George, 25 June 1921, Lloyd George papers, F/25/1.
40. Cabinet meeting, 30 June 1920, CAB 23/21; Middlemass, *Jones* pp. 115–17; Curzon to Grey, 28 November 1919, Curzon papers, vol. 211.
41. *D.B.F.P., Volume XVII*, no. 38; minutes by Tyrrell and Crowe, 16 February 1921, FO 800/157; Hankey diary, entry 31 December 1920; Cabinet meetings, 19 April 1921 and 24 May 1921, CAB 23/25; 18th Imperial Conference meeting, 7 July 1921, CAB 32/2; H.A.L. Fisher diary, entry 30 December 1920.
42. Air Attaché, Paris, to Air Ministry, 18 January 1919, AIR 1/35/15/1/223; CID paper, no. 280–B, CAB 4/7; CID paper no. 102–A, CAB 3/3; 145th CID meeting, 14 October 1921, passim, CAB 2/3.
43. 150th CID meeting, 23 November 1921, CAB 2/3.
44. CP 3619, CAB 24/132; ibid.
45. Hines H. Hall III, 'British Air Defence and Anglo-French Relations, 1921–1924', *Journal of Strategic Studies*, vol. 4 (1981).
46. Cabinet meeting, 1 November 1921, CAB 23/27; Cabinet meeting, 10 January 1922, CAB 23/29; Orde, *Britain* pp. 11–15; memoranda by Crowe and Curzon, 26 and 28 December 1921, FO 371/7000; Curzon to Lloyd George, 28 and 30 December 1921, Lloyd George papers, F/13/2.
47. Cabinet meeting, 23 May 1922, CAB 23/30; minutes by Tyrrell and Curzon, 29 April 1922, FO 371/7567; minute by Crowe, undated but *ca.* May 1922, FO 371/8251.
48. Tyrrell to Curzon, 27 April 1922, Curzon papers, vol. 227; FO 371/8190, FO 371/8187, FO 371/8191, passim.
49. Minute by Curzon, 24 April 1922, FO 371/8188..
50. Cabinet meeting, 28 October 1921, CAB 23/27.

7 The New Strategic Policy of 1922

1. Austen Chamberlain to Lloyd George, 23 March 1922, Horne to Lloyd George, 23 March 1922, Lloyd George papers, F/7/5, F/27/6; Wedgewood Benn diary, entries 24 February and 8 March 1922, Stansgate papers, St 66.
2. Minute by Churchill, 16 November 1920, AIR 5/216.
3. CPs 3551, 3552, CAB 24/133; memorandum by Barstow, 10 February 1922, T 172/1228.
4. Memorandum by air staff, January 1922, CAB 27/164.
5. Memorandum by naval staff, January 1922, ibid.
6. Memorandum by general staff, January 1922, ibid; Army Council meeting, 3 November 1921, WO 163/27; Chetwode to Wilson, 30 December 1921, Wilson papers 73/1/16/58 B.
7. Second Churchill Committee meeting, 10 January 1922, passim, CAB 27/164; Churchill to Horne, 31 January and 11 February 1922, passim, T 172 /1228.
8. Report of Churchill Committee, 4 February 1922, CAB 27/164.
9. Memorandum by Barstow, T 172/1228; Cabinet meeting, 17 February 1922, CAB 23/29; 11th Churchill Committee meeting, 23 February 1922, CAB 27/164.
10. Memorandum, undated, 'Tentative Balance Sheet 1923/4', T 171/205; memoranda by Niemayer, 15 March 1922, passim, T 171/211; CP 3997, CAB 24/136.
11. Report of the Churchill Committee, 4 February 1922, CAB 27/164.
12. Cmd 1603.
13. CP 3765, CAB 24/133.
14. Cmds 1941, 2114; Chetwode to Cavan, 3 February 1922, passim, WO 32/5297.
15. War Office to India Office, 23 November 1920, passim, L/MIL 7/5465; War Office to India Office, 28 April 1920, L/MIL 7/5474; Keith Jeffery, 'An English Barrack in the Orient Seas? India in the Aftermath of the First World War', *Modern Asian Studies*, vol. 15 (1981); CP 3701, CAB 24/133.
16. Cabinet meeting, 21 February 1922, CAB 23/29; CAB 16/38, passim; Memorandum by Indian general staff, no. 8886, WO 33/1011.
17. Cabinet meeting, 17 February 1922, CAB 23/29.
18. Cmd 1607.
19. Board meeting, 14 March 1922, ADM 167/65; Domville diary, entry 15 February 1922; Cabinet meetings, 7 and 15 March 1922, CAB 23/29.
20. Trenchard to Churchill, 6 March 1922, Trenchard papers, 11/27/50.
21. Trenchard to Churchill, 9 March 1922, ibid.
22. Report of the Churchill Committee, 4 February 1922, CAB 27/164.
23. Memorandum by general staff, January 1922, third Churchill Committee meeting, 12 January 1922, CAB 27/164; 'Conversation', pt. 1, S–47, CAB 23/36; 147th CID meeting, 31 October 1921, CAB 2/3.
24. David Walder, *The Chanak Affair* (1969), although flawed, is the best account of the crisis. David Lloyd George, *The Truth About the Peace*

Treaties, Volume 2 (1938) pp. 1349–50; Winston S. Churchill, *The World Crisis: Volume 5, The Aftermath, 1918–1928* (1929) pp. 419–37.
25. Lord Beaverbrook, *The Decline and Fall of Lloyd George* (1963) p. 162; Clarke, *Innings* p. 229; Curzon to Hardinge, 10 October 1922, Hardinge papers, vol. 45; minute by Hankey, 4 November 1927, CAB 21/334.
26. Harington, telegrams to War Office, nos. 2448, 2451, 26 September 1922, FO 371/7895; same to same, no. 2458, 26 September 1922, FO 371/7896; same to same, no. 2486, 28 September 1922, passim, WO 106/1441; Cabinet meeting 10 November 1922, appendix, CAB 23/32.
27. Conference of ministers, 25 and 28 September 1922, CAB 23/39.
28. Order of Battle in the Near East Theatre, 2 October 1922, AIR 8/59.
29. Memorandum by general staff, 26 September 1922, WO 106/709; Lloyd George, telephone call to Hankey, 22 September 1922, CAB 21/241.
30. Order of Battle, AIR 8/59; Harington to War Office, telegram no. 2525, 30 September 1922, WO 95/4961.
31. Trenchard, telegrams to A.O.C. Constantinople, 26 and 27 September 1922, AIR 8/51.
32. Memorandum by air staff, 21 September 1922, passim, AIR 5/267; AIR 5/297, AIR 5/245, AIR 5/847, AIR 5/853, AIR 5/854B, passim.
33. Memorandum by general staff, 17 September 1922, WO 106/1503; WO 106/709, passim.
34. War Office, telegram to Harington, no. 91247, 28 September 1922, WO 106/1441; Marden telegrams to Harington, 29 and 30 September 1922, WO 95/4964.
35. Memorandum by general staff, 26 September 1922, WO 106/709; Conference of ministers, 27 September 1922, CAB 23/39.
36. Informal Army Council meeting, 25 September 1922, WO 106/1442; memorandum by A.M.P., 29 September 1922, AIR 8/56; AIR 5/234, passim.
37. Conference of ministers, 18 September 1922, CAB 23/39; minute by Orde, 15 February 1923, FO 371/9418; memorandum by Hankey, 4 November 1927, CAB 21/334; John Ferris 'Whitehall's Black Chamber: British Cryptology and the Government Code and Cypher School, 1919–29', *Intelligence and National Security*, vol. 2 (1987).

8 Service Policies and Financial Policy, 1922–24

1. Horne to Lloyd George, 27 April 1922, Lloyd George papers, F/27/6; Cabinet meeting, 13 June 1922, CAB 23/30.
2. Minute by Barstow, 18 November 1922, T 161/206 S.19717.
3. Cabinet meetings, 7 and 15 March 1922, CAB 23/29; Roskill, *Naval Policy* pp. 365–70; Trenchard to Churchill, 23 March 1922, passim, AIR 8/17; CAB 21/258, CAB 21/225, passim.
4. Cabinet meeting, 7 March 1923, CAB 23/45, 1st Salisbury Committee meeting, 15 March 1923, report of the Salisbury Committee, July 1923, AIR 8/63.
5. Baldwin to Derby, 17 August 1923, WO 137/7; CP 4330, CAB 24/140.

6. Cabinet meeting, 6 February 1924, CAB 23/47.
7. Typescript memoirs, *Recollections Happy But Hazy,* undated by *ca.* 1940, chapter Washington 1921, Cavan papers.
8. Army Council meeting, 28 June 1922, WO 163/28.
9. Derby to Salisbury, 12 March 1923, WO 137/10; CP 200, CAB 24/159; Derby to Baldwin, 28 May 1923, Baldwin papers, vol. 1, Defence; same to same, 30 May 1923, WO 137/10; Cabinet meeting, 13 June 1923, CAB 23/46.
10. Cavan to Godley, 28 November (1924 or 1925), Alexander Godley papers, Series 3.
11. Army Council meeting, 29 September 1925, WO 163/31; Report of the Territorial Army Expansion Committee, July 1925, WO 33/1088.
12. Cmds 1829, 2061, 2598; memorandum by general staff, 1922, AIR 5/1382; memorandum by Aldershot Command, 14 November 1925, Kirke papers (KCL).
13. John Ferris, 'The Theory of a "French Air Menace", Anglo-French Relations and the British Home Defence Air Force Programmes of 1921–1925', *Journal of Strategic Studies,* vol. 10 (1987).
14. Ibid.
15. Ibid.
16. Neville Chamberlain diary, entry 27 July 1923, passim, Neville Chamberlain papers; Crowe to Phipps, 24 November 1923, Tyrrell to Phipps, 18 December 1923, Eric Phipps papers, vols. 2/3, 2/12.
17. Fisher to Baldwin, 19 July 1923, T 172/1309.
18. Cabinet meeting, 3 August 1922, CAB 23/30; 1st and 10th Salisbury Committee (SC) meetings, 15 March 1923, 16 May 1923, AIR 8/63.
19. 10th SC meeting, 16 May 1923, Air 8/63. 173rd CID meeting, 29 June 1923, CAB 2/3; Derby to Salisbury, 2 July 1923, passim, WO 137/6; Salisbury to Curzon, 30 June 1923, memorandum by Villiers, 17 April 1923, Curzon papers, vols. 231–B, 242; Neville Chamberlain diary, entry 15 July 1923; MacDonald to Crewe, 28 February 1924, FO 371/9812; minute by Barstow, 9 May 1923, T 161/184 S.16984.
20. Memorandum by Barstow, 15 February 1924, T 161/228 S.23285; Cabinet meeting, 9 May 1923, CAB 23/45; Cabinet meeting, 18 February 1924, CAB 23/47.
21. Ferris, 'French Air Menace'.
22. Ibid.
23. Ibid.
24. Ibid; Smith, *Air Strategy* p. 32.
25. Ferris, 'French Air Menace'.
26. Lee to Curzon, 12 October 1922, FO 371/7527.
27. Memorandum by Sperling, 1 February 1924, FO 371/9616; Washington Embassy despatch, no. 984, 6 June 1924, FO 371/9618.
28. Preston, *Cruisers* pp. 69–71; Alan Raven and John Roberts, *British Cruisers of World War Two* (1980) pp. 105–06; Friedman, *U.S. Cruisers* pp. 4, 109–10; memoranda by Dreyer and Chatfield, 7 May 1921, 23 June 1921, ADM 1/8653.
29. Tokyo Embassy, despatch no. 395, 6 July 1922, FO 371/8044; memorandum by Pound, 14 September 1922, ADM 1/8653; 165th CID

meeting, 30 November 1922, CAB 2/3.
30. Minutes by Tyrrell and Wellesley, 8 March 1923, FO 371/9226; minute by Wellesley, 4 August 1922, FO 371/8044.
31. Memorandum no. 2064, ADM 167/72; Board meeting, 13 July 1922, ADM 167/65.
32. 161st CID meeting, 28 July 1922, CAB 2/3; memorandum by Treasury, October 1922, T 161/119 S.9627/01; memorandum by Hurst, 9 October 1922, FO 371/7257.
33. Barnes and Nicholson, *Amery Diaries* p. 310; 168th CID meeting, 14 December 1922, CAB 2/3; minutes by Warren Fisher, 25 October and 16 November 1922, T 161/119 S.9627/01; Cabinet meetings, 7 and 11 December 1922, CAB 23/32; Cabinet meeting, 21 February 1923, CAB 23/45.
34. Board meetings, 13 December 1923, passim, ADM 167/67; memorandum no. 1760, ADM 167/68.
35. Memorandum by Pound, 12 June 1923, ADM 1/8702.
36. Raven and Roberts, *British Cruisers* p. 103; Paul G. Halpern (ed.), *The Keyes Papers, Volume II: 1918–1939* (1980) pp. 60–1; Admiralty, telegram to Beatty, 17 November 1921, ADM 116/3445.
37. Appendices to memorandum by Pound, 30 January 1924, ADM 1/8672.
38. Memorandum by D.C.N.S., 18 March 1919, ADM 167/57; memorandum by Jellicoe, 3 March 1919, John Jellicoe papers, Add. Mss 49045; CID papers nos. 290–B, 295–B, CAB 4/7.
39. Memorandum by Bellairs, 24 May 1928, ADM 116/2423.
40. Barnes and Nicholson, *Amery Diaries* pp. 349–52; Middlemass, *Jones* p. 248; Cabinet meeting, 22 October 1923, CAB 23/46; memorandum by Pound, 27 October 1923, passim, ADM 1/8653.
41. Board meeting, 21 November 1923, ADM 167/67; memorandum no. 1754, ADM 167/68; minute by Murray, 9 January 1924, ADM 1/8672; minute by Barstow, 23 October 1923, T 161/217 S.21914; Cabinet meeting, 17 January 1924, CAB 23/46.
42. Board meetings, 3 August 1923, passim, ADM 167/67; memorandum 9 July 1923, ADM 167/68; memoranda by air staff, March and May 1924, AIR 9/38; meeting of sea lords, 28 January 1924, Beatty papers, vol. 8, no. 5; Trenchard to Churchill, 23 March 1925, T172/1440.
43. Memorandum on Gunnery Armament Stores, 1922, ADM 116/3300; memorandum no. 1710, ADM 167/68; minute by Egerton, 30 March 1925, ADM 116/3862; Egerton to Richmond, Richmond papers, 17 January 1925; RIC 7/3e; Hans Lengerer and Tomako Rehm-Takahara, 'The Japanese Aircraft Carriers Junyo and Hiyo', *Warship*, vol. 33 (1985), citing the Japanese Imperial Defence Committee in 1923. The IJN's actual strength between 1923 and 1927 differed from this figure. (Memorandum by Naval Attaché, Tokyo, 18 February 1924, FO 371/10309; memorandum by same, 24 February 1927, FO 371/12523).
44. Hector C. Bywater, *Navies and Nations, A Review of Naval Developments Since the Great War* (1927).
45. Richmond to Haldane, 16 April and 24 June 1924, Haldane of Cloan papers, vol. 5916; Haldane to Richmond, 19 May 1924, Richmond papers, RIC 7/3e.

46. Beatty to Brock, 13 March 1923, de Robeck papers, vol. 8/7.
47. Fourth meeting of Salisbury Committee, 19 April 1923, AIR 8/63; second meeting of Singapore Committee, 3 March 1924, CAB 27/236.
48. Memorandum by Snowden, June 1924, FO 371/9671.
49. CP 4330, CAB 24/140; minute by Niemayer, 27 March 1923, T 171/214; minute by Niemayer, 24 January 1924, T 171/1226.
50. Appendix; Amery to Neville Chamberlain, 1 December 1923, T 161/227 S.23175.
51. Derby to Baldwin, 7 February 1923, passim, WO 137/7; minute by Barstow, 29 January 1924, T 161/224 S.22908; Barstow to Blackett, 26 July 1923, Blackett papers, vol. 3; 15th meeting Salisbury Committee meeting, 22 June 1923, AIR 8/63.
52. Blackett papers, ibid; CP 369, CAB 24/161; memorandum by Barstow, 2 November 1923, T 161/227 S. 23175.
53. Memoranda by Barstow, ibid; minute by Barstow, 20 February 1923, T 161/800 S.18917/1; memorandum by Barstow, 15 February 1924, T 161/228 S.23285.
54. T 161/228 S.23285, ibid; memorandum by Barstow, 1 December 1924, T 161/241 S.25344.

9 The Road to Locarno, 1924–25

1. MacDonald to Chelmsford and MacDonald to Thomson, 10 March 1924, FO 800/219; MacDonald to Chelmsford, 3 March 1924, T 161/264 S.29188.
2. Cabinet meetings, 18 and 21 February 1924, CAB 23/147; second Singapore Committee meeting, 3 March 1924, passim, CAB 27/236.
3. MacDonald to Eliot, 18 March 1924, FO 800/219; minute by Wellesley, 24 June 1924, FO 371/10319; fourth Singapore Committee meeting, 11 April 1924, CAB 27/236; ADMI/8666 and FO 371/9617, passim.
4. Minute by MacDonald, 18 February 1924, passim, FO 371/9813.
5. War Office to Foreign Office, 28 March 1924, FO 371/9813; minute by MacDonald, 20 June 1924, FO 371/9818; Chelmsford to MacDonald, 29 August 1924, ADM 1/8672; CID paper 516–B, CAB 4/11.
6. Minute by Chamberlain, 26 September 1925, FO 371/10939.
7. Minute by Tyrrell, 18 December 1924, FO 371/9620; memorandum by Ashton-Gwatkin, 22 November 1924, FO 371/10299; memorandum by Wellesley about the Singapore base, 1 January 1925, FO 371/10958; minute by Wellesley, 30 April 1925, FO 371/10634.
8. Memorandum by Wellesley on the naval programme, 1 January 1925, FO 371/10958.
9. Austen Chamberlain to Eliot, 17 December 1924, Austen Chamberlain papers, vol. 51/1; 193rd CID meeting, 5 January 1925, CAB 2/4; minute by Lampson, 28 March 1925, FO 371/10633.
10. Eighth Birkenhead Committee meeting, 30 June 1925, CAB 27/273; 215th CID meeting, 22 July 1926, CAB 2/4; CID paper no. 710–B, CAB 4/15.
11. Orde, *Britain* pp. 70–98 and Sybil Eyre Crowe, 'Sir Eyre Crowe and

the Locarno Pact', *English Historical Review*, vol. 87 (1971–72), present sound accounts of the Foreign Office's views but overlook much of the strategic dimensions of this debate.

12. CID paper no. 575–B, CAB 4/12; Lampson to Hankey, 27 January 1925, FO 371/10727; memorandum by Hankey, 23 January 1925, CAB 63/37.
13. 195th and 196th CID meetings, 13 and 19 February 1925, CAB 2/4; CID paper no. 516–B, CAB 4/11.
14. CAB 4/11 ibid; CID paper no. 654–B, CAB 4/14.
15. Minute by Tyrrell, 26 March 1925, FO 371/10729; minute by Lampson, 14 April 1925, FO 371/10730; memorandum by Nicholson, 23 January 1925, FO 371/10065; 195th CID meeting, 13 February 1925, CAB 2/4; COS 36, CAB 53/12; minute by Lampson, 10 March 1925, FO 371/10726.
16. Second Foreign Policy and Security Committee meeting, 28 May 1925, CAB 27/275; 200th and 201st CID meetings, 22 June 1925, 1 July 1925, CAB 2/4.
17. Memorandum by Plans Division, September–October 1924, minute by Trenchard 12 December 1924, AIR 5/605; CID paper no. 518–B, CAB 4/11; CID papers nos. 545–B, 560–B, CAB 4/12.
18. CP 116, CAB 24/172; CID paper, no. 516–B, CAB 4/11; memorandum by general staff, December 1924, WO 155/4.
19. Minutes by Troutbeck and Crowe, 7 and 9 January 1925, FO 371/10711.
20. Minute by Chamberlain, 4 January 1925, FO 371/11064; 196th CID meeting, 19 February 1925, CAB 2/4.
21. Minute by Crowe, 13 January 1925, FO 371/11064.
22. Memorandum by Nicholson, 23 January 1925, FO 371/11065.
23. Memorandum by Crowe, 2 January 1925, passim, CAB 16/56; minute by Crowe, 14 January 1925, FO 371/10726; minute by Crowe, 15 February 1925, FO 371/11051; minute by Chamberlain, 19 March 1925, FO 371/10756.
24. GP (24) 7, CAB 16/56; CID paper, no. 542–B, CAB 4/2; 190th CID meeting, 4 December 1924, CAB 2/4.
25. 192nd CID meeting, 16 December 1924, CAB 2/4; memorandum by Hankey, 23 January 1925, CAB 63/37.
26. Minute by Lampson, 22 January 1925, FO 371/10726.
27. CP 118, CAB 24/172; 195th and 196th CID meetings, 13 and 19 February 1925, CAB 2/4.
28. Chamberlain to d'Abernon, 11 September 1930, Austen Chamberlain papers, vol. 39/3. Orde, *Britain* p. 90, note 1, has shown that this letter is not entirely accurate. However, contemporary evidence demonstrates that by mid-February 1925 Chamberlain began to favour a quadruple pact rather than an Anglo-French alliance. (Chamberlain to Crowe, 16 February 1925, ibid., vol. 52).
29. Ibid; Cabinet meetings, 2 and 4 March 1925, CAB 23/49; Hankey diary, entry 22 March 1925; Hankey to Baldwin, 17 March 1925, CAB 21/433.

30. Crowe to Chamberlain, 12 March 1925, Austen Chamberlain papers, vol. 52.
31. Minute by Lampson, 4 March 1925, FO 371/10728.
32. Hankey diary, entry 22 March 1925; minute by Tyrrell, 19 June 1925, FO 371/10734.
33. Amery to Dominion prime ministers, 9 August 1925, FO 371/10738.
34. Minute by Chamberlain, 21 May 1927, FO 371/12620.
35. Memorandum by general staff, 31 December 1924, FO 371/10403; India Office to Foreign Office, 30 April 1925, FO 371/10984; CP 286, CAB 24/173; Cabinet meeting, 20 May 1925, CAB 23/50; 21st COSC meeting, 3 July 1925, CAB 53/1: Beatty to Hankey, 4 July 1925, CAB 21/286; Hankey to Beatty, 10 July 1925, Beatty papers, 215th CID meeting, 22 July 1926, CAB 2/4.
36. Minute by Tyrrell, 4 December 1926, FO 371/11787; 193rd CID meeting, 5 January 1925, CAB 2/4; minute by Chamberlain, 3 January 1925, FO 371/10984; minute by Gregory, 21 June 1925, FO 371/10943.
37. 187th CID meeting, 28 July 1924, appendix, CAB 2/4.
38. Minute by Trenchard, 12 December 1924, AIR 5/605.
39. Pound to Richmond, 31 August 1924, Richmond papers, RIC 7/4.
40. Minute by Warren Fisher, 16 November 1922, T 161/119 S.9627/01.

10 The Triumph of Treasury Control and the Ten-Year Rule, 1925–26

1. Robert Rhodes James, *Churchill, A Study in Failure, 1900–1939* (1970) pp. 212–17; Keith Middlemass and John Barnes, *Baldwin, A Biography* (1969) pp. 324–39.
2. Churchill to Baldwin, 1 June 1927, T 162/134 E.18420.
3. Air Council meeting, 22 January 1925, AIR 6/15; memorandum AM 532, AIR 6/22; AE (25) 3, CAB 27/294; ND (25) 8, passim, CAB 27/273.
4. Warren Fisher to Baldwin, 3 February 1925 (two letters), Baldwin papers, vol. 2, Defence; same to same, 26 May 1925, vol. 3.
5. Cabinet meeting, 26 November 1924, CAB 23/49.
6. First Birkenhead Committee meeting, 2 March 1925, CAB 27/273.
7. CPs 38, 67, CAB 24/171.
8. Ibid; minute by Keyes, 22 December 1923, ADM 1/8702; ND (25) 8, first Birkenhead Committee meeting, 2 March 1925, CAB 27/273.
9. Hankey to Balfour, 6 September 1925, CAB 21/287; minute by Chamberlain, 11 August 1926, FO 371/11233.
10. 193rd CID meeting, 5 January 1925, CAB 2/4.
11. Eighth Birkenhead Committee meeting, 30 June 1925, CAB 27/273.
12. Note 4, above.
13. Churchill to Bridgeman, 15 December 1924, William Bridgeman papers, vol. 3, (S.R.O. 4629) Churchill to Baldwin, 15 December 1924, Baldwin papers, vol. 2, Defence; CPs 39, 71, CAB 24/171; First Birkenhead Committee meeting, 2 March 1925, passim, CAB 27/273.

14. Memorandum by Churchill, undated, January–February 1928, Hankey papers, vol. 5/1.
15. Roskill, *Naval Policy* pp. 445–53; Rhodes James, *Churchill* pp. 213–14; Martin Gilbert (ed.), *Companion* to *Winston S. Churchill, 1874–1965, Volume V, 1922–1939* (1976) pp. 373–76; CPs 39,71, CAB 24/171.
16. Baldwin to Bridgeman, 30 May 1925, Bridgeman papers, vol. 3 (S.R.O. 4629).
17. Robert Clive Bridgeman (typescript) *William Bridgeman, his family and his home. The Country Gentleman in Politics* (undated) pp. 572–576, Bridgeman papers (S.R.O. 3820). Cabinet meetings, 12 and 18 February 1925, CAB 23/49.
20. Memorandum by naval staff, 31 July 1924, ADM 1/8672; ND (25) 7, passim, CAB 27/273.
21. First and second Birkenhead Committee meetings, 2 and 5 March 1925, CAB 27/273.
22. Austen Chamberlain to Howard, 18 March 1925, FO 371/10637. B.J.C. McKercher, *The Second Baldwin Government and the United States, 1924–1929, Attitudes and Diplomacy* (1984) pp. 34–42, has overlooked this event.
23. Cabinet meeting, 18 March 1925, CAB 23/49; 198th and 199th CID meetings, 30 March 1925, 2 April 1925, CAB 2/4; memorandum by Hankey, 31 March 1925, AIR 8/70.
24. Cabinet meeting, 6 May 1925, CAB 23/50.
25. Memorandum by Egerton, 1 April 1925, ADM 1/8685; ND (25) 26, CAB 27/273.
26. Seventh and eighth Birkenhead Committee meetings, 25 and 30 June 1925, CAB 27/273.
27. Ibid.
28. Ibid and ninth Birkenhead Committee meeting, 2 July 1925.
29. Report of Birkenhead Committee, July 1925, CAB 27/273.
30. Bridgeman, *Bridgeman*, Bridgeman papers (S.R.O. 3820). p. 590; Rhodes James, *Memoirs* pp. 211–12; John Ramsden (ed.), *Rearl Old Tory Politics, The Political Diaries of Robert Sanders, Lord Bayford, 1910–1935* (1981) p. 221.
31. Cabinet meetings, 15 and 16 July 1925, CAB 23/50; various memoranda by Bridgeman, July 1925, Baldwin papers, vol. 2, Defence; pp. 583–93, Bridgeman, Bridgeman, pp. 583–93, Bridgeman papers (S.R.O. 3820).
32. Roskill, *Naval Policy* pp. 451–53.
    August 1925; Cabinet meeting, 22 July 1925, CAB 23/50.
34. Minute by Trenchard, 31 December 1924, AIR 8/70.
35. Memorandum by Trenchard, January 1925, AIR 8/45; Trenchard to Chamier, 31 August 1925, AIR 5/608.
36. AIR 8/45, ibid.
37. Neidpath, *Singapore* pp. 93–101; minute by Hoare, 25 December 1924, AIR 8/70; Trenchard to Churchill, 6 February 1925, Trenchard papers, 11/27/50.
38. Minute by Barstow, 2 December 1924, passim, T 161/241 S.25344.
39. CP 421, CAB 24/175.
40. Hankey to Balfour, 6 September 1925, passim, CAB 21/287; CP 437,

214 *Notes*

CAB 24/175; Cabinet meeting, 11 November 1925, CAB 23/50; memorandum by air staff, December 1925, AIR 8/73; first meeting of the Air Expansion Committee, 20 November 1925, CAB 27/294.
41. Minute by Trenchard, 12 December 1924, AIR 5/605.
42. CP 437, CAB 24/175.
43. Colwyn Committee to Admiralty, *ca*. October 1925, ADM 1/8692.
44. Memorandum no. 2064, ADM 167/72; 210th and 215th CID meetings, 25 February 1926, 22 July 1926, CAB 2/4.
45. CID paper, no. 599–B, CAB 4/12; memorandum by Niemayer, 6 April 1925, T 176/21.
46. Warren Fisher to Baldwin, 3 July 1925, Baldwin papers, vol. 3; Warren Fisher to Churchill, 16 October 1925, T 176/21.
47. Gilbert, *Companion* to *Volume V* pp. 548–51; Warren Fisher to Churchill, 16 September 1925, T 176/21; first and second meetings of the Cabinet Economy Committee, 14 and 20 October 1925, CAB 27/303.
48. Colwyn to Bridgeman, 18 November 1925, ADM 116/2374; Gilbert, *Companion* to *Volume V* pp. 548–51, 553–56.
49. Army Council meeting, 16 November 1925, WO 163/31; Board meeting, 11 November 1925, ADM 167/71.
50. Bullock to Fraser, 2 December 1925, AIR 8/78; Hoare to Chalmers, 18 December 1925, AIR 19/120.
51. Report of the Colwyn Committee, January 1926, CAB 27/305.
52. Memorandum by Admiralty, 21 January 1926, ADM 181/107.
53. 209th CID meeting, 11 February 1926, CAB 2/4; memorandum by Egerton, ADM 1/8700; memoranda nos. 2088, 2016, ADM 167/72; Board meetings, 1 October and 2 November 1925, ADM 167/71; memoranda nos. 2150, 2158, ADM 167/74; Board meeting, 14 January 1926, ADM 167/73; Chatfield to Murray, 4 December 1925, ADM 116/2269; minute by Dreyer, 19 February 1926, ADM 116/2550.
54. 30th COSC meeting, 30 May 1926, CAB 53/1.
55. AIR 5/608, CAB 16/77, passim.
56. Report of Colwyn Committee, January 1926, CAB 27/305; Seventh Colwyn Committee meeting, 14 October 1925, AIR 19/120; memorandum by Trenchard, 28 October 1925, AIR 8/78; 211th CID meeting, 29 March 1926, passim, CAB 2/4.
57. 24th COSC meeting, 3 December 1925, CAB 53/1; CID paper no. 640–B, CAB 4/13.
58. Gilbert, *Companion* to *Volume V* pp. 672–74; 211th CID meeting, 29 March 1926, CAB 2/4; Hankey to Tyrrell, 12 March 1926, FO 371/11233; Hankey to Churchill, 19 March 1926, CAB 21/469.
59. Memorandum no. 36, CAB 53/12.
60. 28th COSC meeting, 22 April 1926, CAB 53/1; Hankey to Beatty, 26 May 1926, Beatty papers.
61. Memorandum no. 41, CAB 53/12.
62. 215th CID meeting, 22 July 1926, CAB 2/4; Cabinet meeting, 28 July 1926, CAB 23/53.
63. 235th CID meeting, 22 May 1927, CAB 2/5; Cabinet meeting, 20 July

1927, CAB 23/55; CP 207, CAB 24/188.
64. 236th CID meeting, 5 July 1928, CAB 2/5.

11 Conclusion: Men, Money and Diplomacy, 1919–26

1. Cmds 3499, 3506, 3509, 4259, 4262, 4266.
2. Watt, *Personalities* p. 27; Watt, *Succeeding,* passim.
3. Circular letter by Malmesbury, 8 March 1858, FO 83/185.
4. Army Department to India Office, 14 June 1928, Kirke papers, vol. 17 (IORL), E. 396.

Appendix: Service Estimates, 1919–26

TABLE A.1: *Formal Service Estimates**

Year	Naval Estimates		Army Estimates		RAF Estimates	
	Net	Gross	Net	Gross	Net	Gross
1919–20	£157 528 000	£172 798 776	£405 000 000	£492 473 000	£54 030 850	£56 035 950
1920–21	£ 84 372 300	£ 96 590 181	£125 000 000	£148 227 130	£22 992 600	£25 202 319
1921–22	£ 82 479 000	£ 91 186 869	£106 500 000	£120 224 500	£18 411 477	£19 782 967
1922–23	£ 64 884 000	£ 69 476 657	£ 62 300 000	£ 79 251 500	£10 895 000	£15 666 500
1923–24	£ 58 000 000	£ 61 401 165	£ 52 000 000	£ 61 631 500	£12 011 000	£18 605 000
1924–25	£ 55 800 000	£ 59 693 251	£ 45 000 000	£ 54 480 000	£14 511 000	£19 392 000
1925–26	£ 60 500 000	£ 64 443 000	£ 44 500 000	£ 54 333 000	£15 313 010	£21 319 310
1926	£ 58 100 000	£ 62 313 728	£ 42 500 000	£ 52 420 000	£16 000 000	£20 864 500

*Cmds 378, 436, 451, 565, 566, 619, 1166, 1170, 1191, 1603, 1604, 1607, 1818, 1826, 1829, 2061, 2070, 2071, 2348, 2359, 2366, 2595, 2589, 2598. The Services' net Estimates of 1919–20 to 1922–23 cannot be crudely compared with those following 1922–23 because the former were swollen by very large charges for war aftermath, operational and Middle Eastern expenditures.

TABLE A.2: *Current Effective Net Estimates*

Year	Navy	Army	RAF
1921–22	£76 671 900	£62 690 700	£18 305 477
1922–23	£53 569 200	£46 682 800	£10 738 000
1923–24	£50 213 100	£40 894 000	£11 800 000
1924–25	£47 824 400	£36 091 000	£14 378 000
1925–26	£52 369 200	£36 248 300	£15 376 010
1926	£49 880 400	£34 462 500	£15 755 000

TABLE A.3: *Amount of Estimates not Spent*

Year	Navy	Army	RAF
1921–22	£5 514 176	£ 5 096 002	£ —
1922–23	£4 072 702	£12 434 376	£1 912 000
1923–24	£ —	£ 5 770 320	£1 500 000
1924–25	£ 45 852	£ —	£ 831 000
1925–26	£ 495 552	£ 283 329	£ 630 000
1926	£ 800 130	£ 202 375	£ —

In Tables A2 and A3 the years 1919–20 and 1920–21 have been excluded as they were abnormal because of war aftermath and operational expenses.

This information comes from: T 161/136 S.11661, T 161/239 S.24881, T 161/267 S.28846, T 161/261 S.28819, T 161/272 S.30990. T 161/190 S.17769, T 161/205 S.19532, T 161/242 S.25483, T 161/227 S.23154, T 161/186 S.17212, T 161/275 S.31573, T 161/ 202 S.19035, T161/227 S.23145, T 161/264 S.29224.

The gaps in this series occur because several relevant files have been weeded. These figures include only the unexpended amount of the Services' net Estimates and exclude unexpected increases in their incoming appropriations-in-aid. Moreover, the portions of the Services Estimates which they could not spend declined after 1923–24,, largely because they then accepted shadow cuts, and did not use these sums which they had believed they would in fact be able to spend. The Navy accepted shadow cuts of £2 300 000 in 1924–25, £2 000 000 in 1925–26 and £2 000 000 in 1926, while the RAF accepted one of £500 000 in 1925–26. In earlier years, these sums might have been included in the portions of their Estimates which these two Services would have been unable to spend.

Bibliography

PRIMARY SOURCES

Official Records

India Office Library and Records
L/MIL 5 Compilations and Miscellaneous
L/MIL 7 Departmental Papers: Military Collections
L/PS/10 Departmental Papers: Political and Secret Files, 1902–31
L/PS/11 Departmental Papers: Political and Secret Annual Files, 1912–30

Public Record Office, Kew, London
ADM 1 Admiralty and Secretariat Papers
ADM 116 Admiralty and Secretariat Cases
ADM 167 Board of Admiralty Minutes and Memoranda
AIR 1 Air Historical Branch Records: Series One
AIR 2 Correspondence
AIR 5 Air Historical Branch Records: Series Two
AIR 6 Records of Meetings of the Air Council
AIR 8 Chief of Air Staff
AIR 9 Director of Plans
AIR 19 Private Office Papers
CAB 2 Committee of Imperial Defence Minutes
CAB 3 Committee of Imperial Defence, Home Defence Memoranda
CAB 4 Committee of Imperial Defence, Imperial Defence Memoranda
CAB 5 Committee of Imperial Defence, Colonial Defence Memoranda
CAB 6 Committee of Imperial Defence, Defence of India Memoranda
CAB 7 Committee of Imperial Defence, Colonial/Overseas Defence Committee, Minutes
CAB 8 Committee of Imperial Defence, Colonial/Overseas Defence Committee, Memoranda
CAB 16 Committee of Imperial Defence, *Ad Hoc* Sub-Committees
CAB 21 Registered Files
CAB 23 Cabinet Minutes
CAB 24 Cabinet Memoranda
CAB 53 Chiefs of Staff Committee
CAB 64 Hankey *Magnum Opus* Files

CO 534 King's African Rifles Original Correspondence
CO 535 Somaliland Original Correspondence
CO 537 Colonies, General Original Correspondence
CO 730 Iraq, Original Correspondence
CO 732 Middle East, Original Correspondence
FO 83 Great Britain and General
FO 371 General Correspondence: Political
FO 412 Confidential Prints, Miscellaneous
FO 800 Private Collections: Ministers and Officials: Various
T 1 Treasury Board Papers
T 160 Finance Files
T 161 Supply Files
T 162 Establishment Files
T 175 Hopkins Papers
T 176 Niemayer Papers
T 177 Private Office Papers and Private Collections: Phillips Papers
WO 32 Registered Files: General Series
WO 95 War of 1914 to 1918: War Diaries
WO 106 Directorate of Military Operations and Intelligence
WO 137 Derby, Private Office Files
WO 155 War of 1914–1918: Allied Military Committee of Versailles
WO 163 Army Council Records
WO 190 Directorate of Military Operations and Intelligence: Appreciation Files

Private Papers
Earl Baldwin Papers, Cambridge University Library
Earl Balfour Papers, British Museum
Admiral Earl Beatty Papers, National Maritime Museum, Greenwich
Lord Birkenhead Papers, India Office Library and Records
Basil Blackett Papers, India Office Library and Records
Andrew Bonar Law Papers, House of Lords Record Office
William Bridgeman Papers, Churchill College, Cambridge (copies of papers held at the Shropshire Record Office. The accession number cited in the text of the notes is that of Churchill College, Cambridge. The number cited in brackets is that of the Shropshire Record Office.)
Air Vice-Marshal Brooke-Popham Papers, Liddell Hart Centre for Military Archives
Field Marshal Lord Cavan Papers, Churchill College, Cambridge
Lord Cecil Papers, British Museum
Austen Chamberlain Papers, and University of Birmingham Library
Neville Chamberlain Papers, University of Birmingham Library
Lord Chelmsford Papers, India Office Library and Reocrds
Admiral Cowan Papers, National Maritime Museum, Greenwich
Lord Curzon Papers, India Office Library and Records (two collections)
J.C.C. Davidson Papers, House of Lords Records Office
Guy Dawnay Papers, Imperial War Museum

Lord Derby Papers, Public Records Office (WO 137)
Tennyson d'Eyncourt Papers, National Maritime Museum, Greenwich
Admiral Dreyer Papers, Churchill College, Cambridge
Barry Domville Diary, National Maritime Museum, Greenwich
H.A.L. Fisher Diary, Bodleian Library, Oxford
Admiral Fremantle Papers, National Maritime Museum, Greenwich
Air Commodore P.R.C. Groves Papers, Imperial War Museum and Liddell
    Hart Centre for Military Archives (two collections)
Air Commodore R.M. Groves Diary, Imperial War Museum
Malcolm Hailey Papers, India Office Library and Records
General Aylmer Haldane Papers, National Library of Scotland
Lord Haldane Papers, National Library of Scotland
Lord Halifax Papers, India Office Library and Records
Baron Hankey Papers and Diary, Churchill College, Cambridge
Lord Hardinge Papers, University of Cambridge Library
Lord Ismay Papers, Liddell Hart Centre for Military Archives
Admiral Jellicoe Papers, British Museum
General Jeudwine Papers, Imperial War Museum
Admiral J.D. Kelly Papers, National Maritime Museum, Greenwich
General Walter Kirke Papers, Liddell Hart Centre for Military Archives and
    India Office Library and Records (two collections)
Earl Lloyd George Papers, House of Lords Record Office
Ramsay MacDonald Papers, Public Records Office (PRO 30/69)
Lord Milner Papers, Bodleian Library
Lord Mottistone Papers, Nuffield College, Oxford
Field Marshal Montgomery-Massingberd Papers, Liddell Hart Centre for
    Military Archives
Admiral H.F. Oliver Papers, National Maritime Museum, Greenwich
India Office Permanent Under-Secretaries Collection, India Office Library
    and Records
Admiral Phillimore Papers, Imperial War Museum
Eric Phipps Papers, Churchill College, Cambridge
Field Marshal Lord Rawlinson Papers, National Army Museum
Lord Reading Papers, India Office Library and Records
Admiral Richmond Papers, National Maritime Museum, Greenwich
Admiral de Robeck Papers, Churchill College, Cambridge
Horace Rumbold Papers, Bodleian Library, Oxford
Air Vice-Marshal John Salmond Papers, Royal Air Force Museum
Lord Stansgate Papers, House of Lords Record Office
General Strickland Papers, Imperial War Museum
Frederick Sykes Papers, Royal Air Force Museum
Lord Templewood Papers, University of Cambridge Library
Admiral Thesigar Papers, National Maritime Museum, Greenwich
Marshal of the RAF Lord Trenchard Papers, Royal Air Force Museum
Lord Weir Papers, Churchill College, Cambridge
Admiral Wester Wemyss Papers, Churchill College, Cambridge
Field Marshal Henry Wilson Papers, Imperial War Museum

Published Primary Sources
Documents on British Foreign Policy, 1919–1939, First Series (D.B.F.P.)
House of Commons Debates (P.D.) vols. 112–90
Papers Relating to the Foreign Policy of the United States (F.R.U.S.)
Paris Peace Conference, 1919, vols. IV and XI (Washington, 1943)
1922, Volume 1 (Washington, 1938)

White Papers
Cmd 221 of 1919, Treaty Respecting Assistance to France in the Event of Unprovoked Aggression by Germany
Cmd 378 of 1919, Army Estimates, 1919–20
Cmd 436 of 1919, Air Estimates, 1919–20
Cmd 451 of 1919, Naval Estimates, 1919–20
Cmd 565 of 1920, Army Estimates, 1920–21
Cmd 566 of 1920, Air Estimates, 1920–21
Cmd 619 of 1920, Naval Estimates, 1920–21
Cmd 1166 of 1921, Army Estimates, 1921–22
Cmd 1170 of 1921, Air Estimates, 1921–22
Cmd 1191 of 1921, Naval Estimates, 1921–22
Cmd 1603 of 1922, Naval Estimates, 1922–23
Cmd 1604 of 1922, Army Estimates, 1922–23
Cmd 1607 of 1922, Air Estimates, 1922–23
Cmd 1627 of 1922, Conference on the Limitation of Armaments, Washington, 1921–22
Cmd 1818 of 1923, Naval Estimates, 1923–24
Cmd 1826 of 1923, Air Estimates, 1923–24
Cmd 1829 of 1923, Army Estimates, 1923–24
Cmd 2061 of 1924, Army Estimates, 1924–25
Cmd 2070 of 1924, Air Estimates, 1924–25
Cmd 2071 of 1924, Naval Estimates, 1924–25
Cmd 2169 of 1924, Papers Respecting Negotiations for an Anglo-French Pact
Cmd 2348 of 1925, Air Estimates, 1925–26
Cmd 2359 of 1925, Army Estimates, 1925–26
Cmd 2366 of 1925, Naval Estimates, 1925–26
Cmd 2476 of 1925, Programme of Naval Construction
Cmd 2589 of 1926, Air Estimates, 1926
Cmd 2595 of 1926, Naval Estimates, 1926
Cmd 2598 of 1926, Army Estimates, 1926

PUBLISHED SOURCES

Theses

George Patrick Armstrong, *The Controversy Over Tanks in the British Army, 1919 to 1933* (London, 1976).

Patrick Kitaburaza Kakwenzire, *Colonial Rule in the British Somaliland Protectorate, 1905–1939* (London, 1976).

J. Kenneth MacDonald, *British Naval Policy in the Pacific and Far East: From Paris to Washington, 1919–1922* (Oxford, 1975).

Brian James Cooper McKercher, *The British Foreign Policy-Making Elite and Its Attitudes Towards the United States, November 1924 — June 1929* (London, 1979).

Geoffrey Till, *The Impact of Airpower on the Royal Navy in the 1920s* (London, 1976).

Derek J.P. Waldie, *Relations Between the Army and the Royal Air Force 1918–1939* (London, 1980).

D.R.W.G. Walters, *The Relationship Between British Naval and Foreign Policies in the Far East, 1920 and 1934* (London, 1973).

Articles

Kathleen Burke, 'Great Britain and the United States 1917–1918: The Turning Point', *International History Review*, vol. 1, no. 2 (1979).

Ken Booth, 'The Ten-Year Rule — An Unfinished Debate', *Journal of the Royal United Services Institute,* no. 663 (1971).

N.J.M. Campbell, Washington's Cherry Trees. The Evolution of the British 1921–22 Capital Ships', *Warship. A Quarterly Journal of Warship History*, vol. 1, nos. 1–4 (Jan.–Aug. 1977).

Alan Cassels, 'Repairing the Entente Cordiale and the New Diplomacy', *Historical Journal*, vol. 23, no. 1 (1980).

Général Christienne and Pierre Buffotot, 'L'aéronautique militaire française entre 1919 et 1939', *Revue Historique des Armées,* no. 2 (1977).

Malcolm Cooper, 'A House Divided: Policy, Rivalry and Administration in Britain's Military Air Command 1914–1918', *Journal of Strategic Studies*, vol. 3, no. 2 (1980).

Sybil Eyre Crowe, 'Sir Eyre Crowe and the Locarno Pact', *English Historical Review*, vol. 87, no. 1 (1972).

John G. Darwin, 'The Chanak Crisis and the British Cabinet', *History*, vol. 65, no. 213 (1980).

John G. Darwin, 'Imperialism in Decline? Tendencies in British Imperial Policy Between the Wars', *Historical Journal*, vol. 23, no. 3, (1980).

Roberta Allbert Dayer, 'The British War Debts to the United States and the Anglo-Japanese Alliance, 1920–1923', *Pacific Historical Review*, vol. 45 (1976).

Richard K. Debo, 'Lloyd George and the Copenhagen Conference of 1920:

The Initiation of Anglo-Soviet Negotiations', *Historical Journal*, vol. 24, no. 2 (1981).

M.L. Dockrill and Zara Steiner, 'The Foreign Office at the Paris Peace Conference of 1919', *International History Review*, vol. 2 (1980).

P.G. Edwards, 'Britain, Mussolini and the "Locarno-Geneva' System', *European Studies Review* vol. 10, no. 1 (1980).

George W. Egerton, 'Britain and the "Great Betrayal": Anglo-American Relations and the Struggle for United States Ratification of the Treaty of Versailles, 1919–20', *Historical Journal*, vol. 21, no. 4 (1978).

John Ferris, 'A British "Unofficial" Aviation Mission and Japanese Naval Developments, 1919–1929', *Journal of Strategic Studies*, vol. 5, no. 3 (1982).

J. Douglas Goold, 'Lord Hardinge as Ambassador to France and the Anglo-French Dilemma Over Germany and the Near East, 1920–22', *Historical Journal*, vol. 21, no. 4 (1978).

Hines H. Hall, III, 'British Air Defence and Anglo-French Relations, 1921–1924', *Journal of Strategic Studies*, vol. 4, no. 3 (1981).

Robert Himmer, 'Soviet Policy Toward Germany During the Russo-Polish War, 1920', *Slavic Review*, vol. 35, no. 4 (1976).

Keith Jeffery, 'Sir Henry Wilson and the Defence of the British Empire, 1918–22' *Journal of Imperial and Commonwealth History*, vol. V, no. 3 (1977).

Keith Jeffery, '"An English Barrack in the Oriental Seas?' India in the Aftermath of the First World War', *Modern Asian Studies*, vol. 10 (1976).

Keith Jeffery, 'The British Army and Internal Security 1919–1939', *Historical Journal*, vol. 24, no. 2 (1981).

Hans Lengerer and Tomako Rehm-Takahara, 'The Japanese Aircraft Carriers Junyo and Hiyo', *Warship*, vol. 33 (1985).

J.R. McCrum, 'French Rhineland Policy at the Paris Peace Conference, 1919', *Historical Journal*, vol. 21, no. 3 (1978).

Helmut Mejchen, 'British Middle East Policy 1917–1921: The interdepartmental level', *Journal of Contemporary History*, vol. 8, no. 4 (1973).

F.S. Northedge, '1917–1919: The Implications for Britain', *Journal of Contemporary History*, vol. 3, no. 4 (1968).

Eunan O'Halpin, 'Sir Warren Fisher and the Coalition, 1919–1922', *Historical Journal*, vol. 24, no. 4 (1981).

John D. Rose, 'Batum as Domino, 1919–20: The Defence of India in Transcaucasia', *International History Review*, vol. 2, no. 2 (1980).

Captain Stephen Roskill, 'The Ten-Year Rule — The Historical Facts', *Journal of the Royal United Services Institute*, no. 665 (March 1972).

Paul W. Schroeder, 'Munich and the British Tradition', *Historical Journal*, vol. 19, no. 1 (1976).

Alan J. Sharp, 'The Foreign Office in Eclipse, 1919–22', *History*, vol. 61 (1976).

Peter Silverman, 'The Ten Year Rule', *Journal of the Royal United Services Institute*, no. 661 (1971).

G.H. Soutou, 'La France et les Marches de l'Est, 1914–1919', *Revue Historique*, no. 528 (1978).

Geoffrey Till, 'The Strategic Interface: The Navy and the Air Force in the Defence of Great Britain', *Journal of Strategic Studies,* vol. 1, no. 2 (1978).

Roberta M. Warman, 'The Erosion of Foreign Office Influence in the Making of Foreign Policy, 1916–1918', *Historical Journal,* vol. 15, no. 3 (1972).

Stephen White, 'Communism and the East: The Baku Congress, 1920', *Slavic Review,* vol. 33, no. 3 (1974).

Robert Young, 'The Strategic Dream: French Air Doctrine in the Inter-War Period, 1919–1939', *Journal of Contemporary History,* vol. 9, no. 4 (1974).

Books

Leo S. Amery, *My Political Life, Volume 2: War and Peace, 1914–1929* (London, 1953).

Geoffrey Archer, *Personal and Historical Memoirs of an East African Administrator* (London, 1963).

Lord Beaverbrook, *Men and Power, 1917–1918* (London, 1956).

The Decline and Fall of Lloyd George (London, 1963).

John Barnes and David Nicholson (eds), *The Leo Amery Diaries, Volume One: 1896–1929* (London, 1980).

Correlli Barnett, *Britain and Her Army, 1509–1970. A Military, Political and Social Survey* (London, 1970).

The Collapse of British Power (London, 1972).

Max Beloff, *Imperial Sunset, Volume One, Britain's Liberal Empire, 1897–1921* (London, 1969).

Brian Bond, *British Military Policy Between the Two World Wars* (Oxford, 1980).

Andrew Boyle, *Trenchard, Man of Vision* (London, 1962).

William Braisted, *The United States Navy in the Pacific, 1909–1922* (Austin, Texas, 1971).

D.K. Brown, *A Century of Naval Construction. The History of the Royal Corps of Naval Constructors* (London, 1983).

Elizabeth Burgoyne, *Gertrude Bell, From Her Personal Papers, 1914–1926* (London, 1961).

Kathleen Burke, 'The Treasury: From Impotence to Power' in K. Burke (ed.) *War and the State, The Transformation of British Government, 1914–1919* (London, 1982).

Robert Blake, *The Unknown Prime Minister, The Life and Times of Andrew Bonar Law, 1858–1923* (London, 1955).

Hector C. Bywater, *Sea-Power in the Pacific* (London, 1921).

Navies and Nations, A Review of Naval Developments Since the Great War (London, 1927).

E.H. Carr, *The Twenty Years' Peace, 1919–1939* (London, 1980).

C.E. Callwell, *Field Marshal Sir Henry Wilson, His Life and Diaries, Volume Two* (London, 1928).

John Campbell, *Lloyd George, The Goat in the Wilderness, 1922–1931* (London, 1979).

Rear-Admiral W.S. Chalmers, *The Life and Letters of David Beatty, Admiral of the Fleet* (London, 1951).

Austen Chamberlain, *Down the Years* (London, 1935).

Lord Chatfield, *The Navy and Defence. The Autobiography of Admiral of the Fleet, Lord Chatfield* (London, 1942).

Hosaya Chihiro, 'Britain and the United States in Japan's view of the International System, 1919–37', in Ian Nish (ed.), *Anglo-Japanese Alienation, 1919–1952* (London, 1981).

Randolph Churchill, *Lord Derby, 'King of Lancashire'* (London, 1959).

Winston S. Churchill, *The World Crisis, Volume 5. The Aftermath, 1918–1928* (London, 1929).

The Second World War, Volume One. The Gathering Storm (London, 1948).

Alan Clarke (ed.), *'A Good Innings': The Private Papers of Viscount Lee of Fareham* (London, 1974).

Peter K. Cline, 'Lloyd George and the "Experiment' with Businessmen in Government, 1915–22', in Keith D. Brown (ed.) *Essays in Anti-Labour History, Responses to the Rise of Labour in Britain* (London, 1974).

Maurice Cowling, *The Impact of Labour 1920–1924, The Beginning of Modern British Politics* (Cambridge, 1971).

Gordon Craig, 'The British Foreign Office from Grey to Austen Chamberlain', in Gordon Craig and Felix Gilbert (eds), *The Diplomats, 1919–1939* (Princeton, New Jersey, 1953).

Gordon Craig, *The Politics of the Prussian Army, 1640–1945* (Princeton, New Jersey, 1955).

Viscount d'Abernon, *An Ambassador of Peace. Lord d'Abernon's Diary* 3 vols., (London, 1929–30).

John Darwin, *Britain, Egypt and the Middle East, Imperial Policy in the Aftermath of War, 1918–1922* (London, 1981).

M.L. Dockrill and J.D. Goold, *Peace Without Promise: Britain and the Peace Conferences, 1919–23* (London, 1981).

M.L. Dockrill, 'Britain, the United States, and France and the German Settlement, 1918–1920', in B.J.C. McKercher and D.J. Moss (eds), *Shadow and Substance in British Foreign Policy, 1895–1939* (Edmonton, Alberta, 1985).

Norman Friedman, *U.S. Cruisers, An Illustrated Design History* (London, 1985).

Michael G. Fry, *Illusions of Security, North Atlantic Diplomacy, 1918–1922* (Toronto, 1972).

J.F.C. Fuller, *The Army in My Time* (London, 1936).

John Gallagher, *The Decline, Revival and Fall of the British Empire* (Cambridge, 1982).

Gerald Gibbs, *Survivor's Story* (London, 1956).

N.H. Gibbs, *Grand Strategy, Volume One, Rearmament Policy* (London, 1976).

Martin Gilbert, *The Roots of Appeasement* (London, 1966).

Winston S. Churchill, 1874–1965, Volume IV, 1916–1922 (London, 1975).

Volume V, 1922–1939 (London, 1976);
Companion Volumes I, II and III to Volume IV (London, 1975);
Companion Volume to Volume V, (London, 1976).

Paul Haggie, *Britannia at Bay, The Defence of the British Empire Against Japan, 1931–1941* (London, 1981).

Aylmer Haldane, *A Soldier's Saga* (London, 1948).

Paul G. Halpern (ed.), *The Keyes' Papers, Volume II: 1918–1939* (London, 1980).

Lord Hankey, *Diplomacy By Conference* (London, 1946).
The Supreme Control at the Paris Peace Conference, 1919. A Commentary (London, 1963).

Lord Hardinge of Penshurst, *Old Diplomacy, The Reminiscences of Lord Hardinge of Penshurst* (London, 1947).

Norman Hilmer, 'The Foreign Office, the Dominions and the Diplomatic Unity of the Empire, 1925–29', in David Dilks (ed.), *Retreat from Power, Studies in Britain's Foreign Policy of the Twentieth Century, Volume One, 1906–1939* (London, 1981).

Michael Howard, *The Continental Commitment, The Dilemma of British Defence Policy in the Era of the two World Wars* (London, 1972).
The Causes of War and Other Essays (London, 1983).

Lord Ismay, *Memoirs* (London, 1960).

Robert Rhodes James (ed.), *Memoirs of a Conservative. J.C.C. Davidson's Memoirs and Papers, 1910–1937* (London, 1969).

Robert Rhodes James, *Churchill, A Study in Failure, 1900–1939* (London, 1970).

Keith Jeffery, *The British Army and the Crisis of Empire, 1918–1922* (Manchester, 1984).

Paul Kennedy, *The Rise and Fall of British Naval Mastery* (London, 1976).
The Realities Behind Diplomacy: Background Influences on British External Policy, 1865–1980 (London, 1981).

Aaron S. Klieman, *Foundations of British Policy in the Arab World: The Cairo Conference of 1921* (London, 1970).

Patrick, Kyba, *Covenants Without the Sword, Public Opinion and British Defence Policy, 1931–1935* (Toronto, 1983).

Basil Liddell Hart, *The Tanks, Volume One, 1914–1939* (London, 1959);
The Memoirs of Captain Liddell Hart, Volume One (London, 1965).

David Lloyd George, *The Truth About the Peace Treaties, Volumes One and Two* (London, 1938).

Charles S. Maier, *Recasting Bourgeois Europe* (Princeton, New Jersey, 1975).

Arthur J. Marder, *From the Dreadnought to Scapa Flow: The Royal Navy in the Fisher Era, 1904–1919, Volume V, Victory and Aftermath, (January 1918–June 1919)* (London, 1970).

Sally Marks, *An Innocent Abroad, Belgium at the Paris Peace Conference of 1919* (Chapel Hill, North Carolina, 1981).

David Marquand, *Ramsay MacDonald* (London, 1977).

Frederick Maurice, *The Life of Lord Rawlinson of Trent* (London, 1928).

Arno J. Mayer, *Politics and Diplomacy of Peacemaking: Containment and Counter-Revolution at Versailles, 1918–1919* (London, 1968).

J.K. McDonald, 'Lloyd George and the Search for a Postwar Naval Policy, 1919', in A.J.P. Taylor (ed.) *Lloyd George. Twelve Essays* (London, 1971).

W. David McIntyre, *The Rise and Fall of the Singapore Naval Base, 1919–1942* (London, 1979).

B.J.C. McKercher, *The Second Baldwin Government and the United States, 1924–1929. Attitudes and Diplomacy* (Cambridge, 1984).

Richard Meinertzhagen, *Middle East Diary, 1917–1956* (London, 1959).

Keith Middlemass and John Barnes, *Baldwin, A Biography* (London, 1969).

Keith Middlemass (ed.), *Thomas Jones, Whitehall Diary, Volume One, 1916–1925,* (London, 1969).

A.E. Montgomery, 'Lloyd George and the Greek Question, 1918–1922' in A.J.P. Taylor (ed.), *Lloyd George. Twelve Essays* (London, 1971).

H. Montgomery Hyde, *British Air Policy Between the Wars, 1918–1939* (London, 1976).

K.O. Morgan, *Consensus and Disunity. The Lloyd George Coalition Government, 1918–1922* (Oxford, 1979).

Charles Loch Mowat, *Britain Between the Wars, 1918–1940* (London, 1955).

James Neidpath, *The Singapore Naval Base and the Defence of Britain's Eastern Empire, 1919–1941* (London, 1981).

Harold Nicholson, *Curzon: The Last Phase, 1919–1925. A Study in Post-War Diplomacy* (London, 1934).

Ian Nish, *Alliance in Decline, A Study in Anglo-Japanese Relations, 1908–1923* (London, 1972).

'Japan in Britain's View of the International System, 1919–1937' in Ian Nish (ed.), *Anglo-Japanese Alienation, 1919–1952* (London, 1981).

F.S. Northedge, *The Troubled Giant: Britain Among the Great Powers, 1916–1939* (London, 1966).

Anne Orde, *Great Britain and International Security, 1920–1926* (London, 1978).

G.C. Peden, *British Rearmament and the Treasury* (London, 1979).

Antony Preston, *Cruisers, An Illustrated History* (London, 1980).

John Ramsden (ed.), *Real Old Tory Politics, The Political Diaries of Robert Sanders, Lord Bayford, 1910–1935* (London, 1984).

Alan Raven and John Roberts, *British Cruisers of World War Two* (London, 1980).

Colonel Charles à Court Repington, *After the War, A Diary* (London, 1922).

Admiral Sir Herbert Richmond, *Statesmen and Sea Power* (Cambridge, 1946).

Lord Riddell, *Lord Riddell's Intimate Diary of the Peace Conference and After, 1918–1923* (London, 1933).

Lord Ronaldshay, *The Life of Lord Curzon, Being the Authorised Biography of George Nathaniel, Marquess Curzon of Kedleston, K.G., Volume Three* (London, 1928).

Captain Stephen Roskill, *Naval Policy Between the Wars, Volume One: The Period of Anglo-American Antagonism,* 1919–1929 (London, 1968); *Hankey, Man of Secrets, Volume Two,* 1919–1931 (London, 1972); *Admiral of the Fleet, Earl Beatty: An Intimate Biography* (London, 1980).

Charles Seymour (ed.), *The Intimate Papers of Colonel House, Volume 4:*

The Ending of the War, June 1918–November 1919 (London, 1928).

Malcolm Smith, *British Air Strategy Between the Wars* (Oxford, 1984).

Harold and Margaret Sprout, *Toward a New Order of Seapower* (Princeton, New Jersey, 1940).

Zara Steiner, *The Foreign Office and Foreign Policy, 1898–1914* (London, 1969).

David Stevenson, *French War Aims Against Germany, 1914–1919* (London, 1982).

Frederick Sykes, *From Many Angles* (London, 1942).

A.J.P. Taylor, *Rumours of War* (London, 1952).

H.W.V. Temperly *et al.* (eds), *A History of the Peace Conference of Paris*, 6 vols. (London, 1920–24).

Viscount Templewood, *Empire of the Air. The Advent of the Air Age* (London, 1957).

Christopher Thorne, *The Limits of Foreign Policy, The West, The League and The Far Eastern Crisis of 1931–1933* (London, 1972).

Geoffrey Till, *Air Power and the Royal Navy, 1914–1945. A Historical Survey* (London, 1979).

Seth Tillman, *Anglo-American Relations at the Paris Peace Conference of 1919* (Princeton, New Jersey, 1961).

David F. Trask, *Captains and Cabinets, Anglo-American Naval Relations, 1917–1918* (Princeton, New Jersey, 1972).

David Walder, *The Chanak Affair* (London, 1969).

D.C. Watt, *Personalities and Politics, Studies in the Formulation of British Foreign Policy in the Twentieth Century* (London, 1965);
Succeeding John Bull, America in Britain's Place, 1900–1975 (London, 1984).

Sir Charles Webster and Noble Frankland, *The Strategic Bombing Offensive Against Germany, Volume One* (London, 1961).

Kenneth Young, *Arthur James Balfour, The Happy Life of the Politician, Prime Minister, Statesman and Philosopher, 1848–1930* (London, 1963).

Index